RICHARD GERE

Also by John Parker

King of Fools: A Biography of the Duke of Windsor
Five for Hollywood
The Princess Royal
The Trial of Rock Hudson
Prince Philip: A Critical Biography
The Joker's Wild: The Biography of Jack Nicholson
The Queen: The New Biography
At the Heart of Darkness
Sean Connery
Elvis: The Secret Files
Polanski
Warren Beatty: The Last Great Lover of Hollywood
Michael Douglas: Acting on Instinct

RICHARD GERE

The Flesh and the Spirit

John Parker

HEADLINE

First published in 1995
by HEADLINE BOOK PUBLISHING

10 9 8 7 6 5 4 3 2 1

British Library Cataloguing in Publication Data

Parker, John
Richard Gere
I. Title
823.914 [F]

ISBN 0-7472-1558-8

Typeset by
Letterpart Limited, Reigate, Surrey

Printed and bound in Great Britain by
Mackays of Chatham PLC, Chatham, Kent

HEADLINE BOOK PUBLISHING
A division of Hodder Headline PLC
338 Euston Road
London NW1 3BH

Contents

Chapter One

The Body

'I will not be a piece of meat just so some jerk will pay five dollars to look at an image on a screen. As long as I have the opportunity to work, what do I care if nobody knows who Richard Gere is.' So said Richard Gere of himself in October 1979 when he was just on the brink of crashing into stardom with *American Gigolo*, a film in which he did indeed display a certain amount of meat for those five-dollar punters, a full-frontal shot of revelatory quality never previously seen in a mainstream movie that wasn't depicting African bushmen.

He was never averse to displaying the meat in his early days. Once when a woman reporter from the *Ladies' Home Journal* came to call, and began the interview by asking him what it was like to be a sex symbol, he dropped his trousers to show her. She wasn't impressed. Nor was New York critic Rex Reed, the man to whom Gere insisted he did not want to be flavour of the month, which was, said the critic, a decidedly odd statement from a young man who was being touted by Hollywood as the hottest star since . . . well, you know, the usual list of tormented souls: Brando, Clift, Dean, De Niro, etc. etc.

Reed warned him he was in danger of disappearing into his own contemplation, that no one knew who he was because he didn't know himself. And if he continued pretending to be Greta Garbo he might end up the same, a forgotten man living the life of a recluse.

Reed's prediction almost came true. In the next decade, Gere took a bumpy roller-coaster ride from so-called overnight stardom to virtual oblivion until, half forgotten and unknown by a new generation of five-dollar customers (now paying ten), he jumped naked into a jacuzzi with a prostitute in *Pretty Woman.* And the critics said: Here we go again . . .

At the time, he was in danger of being consigned to the directory of stars of yesteryear, until he was persuaded by his agent to change his mind after his fourth refusal to join the most adored terrestrial being of the moment, Julia Roberts, in what became the proverbial blockbuster, earning $400 million worldwide – and then promptly married that other most famous body of the day, Cindy Crawford, who was far too young to catch him first time around.

Thus he demonstrated that he had lost none of the sex appeal that originally made him famous, and as these words are being written, he is back up among the highest, endowed with the status that he enjoyed when he was a boy, figuring among the top thirty most bankable international stars listed in the May 1995 issue of *Empire* magazine, with a price tag of $8 million a movie.

This meticulous piece of movieland research accorded him an accolade based upon film box office takings of recent movies, and put him alongside a host of other star names who were, by their output and diversification over the past few years, far more deserving of a place in the list – which, incidentally, did not include Robert De Niro, with whom Gere used to be compared in his early days. That he should make such a comeback after his long stroll into the wilderness, contemplating his reason for being, devoting himself to a study of Buddhism and the teachings of his spiritual mentor, the Dalai Lama, was commercially surprising and remarkable in that it happened at all.

It was also ironic.

He rebounded back into public notoriety in *Pretty Woman* and as the psychopathic cop in *Internal Affairs* through his sexual attributes. It was those same qualities, along with very obvious homoerotic undertones, that had forced him down from the pedestal of iconoclastic acclaim that he had reached in the early 1980s, when he discovered that his naked body could no longer stand the heat, and retired from the kitchen into his austere, monastic study to read his books on philosophy and religion.

Aficionados of Richard Gere's early career will have no difficulty in recalling a memorable scene from *American Gigolo* that set him firmly in the 'go' mode as far as Hollywood was concerned, launching him on a career that was in part to be determined by his ability to inspire reaction among a diverse audience, male and female, straight and gay. Some say that scene went on to shape his life, because it gave the mysterious Richard Gere his first screen presence, which was retained in the mind's eye of the audience as the character with whom he would be most popularly identified, the character audiences imagined he really was.

In *American Gigolo* he is first to be glimpsed as the body-beautiful male prostitute Julian Kay as he struts into the renowned Polo Lounge at the Beverly Hills Hotel, brushes off his expensive sports coat, palms the maitre d' some folding money and surveys the scene. He spots a well-dressed woman, apparently wealthy and alone. Noticing that she addresses the waiter in French, he does the same.

Moving quickly to her table, he ingratiates himself with her.

'Excusez-moi,' says the bilingual hooker.

She is startled but then realises it is a pick-up and allows herself to be flattered by the situation – handsome young man takes up with older woman – and eventually is surprised to discover that he wants money. It's a classic hustle but she is happy to go along.

The woman is played by former Revlon model turned actress Lauren Hutton. It remains to this day her best role, and in that respect, the film, filled with its sophisticated sleaze, gave both her and Richard Gere the kind of imprint that is long remembered. As director and writer Paul Schrader said at the time, he aimed to make a movie that, like one of his earlier works, *Taxi Driver*, would have a long shelf life because of its in-depth analysis of a particular aspect of a timely social phenomenon when men began to discover and use their sexuality to change their class and their lives, just as women had done for years. Schrader has a knack of allowing his characters to wallow in the more murky waters of American life.

Gere's performance in this movie was the one which took him into the realms of bankability. He was laid-back and cool, almost shy, and he was said to have put a curious notion in the minds of female filmgoers: that if women weren't paying him for his devoted attentions, Gere, in the character of Julian Kay, would have been paying them. Apparently, the tingling sensations evoked by his love-making, effected with an appealing, vulnerable quality, brought women members of audiences to the edges of their seats, and produced a somewhat unexpected side effect: because of the various undercurrents of gay involvement in the plot, he became similarly attractive to homosexuals.

And thus he became one of the few actors in Hollywood who in his audience appeal crossed the gay-straight divide with ease. As such, he became a media target long before he was a 'world-famous star' and, like Warren Beatty for more traditional reasons, often found himself in the headlines not so much through his roles as for his sex appeal. Rumours that he was gay, or at least bisexual, began after this, his first major movie, when, displaying a lean, well-proportioned body, a soft voice and almost retiring manner, he became the object of fantasy to adoring fans and was immediately deluged with letters offering him assorted pleasures should he care to indulge.

John Travolta, who had originally been cast in the role of Julian Kay, spotted the danger and pulled out of the project, ditching a $1 million fee plus a percentage in the process, for fear of becoming dogged by what was then – and still is for that matter – considered by Hollywood an unwanted fan club of mixed gender. Gere had no such qualms, and once discovered, he went on to capitalise on the situation. The sullen look, the heavy dark eyes, the muscular body and the pouting lips promoted Richard Gere from an interesting career off-Broadway into one of the heartthrob movie actors of the early 1980s.

American Gigolo was a turning point and one in which it is possible to identify the beginnings of Richard Gere's intense study of how to achieve and maintain star status on an acting talent that some have regarded as at best rather restrained. 'It's flattering to be desired,' he once said, 'flattering that people accept the reality of the characters I play. But in the end, the characters that are given life through me have an existence of their own, and I take no responsibility for them outside of their artistic context. It's ridiculous to assume that because I play a gigolo or any other character onscreen, I must play the same role off-screen. I'm an actor. I refuse to give up who I am because of what people expect me to be.'

He found difficulty in hammering down that concept, and it became almost impossible to deflect what he considered intrusive and invasive questioning about his private thoughts, of the kind that stars since Hollywood was invented have been expected to reveal for public consumption. De Niro and Al Pacino, known for their own firm rule of distancing their lives from their art, were positive chatterboxes compared with Gere's guarded defensive and often antagonistic responses to media enquiries. He kept the press at bay, never allowed a writer into his apartment, never let them watch him work, never appeared on television, never ever spoke about his love life. The media responded in the time-honoured tradition. They proceeded to take him apart.

★ ★ ★

The starting point of his journey was not one of usual thespian ambition, burned into the heart through a talent shown at school or encouraged by college tutors who spotted potential acting ability. There was none of that, and in fact he did not even contemplate in his youth that his working life might take him in that direction. At best, the performing arts was a possible career attraction only through his proficiency on the cornet, as well as several other instruments, and his interest in composing. Gere slid into acting almost accidentally and his elevation to superstar status was not only an unexpected achievement from his own point of view but came as a shock to his staunchly Methodist middle-class family.

He was born Richard Tiffany Gere in Philadelphia on 29 August 1949. In his early childhood his parents moved to the outskirts of Syracuse, in the northerly reaches of New York state, close to Lake Ontario, a superb location for his formative years. The countryside was and is idyllic and the city of Syracuse itself, with a population of more than 600,000, offered fine facilities and a diverse spread of cultural activities, even if the young Richard Gere did not avail himself of them as he later wished he had.

The University of Syracuse, with some 20,000 students, has always been a major focal point of the area. The city was known for its cultural possessions, such as a symphony orchestra, two excellent museums and a theatre specialising in European films. It attracted several major multinational industrial conglomerates, among them General Electric, but the environs were generally unspoiled, with mile upon mile of farmland and attractive countryside leading down to the shores of Lake Ontario an hour's drive away.

Homer Gere, Richard's father, was an insurance salesman who managed to maintain a decent standard of living for his growing family. He was a man of God-fearing principles and a regular church-going habit, to which he ensured his children adhered.

Richard Gere himself likened his father to a minister who was always ready to lend a helping hand. His parents were strict in terms of the principles and standards that they expected of their five children but otherwise, in Gere's own words, were 'sweet and loving'. It was, by all accounts and his own recollections, a typical middle-class American family existence with few untoward events, and in that regard somewhat unusual for a Hollywood superstar. Those without some kind of quirkiness to their upbringing are certainly in the minority. Quite often in film biographies – especially those written by studio publicists – childhood is punctuated by colourful and even dramatic events or parents with abusive tendencies or addictions that provide modern therapists with areas for deep soul-searching.

Gere's childhood was normality personified. He stayed out of trouble, had a half-decent school record, was a regular churchgoer, attended Bible class and the boy scouts, and so on. His family all shared common interests, although his sister Susan remembers, 'If you look at his baby pictures, you would see that he was brooding at the age of two.'

The Gere children all progressed through their early life uneventfully. Homer was a good provider and the family, within limits, enjoyed good times, pleasant holidays and a fairly regimented but homely atmosphere. At school, Richard was the lesser performer among his brothers and sisters in terms of academic results, and as Gere himself pointed out, they were all quite unlike their parents, although they grew up from a common cultural base. This in turn he believed was inherited from his mother's side of the family. 'The Gere side,' he recalled, 'were all earth-oriented people. My mother, on the other hand, came from a very neurotic, petit-bourgeois family.' His older sister studied psychology, using what Gere described as 'Zen and dance therapy'. A younger sister studied ballet while one brother became a concert pianist and the other a dance critic.

Music was a constant presence in the Gere family and it captured Richard's interest from the age of thirteen, at a time when the great bands and rock performers of the sixties were emerging, although at the time he was steered by his tutors to the classical side. He played trumpet initially, and later switched instruments, becoming versatile in several, notably the guitar.

If there was any early indication that he might follow a career in the theatre it occurred only briefly when, in his early teens, he and Susan would entertain the family after dinner with their impersonations. However, like thousands of other teenagers, inspired by the Beatles and Bob Dylan, as well as modern jazz groups and blues bands like B.B. King, he formed a small group to play rock for themselves and more standard music for weddings and social events.

At sixteen, he was proficient enough on the trumpet to be invited to appear as a soloist for the Syracuse Symphony Orchestra in a performance of Handel's *Messiah*. By then, he was also a capable performer on piano, guitar, banjo and sitar, and it was his interest in music that first brought him into contact with the theatre. Unlike many of his contemporaries in the acting profession, he did not step out on to the boards straightaway as an actor. He began by writing the music for school productions, although eventually he was persuaded to take minor acting roles, too. From that point, he had no trouble winning leading roles.

At the time, he was just as interested in sports, especially gymnastics, and it was then that he developed something of an obsession about getting his body in good shape. William Fisher, a contemporary of Gere's at high school, and who grew up to become a NASA astronaut, remembers the actor as someone who was never pushy, never put his head above the parapet. 'He was very quiet most of the time,' said Dr Fisher. 'And he was certainly not a joker. On a scale of one to ten, I'd rate his sense of humour at three. To me, he was just another ugly guy.'

Gere was also a product of the age, coming into his early maturity and graduating from high school at the time of the great undercurrents of activity that were grasping the attention of the youth of the American nation, although emanating as much from Europe, through the British music scene, the French student riots and the emerging revolutionary groups in Germany and Italy, which all had their effect on the world's counterculture movement.

The explosion of protest and violence had seen the assassinations in 1968 of Robert Kennedy and Martin Luther King, the upsurge of black power, the Vietnam war claiming its 40,000th American victim, fever-pitch anti-war demonstrations, draft-card burning and draft dodgers escaping to Canada and other shores.

Liberalism blossomed, much to the chagrin of the guardians of the public morals, J. Edgar Hoover, head of the FBI, and President Nixon, who gazed in horror upon the American west coast, home of the 'tune in, turn on, drop out' philosophy. Meanwhile, film and theatre were pushing out their own boundaries. Stage censorship in London ended in 1969 and the musical *Hair* was playing to packed houses, as did Kenneth Tynan's *Oh Calcutta!* when it opened in New York the same year. John Lennon and Yoko Ono allowed the world's media to attend their bed-in to protest at the war, and Jack Nicholson, Peter Fonda and Dennis Hopper smoked real dope in the 1969 anthem to the era, *Easy Rider*. The prevailing social culture as Gere was about to leave home was a confusing mess of psychedelic fads, fashions and philosophising.

Syracuse, close to the Canadian border, was hardly the centre of the universe in this era of protest and new-found freedom. If anything it was well behind the times. Gere describes his late teens as being 'full of punks, motorcycles, leather jackets, knives, violence, the whole James Dean–Brando bit.' That was the uniform of a bygone era, and the once stylish leaders of the pack were decidedly out of fashion as the kaleidoscopic, acid-dropping age of flower power and meditation caught hold. But in Syracuse, Gere was seen as a rebel. Robert Strother, his junior high school geometry teacher, said he stood out because of it. 'This area is very conservative and so when Dick [as he was known in those days] went to the long hair, the leather jacket and dark glasses, it was seen as rebellious. I don't doubt that he's done some bizarre things since . . . but he is not an open person. He's very within himself. He won't walk across the living room to say hello.'

Charles Parry, a religious scholar in Syracuse, was one of Gere's best friends at school. 'We got up to the usual pranks. At our school, fraternities were very important. But Dick and I thought that the initiation ceremonies for new members were awful. Some involved urinating over the pledges to join the fraternity. In protest, we formed our own joke fraternity, called the Royal Order of the Mystic Carp – and nearly got expelled because they thought we were starting a religious cult.'

Otherwise, said Parry, their schooldays passed without great incident. 'Dating was never a big thing with Dick and he was pretty shy around girls. In many ways, he was an introspective, modest kid and some people mistook this for surliness or coldness, but he wasn't like that at all.' This was to be the story of his life.

Even so, Gere did usually manage to run against the grain, one way or the other, to make himself stand out. An athletics colleague, George Hobbs, recalled that the school team always wore a maroon jumper with a white initial G emblazoned on it, for Gymnastics. 'Dick ordered one in white, with a maroon G,' said Hobbs. 'That was Dick's way of expressing himself and, also, when the county gymnastic competition came up, he won top prize.' He'd begun too to take leading roles in the school plays, and was cast as the King of Siam in their version of *The King and I*, which gained him his first review in the local newspaper.

With his attentions diverted by these extracurricular activities, his school grades never made encouraging reading for his parents, who hoped their son would seek a profession. Even so, he remained on the path of conformity for the time being, by getting a place at the University of

Massachusetts, in Amherst, an achievement which owed more to his prowess in gymnastics and athletics than to his academic qualifications. He was never certain that he even wanted to go to university. He did not make friends easily outside his own circle and had always been something of a loner.

His aimless two years on the Amherst campus shed a half-light on his acting talent. He began to turn towards the smell of greasepaint, edging cautiously towards the college drama group. Soon he was in the thick of things, appearing in Pinter plays like *The Birthday Party* and *The Caretaker*. 'I found it a liberating experience,' Gere recalled, 'and I suppose that's what it's all about in acting, that you discover as I did for the first time that you can get outside yourself and become another jerk you're not responsible for.' But still at that stage he never contemplated it seriously as a part of his future.

He chose to major in philosophy, which was the first demonstration of his tendency towards deep thought and soul-searching that would remain with him down the years and lead him to spiritual contemplation and, eventually, his contact with the Dalai Lama.

He took quite seriously the examination of his personal attitudes and sensitivities. He filled his college hours reading up on Freud and Jung, and like most people of that age, confronted himself with questions that were as much about self-discovery as about the world at large. He admitted: 'There were all those things I couldn't answer. I kept asking why, why, why? But the answers I got from courses seemed to be meaningless. And so in that respect, my first two years at college seem to me now to have been a destructive experience.'

Even so, he did come to local attention in 1969 for his appearance in a university production of *Hamlet*. The drama critic for the *Greenfield Recorder* wrote: 'Richard Tiffany Gere did what he could to put life and conviction into the role, but he raised very little sympathy.' How often

Gere was to read that latter phrase.

The notice did nothing to inspire him, although a quality that set him apart was noticed by Vincent Brann, who directed the production: 'He would always sit way back in the darkness when I was discussing a day's work with the cast. He wore sunglasses even at night. The other kids in the company were in awe of him.' But it was the university's drama professor, Doris Abramson, who pinpointed the aspect that would eventually be the making of him: 'Although I felt he was very talented, what he stood out for was his body . . . the girls fainted at it. He was always very, very serious and aloof but he was a very beautiful youth.' When he first became famous, Doris used to boast that she taught him 'everything he knows', but she dropped the claim after seeing him in *American Gigolo*.

Gere began to seek escapism rather than continue his studies, and this led to him spending more and more time in the local picture palaces, usually alone. 'I would walk around puzzling things out in my brain and then disappear into the movies,' he said. 'I did not have too many friends, so I would often sit there for five or six hours, often watching the feature twice so that eventually I found I was actually studying the films rather than watching them for pleasure, especially when it was an Antonioni movie – like *Blow-Up* – and I began to seek out non-Hollywood films, like those by Robert Bresson who was especially prolific in the late sixties and early seventies.'

There was, however, still no plan forming in his mind about future employment. At the end of his second year he left college feeling depressed and unsure of himself. He found the course hard going and somehow could not envisage completing it. Nor would he. That summer, events fell into place that would change his life and provide him at last with a goal.

One of his few college pals had arranged to have an audition to become a member of the cast of the renowned summer stock company based at the Provincetown Playhouse at Cape Cod.

Needing some moral support, Gere's friend invited him along for the trip, and they agreed that he might as well audition too.

Gere, at this stage, looked every inch the modern James Dean. He was a naturally shy person who was always softly spoken except in a rage or on the sports field. His personality was one of restrained politeness, though he was often caught with a sullen expression which many read as mean and moody arrogance – hence his lack of friends. He had thinner features then, high cheekbones above pinched cheeks, and a darkly handsome face beneath a mop of unkempt, shoulder-length hair.

He attended his audition in the only clothes he had taken, Brandoesque torn jeans, leather jacket and sweaty T-shirt. One of the resident directors at the Cape Cod theatre that summer, Bill Roberts, listened to him from the stalls as he gave his offering. 'To be brutally frank,' said Roberts, 'when I first saw him, I thought . . . punk! He did not seem that interested in what was going on. Then he gave his reading, which I thought was brilliant. Even so, Richard still did not seem that enthused by the task at hand. In fact he appeared quite indifferent. I decided to take a chance, because his audition so impressed me, and I then witnessed his true excitement when I posted the cast list with his name on it. Looking out of my window, I saw him run down the beach and hurl himself into the sea.'

The theatre signed him up for the summer for the princely salary of $28 a week. It was the beginning of an impressive, if fitful, theatrical apprenticeship. He had no training as an actor apart from a couple of college plays. He had not taken any university subjects which were allied to the performing arts, and his knowledge was limited to what he had learned in the only place that had managed to attract his regular attendance, the cinema.

He would, in fact, learn his craft directly by working at it, without tutors, long lectures from worthy professors or meaningful debates on the subcurrents of Chekhov, Ibsen or Ionesco, or hours spent studying acting techniques. He would be pushed on to the stage before a notoriously critical audience, equipped only with a desire to succeed and the basic instruction to speak loud and clear and 'make sure they can hear you at the back'.

But in the eyes of many, there was no better place to start out than where Richard Gere found himself that summer of 1969 – in a tight-knit company in which there was no room for temperament, prima donnas or special favours. They were set a punishing schedule of plays which each ran for two weeks, so that while one was being played nightly, with a matinée on Saturdays, the company had to rehearse during the day to prepare the next one.

The plays listed for production were diverse and never easy. The six performed that summer included Tom Stoppard's celebrated *Rosencrantz and Guildenstern Are Dead*, with which the playwright had made his name at the Edinburgh Festival two years earlier, and Tennessee Williams's *Camino Real*. By the second or third production, Gere was taking leading roles and his learning curve shot off the graph. As he recalled for a 1990 interview with *Vanity Fair*, the homoerotic subtext to his career also began there: 'At that point, Provincetown was the gay capital of the world, so that was a whole new learning experience.'

Nothing, apart from music, had retained his interest and attention in the same way as the theatre did, and by the end of the season he was already thinking in terms of an acting career. He even had a ready-made opportunity present itself. Director Bill Roberts had taken a new post for the winter season as production designer with the Seattle Repertory Company. He invited Gere to go along with him.

Crunch time came when Gere went home to Syracuse to tell his parents that he intended to drop out of university. They were dumbfounded by his decision, and came out with the cautionary words that the parents of performers since time immemorial have recited: The world is full of unemployed actors – can't you think of something more constructive to do with your life?

Gere admitted that he did not begin to understand his father's fears: 'At the time I just thought they were bourgeois. My father knew what I refused to accept . . . that I would have to go through hell and he just didn't want to see it. I was at that stage of my life when I could not face going back to the boredom of being talked down to; I didn't want what I thought was that amorphous middle-class nowhere status. I wasn't even sure I wanted to make a career in the performing arts, but once I had decided to take a look, my parents were loving and supportive, although I don't think they ever understood what I was going through.'

That autumn, he joined Roberts in Seattle, enjoying the status of a breadline actor on $75 a week, which was barely enough to feed himself after paying the rent, light and heat on his room. He took part-time jobs in bars and played the piano at fashion shows to supplement his wages, and kept telling himself that it would all be worthwhile because, as everyone else kept reminding him, he was getting the best training possible for an actor. He might well have convinced himself had he also found enjoyment in his new life in Seattle.

The fact was, he didn't. The repertory company was a much more commercially disciplined organisation, changing productions every month, and sooner if they weren't doing the business. Gere did not get the kind of roles he had been awarded in summer stock, although he was cast in the challenging lead in *Volpone* and wrote some incidental music.

After the pleasant summertime experience at Provincetown, he rather precociously felt he was not getting the kind of breaks he deserved, and the whole experience began to challenge his belief that his future lay in the theatre. As the weeks and months dragged by, he became increasingly disillusioned, and by the summer of 1970 he and the Seattle repertory had parted company. He used what little money he had been able to set aside to buy a second-hand van, equipped it with a sleeping bag and took to the road, setting off across country, past his home state and into Vermont.

He ended up in a small commune of like-minded souls of that post-hippie age, camped on the side of a mountain. There he teamed up with a group of other youngsters to form a rock band. They called themselves The Strangers and wrote songs and rehearsed for six weeks, with Gere himself on guitar and lead vocals. However, their enthusiasm soon evaporated as they discovered their incompatibility. The dream ended as abruptly as it had begun and Gere climbed back into his wagon and hit the road again.

At that point, he had no idea what he was going to do with his life. At twenty years old, he felt that he had three options. He could go back home and resume his education, or look for a job locally. Or he could head south to New York. He surmised that if he was going to get serious about acting, he had only one choice . . . to make for the great metropolis. He was well aware of all the horror stories about what life could be like in the loneliest city on earth. But as many before and since have discovered, it is the best place to be taken seriously as an actor. In Hollywood, as he would discover later, they look for 'stars' as opposed to actors, and those who have that potential become commodities.

There was also no longer any real training ground in the film capital. The much derided and hated studio system had finally collapsed a decade earlier. Long gone were the days when young hopefuls could turn up at the studio gates and hang around until they were discovered, or succeed in attracting the eye of a casting director for minor parts in a B-movie that might lead to greater things.

New York had to be the starting point for kids without contacts or training, and anyway Gere was aiming at the theatre, not films or television, and so Broadway and its surrounds remained the only sure route for a young performer to test himself against the uncertainties of an actor's life. If only he'd known it, the place was teeming with triers – but it was also a good time to be there.

New York in the early 1970s was buzzing with a new breed of actors, writers, directors and film-makers ready to make their mark. The period was almost a rerun of the late forties and early fifties when the city produced a batch of great new actors, like Brando, Clift, Dean, Monroe, Newman and McQueen, along with boundary-moving directors like Elia Kazan, Stanley Kubrick, Sidney Lumet and Arthur Penn, many of them emanating from the Actors Studio and its associated tutors of the American method style of acting, which in turn inspired the quest for new realism by writers and directors.

As Gere headed for New York, a whole new generation of actors and film-makers was emerging, notably a group who were to become most influential in the modern cinema, Steven Spielberg, George Lucas, Brian de Palma and Martin Scorsese. Among the budding actors, Robert De Niro and Al Pacino had already spent half a decade trying to find a toehold on the climb to fame. They, at least, had knowledge of the city, and a home. They were both New York born and bred and unlike Gere had proceeded through the more conventional route of intensive training in acting academies to reach the early rungs of the ladder.

Pacino, hungry and struggling for recognition, spent his days and nights during the late 1960s at the Actors Studio, that most controversial of institutions which produced a generation of America's most stylistic method actors. According to the official history of the studio, it was Pacino's 'home and family' and for a time even assisted him financially with a grant from the James Dean Fund, set up to aid new actors in dire financial straits.

De Niro, meanwhile, was among many famous students of Stella Adler, a rigid exponent of the Stanislavski method, whose directives he has applied throughout his career. But apart from being places of learning, these academies of acting were also familial in outlook, and the camaraderie among their students helped many struggling actors through hard times – a fact which Pacino recognised some years later when he anonymously donated $25,000 to set up a new fund at the Actors Studio to enable it to continue its tradition of 'family' help.

Richard Gere had no access to these centres of excellence for his craft, where would-be actors could meet, practise and, if they were lucky, get noticed by producers and directors who came to watch their productions. Anyway, at the time he was not even sure that he had either the stamina or the ability to go for mainstream acting, and so began to use his talent for music as a starting point.

Chapter Two

London Calling

New York has a special place in the hearts, minds and memories of many of the most iconoclastic movie stars of the recent past. Maureen Stapleton, the Oscar-winning character actress, once told me how she and Marlon Brando lived in a seedy apartment building equipped with only cold running water. Michael Douglas and Danny DeVito shared a less than salubrious bedroom when they were starting out. Warren Beatty left the comfort of his middle-class home to take up residence in a stinking single room in a rat-infested building. James Dean recalled his early days in the city: 'The first few weeks I was so confused that I strayed only a couple of blocks from my room . . . I would watch three movies a day to escape from my loneliness and depression.'

So the tale is a familiar one, and nothing had changed when Richard Gere arrived. New York was still the same hostile place, and desperately competitive for anyone starting out in the performing arts. Struggling actors with high hopes and ambitions invariably find themselves waiting on tables, peeling potatoes, cleaning cars and living in rotting squalor in unsalubrious areas while they try to make a go of it. Only a tiny percentage make it through the maze: as Kirk Douglas pointed out to his son when he decided to make acting his career, at any one time 85 per cent of American actors are unemployed.

Initial enthusiasm is seldom dulled by such warnings and the routine never changes: find a contact, spend your last few dollars on some photographs, search the listings and begin the endless round of auditions. Rejection becomes a way of life. The lucky ones might get a place in a play, way off Broadway, that attracts a small crowd nightly, and then folds after a week. They soldier on, hoping that one day the spotlight will shine upon them, disregarding the statistical truth that only half a dozen youngsters in any given decade will make it into the big time.

Gere was no different from the rest. There were dozens of talented kids on the streets of the Big Apple with exactly the same aspirations that he possessed, and many of them with a good deal more commitment and talent. He took a room in a ruin on the Lower East Side – a place where 'they don't deliver mail and the Fire Department doesn't even answer an alarm'. Like James Dean, he discovered that the only benefit of being out of work was that it gave him the chance to see a lot of movies, and he sought out the unusual, mostly the European films which were very much the rage at the time. He remembered seeing a couple of movies by Rainer Werner Fassbinder, the fashionable German director whose work was just being noticed in the US for its despairing commentary on the state of modern society, along with the latest from Werner Herzog, Fassbinder's compatriot.

There was ample time to take in the movies because work was hard to find. Gere could offer little more than a handsome physique, a musical talent and a sparse CV padded out slightly by his few months' experience in rep. He had virtually no contacts or friends. 'I looked up an old girlfriend, but she did not want to know I was alive,' he recalled. There was only one person he could turn to – Janet Roberts, wife of Provincetown director Bill, who was a literary agent in the city.

She was at least welcoming and offered a haven in times of need and depression. She also put him in touch with a theatrical agent, Ed Limato, then with one of the largest managers of star names, International Creative Management, an organisation so vast that it seldom looked at any clients who were not already established. In fact, the introduction turned out to be Gere's lucky break, one that few actors at the start of their careers could ever hope to meet.

It was also the beginning of a long-running association. 'I had never seen him work,' Limato recalled, 'but then let's face it, hardly anyone had. But I was impressed by his manner. Oh, sure enough he looked like another long-haired rebel with a guitar, and there were plenty of them around. But he was a different-looking guy. Beneath the uniform I could envisage the quality of a leading man. He was handsome, and he had a hint of unpredictability, even danger, to him.'

Weeks passed before Limato found him work, but when he did, it suited Gere's talents exactly, because it focused more on music than on pure acting ability. A new rock opera called *Soon*, whose producers had hopes of it mirroring the success of *Hair*, was opening in a near-Broadway theatre.

The cast included several new stars, including actor Barry Bostwick, noted for his uncanny resemblance to James Stewart. Bostwick had just made his big-screen début in a film entitled *Jennifer On My Mind*, in which Robert De Niro had a bit part, and would later star in the movie version of *The Rocky Horror Picture Show*, with Tim Curry and Susan Sarandon. Also in among the leads in *Soon* was the singer and comedy actress Nell Carter, who was also in the film version of *Hair*.

From Gere's point of view this was a decidedly good start, from nowhere to near-Broadway within such a short time. For one who did not make friends easily, he also found the companionship that goes with every production enjoyable, and the work was doubly encouraging because it gave him the opportunity of bringing the more established side of his talent, the music, into play.

The cash-starved producers were quick to take advantage when they discovered that they had in their midst a young singer-actor who could compose music as well as play. They commissioned him to write a couple of new songs, and he was also assigned to play several instruments on stage – 'more instruments than the entire band, and for less money than anyone else,' he recalls.

Director Robert Greenwood remembers Gere for his energy and enthusiasm: 'He was a real worker, came early and was always the last to leave. He was very green then, of course, but he had a special quality, never pushy or over-the-top, and I had no doubt in my mind he would become a star.' Rehearsals began as New York's renowned icy December winds began to swirl around the skyscrapers. Gere returned home for Christmas with tales to tell and full of hope for a successful opening.

However, like so many well-intentioned productions, the musical did not take long to fall into New York's showbiz graveyard. *Soon* opened on 11 January 1971 at the Ritz Theatre – and closed the following night. The torment was all the greater for Gere because it was his first big job. 'It was a painful time,' he admitted, 'and my family shared my disappointment. In the months afterwards, I found myself on the railing of the East River – trying not to jump in.'

The loneliness and the social undercurrents of New York hit him badly, and were relieved only when he became friendly with a dance student and began to attend classes at the American Ballet Theatre as an observer. Although he did not participate, he studied ballet movements and disciplines with rapt attention. He filled the rest of his time searching for work and taking odd jobs to keep himself at survival level. Gere reckons it took him two years to get the lie of the land in New York, gradually learning that the complexities of the city's 'geography' had nothing whatsoever to do with the street map of New York.

Life in the Big Apple was far more intricate than simply negotiating Manhattan's fairly straightforward grid system. The long avenues and the crisscrossing streets were simplicity itself to manoeuvre. Deeper knowledge, however, was necessary to understand the social and professional scene, which altered dramatically through each section and district, from the stigma of living on the Lower East Side, on through the artiness of SoHo and Greenwich Village, into the seedy red-light zones around 42nd Street, the commerce of midtown Manhattan and finally the snobbishness that abounded uptown around Central Park. For Gere it was really a case of careful selection, guiding himself towards the areas which were likely to give him what he wanted. New York, as Truman Capote once described it, is a place that once mastered 'can become anything you want . . . you can hide, have secrets and have friends that your friends don't know that you have'.

It was a process that did not occur to Richard Gere overnight; it took several years before he mastered the elements of the city, until it had become what he wanted. To begin with he was unsure of himself and his ability. He made no bold steps and did not venture towards the better-known acting establishments that might have placed him in the direct line of fire, where he would have had no alternative but to test himself in front of people who could judge – like the high priests of New York method acting who had witnessed the evolution of several generations of actors, to whom, later in his career, Gere would be compared.

It was Robert Greenwood, director of the ill-fated *Soon*, who also gave Gere his next role, which allowed him to maintain a foot in both the acting and music camps. Greenwood had been hired to put together another off-Broadway musical drama and asked Gere to audition for the leading role.

The production was based upon the life of 1960s American cult figure Richard Farina, who made his name as a singer, songwriter and poet and recorded several albums featuring his own darkly evocative lyrics about life and death which he wrote with his wife Mimi, sister of Joan Baez. In the last months of his life, he also wrote a novel entitled *Been Down So Long It Looks Like Up To Me*.

Farina did not live to see his book reviewed. He was killed in a motorcycle accident one night in April 1966, returning home from a publishing party to launch the novel. As a theatrical project, his story was at best a low-budget village proposition, and the title of the show, *Richard Farina: A Long Time Coming and a Long Time Gone*, barely aided audience arousal. From Gere's point of view, however, it was a heaven-sent opportunity, not just for the work, but in the progression of gaining stage experience, even though it was far off Broadway in one of the smaller theatres of Greenwich Village.

The role also called for some exacting research, because the work of the character he was playing was well within the recent memory of the audience, and those attracted to the show would doubtless be there because of their fascination for the subject. Farina had developed a very personal and unusual backing to his songs, using the popular folk instrument the dulcimer, as well as guitar. Gere found it both challenging and a joy to combine his musical ability with a further step in his experience as an actor.

Unfortunately, this show did not last either, opening in the autumn of 1971 and folding in less than a month. Gere was back on the streets, and more than a year would pass before he found work in the theatre again. He had, however, made two good friends to share the pain of his ill-fortune. One was a would-be photographer named Herb Ritts, who would feature in some of the most important stages of Gere's career and with whom he lodged for a while. The other was a young actress who had a role in the Farina play, twenty-year-old Penelope Milford.

Penelope, whom Gere once described as 'eccentric', was on the fringes of the New York scene, and thrown together by their joint struggle for survival, the friendship developed into a relationship which lasted more than six years. Penelope's own work was even more spasmodic than Gere's, and she achieved little film recognition until 1978 when she received an Academy nomination for best supporting actress for the anti-war movie *Coming Home*. 'Richard was not like some of the other more ebullient people who were around at the time, who were loud and trying to bolster their confidence and importance,' she recalls. 'Neither of us were known in the business and it was a time of transition for both of us. To me, the thing that attracted me most was that he makes it obvious that he needs you to love him. It is something, I think, that comes across in his movies and that's what I saw in him in those early days in New York.'

For the time being, however, the closure of the Farina project once again put him in line for unemployment benefit, and months passed before he was working again. He and Penny survived on occasional support from home and what money they could rustle up between them from odd jobs around New York. It was, as Gere describes it, a most debilitating time, a period that he has seldom referred to in the limited discussions he has allowed himself on his early attempts to formulate his career, other than to confirm that it was a stage of his life when 'obviously the whole universe was against me'.

The harsh lessons of that period were more about how to survive on a dollar a day, and like many of those in the same position – and there were hundreds – he did the usual round of temporary employment opportunities, largely the restaurants and eating houses around Greenwich Village. But his middle-class upbringing had instilled a curious pride that stopped him from taking 'front-of-house' jobs where he might be seen and recognised. He usually refused to wait on tables, and instead preferred the anonymous backroom role of washing dishes in the hot, steamy kitchens of Hungry Charlie's. He said he was too embarrassed to risk being spotted 'because people would know I was doing it for the money . . . back there by myself with the dishes and the steam, I could think. No one was hounding me because no one else wanted to do that job.' On one of the few occasions he did work waiting on tables, he found himself serving coffee and doughnuts to Robert De Niro, who still spent most of his time in New York and lived not far away in Greenwich Village. Gere went home that night swearing that one day he would get where De Niro was.

There is little from this whole period that he would discuss in the future, other than to confirm that these were his 'wrist-slitting days' in Manhattan. But though it may have seemed like an eternity arriving, help was at hand – in the shape of Barry Bostwick, with whom Gere had worked in *Soon*.

Bostwick, after his appearance in a couple of low-budget movies in the early seventies, went on to become the creator of the role of the macho gang leader Danny Zuko when the long-running nostalgic teenage musical *Grease* opened on Broadway. It was the role that John Travolta played in the film version of the musical opposite Olivia Newton-John. In late 1972, Gere became understudy to Bostwick and then learned that another company was being put together to open the show in London.

Gere auditioned successfully for the part of Danny Zuko for the British production, and by the year's end was in London for the West End rehearsals. Whilst there, he was also attracted to the renowned Chichester Festival Theatre and it was in that town that he equipped himself with a high-powered Triumph motorcycle. After the curtain came down on *Grease* each night, he put on his leather jacket and went off riding with a gang of real greasers, partly for enjoyment and partly to stay in character.

Gere had a decent reception in London for the West End run of *Grease*, although the show was never received there with the same enthusiasm as in the US. He was also introduced to the local scene by contacts he'd made in New York, and was soon being shown around the Chelsea area by a new pal, photographer, Michael Roberts.

Roberts discovered, however, that Gere had 'an amazing attitude problem' at the time. 'He was just incredibly rude to everyone I introduced him to, acting out his James Dean prototype. I'd take him to Tramps where Bianca Jagger and lots of our friends were dying to meet him. He'd turn up in his leather jacket and act around like a street kid.' The London crowd, to his surprise, found his eccentric behaviour amusing, and put it down to him coming straight from New York.

The London sojourn had a far more beneficial effect than simply achieving a starring role in a rock musical. Gere made the best possible use of his time there, meeting a number of British actors who in turn introduced him around. Among those he met was Frank Dunlop, one of Britain's most respected veterans of the classical stage. He was associate director of the National Theatre and its administrator until 1971. In 1970, he founded the prestigious Young Vic theatre company and was its long-time director.

Dunlop gave Gere a reading and then hired him for a production of *The Taming of the Shrew.* Gere thus became the first American actor to join the Young Vic company – a career highlight which overnight made a significant entry upon his CV, one that was to impress directors and producers in New York. He was cast in the role of Christopher Sly, the drunken victim of practical jokes in the two-scene prologue that sets up the story of Petruchio and Katherina.

London proved to be fertile ground, and his success in the role was repeated back in America when the Young Vic brought a touring company to packed houses in a Brooklyn theatre. Reviewers who came to take a look at the production by one of London's finest companies naturally paid some attention to the only American actor in the cast and gave him decent notices, describing his performance as funny and imaginative.

By then luck was running his way. The London experience had opened up a period in the New York theatre which would include some of his most interesting work. He took over from Barry Bostwick in the Broadway production of *Grease* and completed over 200 performances in the role. He secured a bit part in the TV series *Kojak,* which was followed by other TV offers, including a small role in a TV movie called *Strike.* But he dropped out of TV completely after appearing in a television special for the actress Marlo Thomas. In it he had to say one word – hello – but when it came to it, he froze completely. He declared that he would never do television again, because it was the 'most disgusting, humiliating experience of my life'.

The kind of recognition he really sought came when his agent Ed Limato was contacted by Judy Lamb, casting director for the famous Joseph Papp's Public Theatre. Lamb was one of the few people to have seen Gere in the single performance of *Soon,* while Joe Papp was the New York equivalent of Frank Dunlop – the man every actor would work for, often for virtually nothing. Pacino, De Niro, Dustin Hoffman, Meryl Streep and many others willingly joined his productions which brought them right back to the grass roots of New York theatre audiences.

Papp, born in Brooklyn in 1922, had formed a Shakespearian workshop at the Emanuel Presbyterian Church on the Lower East Side in 1952. Two years later, the workshop started performing free shows during the summer months in Central Park, and in 1962 it transferred to a permanent home in Central Park, the open-air theatre known as the Delcorte. In 1967, Papp opened his public theatre off Broadway with the American production of *Hair.* Later, he became director of the Lincoln Center.

By being selected for the part of Demetrius in Papp's production of *A Midsummer Night's Dream,* Gere had moved into upwardly mobile mode. The play was performed at the Lincoln Center and Gere's contribution was marked once again by some worthwhile notices. More importantly, it was exactly the right area for his own way of thinking.

At the time, according to those close to him, in spite of the 'punk' uniform he always wore his outlook remained decidedly middle class. He was a deep thinker, always trying to pull together the threads of his own existence, along with pondering the wider meaning of life. His preoccupations were more to do with the spiritual than the factual, and social concerns seldom entered his conversation. 'Richard could, in fact, be an absolute turn-off at times,' recalls one person who was close to him in those early days. 'I mean, we were all starting to look at moral issues at the time, but he would not get involved. He wasn't a social kind of person or even a pleasant person to a lot of people. He was definitely quite selective in who he became friends with and if you didn't become part of his mind's-eye scenario, he just ignored you. He was probably the rudest person I knew at that time. The point was that if he didn't like you, he would not even give you a reaction – as far as he was concerned you weren't there. It was odd. I suppose everyone is categorised – decent person, horrible or whatever – but with Richard it was difficult because actually very few people got to know him. He was always off to the left somewhere, never quite joining in. At the same time, his face could suddenly be taken by this amazing look of vulnerability that actually made you feel sorry for him and blame yourself that he wasn't part of the group. You'd want to go over and say, "Come on, Rich . . ." but then you'd remind yourself that he was just as likely to spin on his heel and walk away. He was the cause of his own isolation.'

Though still poor, nowhere near comfortable financially, Gere's run of good fortune did enable him to move from his dive on the Lower East Side to larger, more suitable accommodation. He took over an abandoned storefront in the West Village and set about converting it to a habitable abode. It was a plumber's shop before he moved in, ten feet wide and about twenty feet long, and divided into three rooms with two lofts and a fireplace. He filled the huge window on the street front with plants.

The only problem with the area was that after midnight, it tended to get rowdy, with clients leaving a raucous strip of gay bars taunted and sometimes attacked by gangs of teenagers who came to the area specially for the 'sport' of gay-bashing. One night, Gere himself was attacked. 'They probably thought I was gay,' he explained afterwards, 'because I had on a leather jacket and motorcycle boots. I've always worn that. I've been into motorcycles for years.'

Penelope Milford remained in his life, and had been his 'soul' girlfriend, she said, almost since they met. She was still 'a struggling actress' but with Gere experiencing better times, she shared the new apartment. There was no rigid routine to their relationship, nor was it one that relied upon total commitment. What Penelope saw in him was 'a single-minded devotion to making it in his career, and that meant theatre which he was absolutely in love with when he returned from London.'

If there was a turning point in Gere's career, that metaphorical fork in the road which leads a performer on to greater things, Penelope Milford believes it was the invitation to perform a new one-man, one-act play by Sam Shepard called *Killer's Head*. This was being staged at the American Place Theater, under the directorship of Wynn Handman.

The theatre was another prestigious showcase for up-and-coming actors. It was an intimate, in-the-round venue run on a subscription basis which ensured reasonably full houses and a guaranteed run for a specified time for any play staged. Shepard, born in Illinois, had moved to New York in 1960 and had also recently been in London, where his rock drama *The Tooth of Crime* was staged at the Royal Court Theatre in 1974.

His new work was a theatrical *tour de force* for Gere, who played the role of a convicted killer delivering a meandering monologue about his nonexistent future. Throughout the play Gere was strapped into an electric chair with a blindfold over his eyes. Few modern American playwrights have the sensitivity of Sam Shepard and few can match his intensity. This work was no exception and was as demanding for the audience as it was for Gere himself, who described it as a bizarre play but one with which he felt totally connected, yet in another way totally disconnected because of the blindfold. 'It was an absolutely non-narcissistic thing . . . I had to manufacture energy outside of my body. It was as though my body did not exist.'

He could not move a muscle while strapped to the chair, nor could he see through the blindfold and thus had no visual contact with his audience. Wynn Handman gave Gere the benefit of his personal coaching for the role, one of the few occasions Gere has actually received, or accepted, tuition. Handman said of Gere: 'He is serious, a devoted actor and an adventurous one. He goes very deeply into character and was spectacularly good in *Killer's Head*. It was no easy thing to do, holding the attention of the audience with just voice changes and expression from a half-hidden face.'

Reviewers well used to the experimental nature of many of the productions at the American Place had some complimentary things to say about his 'garrulous, virtuoso performance'. And as he finished the run, a movie offer arrived, the first of several that initially had him type-cast in roles that, to use his own description at the time of the Sam Shepard play, were bizarre. News of this young actor who could let loose some near-pathological intensity on stage had begun to filter into Hollywood.

He was cast in a small though noticeable role as a pimp in a United Artists movie, *Report to the Commissioner*, which showcased the winsome talents of Michael Moriarty in the starring role. It was a police melodrama of B-movie calibre, and hardly did justice to the abilities of Moriarty, who had recently co-starred in the film that launched Robert De Niro, *Bang the Drum Slowly*. But whereas De Niro had taken off, Moriarty, enigmatic and overly pleasant in every regard, had not made a major impact. Now he would see the same thing happen again – his movie launching an actor who was destined to become a much bigger star than himself.

Gere was never overkeen on the role he played in *Report to the Commissioner* and he excused himself by telling everyone that he'd done it just for the money. He wasn't keen on the picture itself either, a view which was shared by audiences everywhere. It was not a major production, and Gere was happy to return to the stage, still unsure that he was ready for the movies.

The money was good, even for a bit part, but he had found this first outing a thoroughly unsettling experience, almost as bad as television. In one of his first media interviews he trotted out a rather well-worn explanation that 'there are layers of energy between the people on stage and in the audience. It's also riveting to know that something might go wrong, whereas in film you just do it again.'

He completed filming in time to audition for a new Broadway opening – a sex farce by Alan Bennett, *Habeas Corpus*. Gere, in the role of a travelling falsies salesman, was cast opposite the British actress Rachel Roberts, who was currently living in America and doing a television series with Tony Randall. The play went into rehearsal in the autumn of 1975 but although it was decently received by the critics, American audiences did not take to this particular line in British humour and the play closed after ninety-five performances in February 1976.

Gere was immediately signed up by the well-known McCarter Theater, Princeton, New Jersey, to star in a revival of Clifford Odets' 1930s play, *Awake and Sing*. The work, one of the three most popular of Odets' important plays from this era, was first produced on Broadway in 1935 and its message of social conscience about a Jewish family fighting for survival during the Depression had barely dated. Gere's role of Ralph, the ambitious young son who longs for better days, was originally played by John Garfield, with whom Gere would often be compared. The producers in reviving this major hit of the 1930s even went so far as to find veteran actor Morris Carnovsky to recreate his role of Grandpa.

Media interest in Gere had so far been limited to occasional mentions, and he admitted that it was a low-profile life he was leading. 'You don't get your name in the papers,' he said, 'and you don't make any money. The pleasure is in the work, and in the learning, learning, learning.' It was also derived from the good reviews which he received for the New Jersey production, viewed by leading critics who gave him generous applause for his performance.

He auditioned almost immediately for a new off-Broadway production of Albert Innaurato's play *Earthworms*. It was a courageous move at that particular point in his career because the role he read for was the homosexual soldier lover of the character portrayed by art critic and Greenwich Village doyen, Rene Ricard. Gere's reading for the part was described by one person present as 'brilliant – we all sat there with our mouths gaping when he had finished, you know, like a star is born.' But audiences never got to see him in that play. It was already in rehearsal when he received a call from his agent: a bigger and better film opportunity was coming his way. At a time when he was on the brink of greater acclaim in the New York theatre, Gere moved on, and in fact after New Jersey would not appear on stage again for almost four years. At that moment, Hollywood was finally beckoning and his life was on the turn towards the movies that made him a star of the eighties.

Chapter Three

Heaven-Sent Opportunity

By the mid-1970s Gere had tested his talent in the competitive world of New York theatre and was surveying a changing scene on Broadway and its surrounds, in which serious drama was taking a back seat in the trend towards frothy stage entertainment. In a way, Gere had travelled the wrong way around the circle. He had started out in the froth of rock musicals and finished up playing Shakespeare, Clifford Odets, Tennessee Williams, Alan Bennett and Sam Shepard. He had mastered the art of survival in the city that gave him his start, but he was still never more than a few steps from the breadline and the unemployment office. He surmised that the situation would not improve.

Movies were stealing the thunder of the theatres, producing hard-hitting topical drama as the new breed of directors began to push into mainstream Hollywood. That period of the mid-seventies saw a collection of brilliant movies that would become time-tested successes – Sidney Lumet's *Dog Day Afternoon*, which he followed with *Network*, Milos Forman's *One Flew Over the Cuckoo's Nest*, Robert Altman's *Nashville*, Martin Scorsese's *Taxi Driver*, Stanley Kubrick's *Barry Lyndon* and Steven Spielberg's *Jaws*.

The male stars who came up for Oscar nominations at

this time included several with whom Gere had been compared, like Al Pacino, Robert De Niro and Jack Nicholson. As he looked around Broadway, with its declining attention to good drama, Gere made a conscious decision that it was time to move on, head west and make a serious attempt to break through into the movies – although as with most of his decisions, it was not an absolute declaration of intent.

For the time being, he wanted to retain a presence in New York, which would remain his home and his base. His own assessment of the situation was that: 'The theatre is not in a healthy state. A lot of what theatre has been doing for centuries is being done better in movies.' That was a somewhat broad statement to make and not entirely true. The truth lay in a more personal dimension, that of the ambition that eventually grabs hold of every budding star who is encouraged to believe that he has a particular talent.

The vehicle that would launch him was not an especially good example of the point he was trying to make, but it served its purpose. In the winter of 1975, his agent Ed Limato secured an audition with the New York director John Hancock, who was casting for a new movie being financed, among others, by Aaron Spelling, the brash new Hollywood mogul and creator of such soaps as *Dynasty*. Hancock was largely credited with launching the movie career of Robert De Niro in his excellent 1974 baseball tear-jerker, *Bang the Drum Slowly*. This, in turn, secured De Niro his memorable role in Francis Ford Coppola's *The Godfather Part II*, after which he took off.

Now Hancock had been charged with bringing to the screen a movie entitled *Baby Blue Marine*, a slight tale about the adventures of a World War II soldier who returns home pretending to be a hero. This role was played by Jan Michel-Vincent who had just appeared in Richard Brooks' *Bite the Bullet* with Gene Hackman and Candice Bergen.

Gere's relatively small part in the drama was a shell-shocked, psychopathic marine who forcibly trades uniforms with the 'hero'. His performance, however, was among the better moments of the film and gave sustenance to the green shoots of his growing reputation for moody characterisation. Largely on the strength of it, he moved on to the next level, and an important role in establishing his name among the people who mattered in Hollywood.

Among them, coincidentally, was a face from his past, Judy Lamb, who had hired him for his appearance in Joe Papp's production of *A Midsummer Night's Dream* and who had since joined Paramount Studios as a casting director. She was currently associated with a project which was earmarked for another hot new director, Terrence Malick, who had signed with Paramount for his second film after the unexpected huge acclaim for his 1973 début, *Badlands*.

The enigmatic Malick in fact directed only two movies – *Badlands* and this new project, *Days of Heaven* – before he left Hollywood, disillusioned, for Paris in 1979 and never returned. Over the years there have been rumours now and again that he was planning a comeback, but he never has, which is a great pity.

His directorial début with *Badlands* was heralded as an event of some significance and excitement. He wrote, produced and directed the film, which was based upon the true story of two young delinquents of the midwest of the 1950s who embark on an orgy of killings. The film, which showcased the talents of Martin Sheen and Sissy Spacek in their first major starring roles, was a masterpiece of narrated cinema, widely compared with Orson Welles and Abraham Polonsky.

His next movie was awaited with bated breath by critics and moguls alike. The latter were so enthusiastic that Malick merely had to outline his next screenplay, *Days of Heaven*, to Paramount to receive their go-ahead. He went on to complete the story, a superb evocation of human despair about a handful of people marooned together in a Texas panhandle in the year 1916.

At the heart of the story is a festering love triangle filled with deceit and betrayal. It is a very basic plot, concerning a young itinerant worker who arrives with his two sisters, except that one of them is not his sister at all but his girlfriend. He is hired for the grain harvest by a young, wealthy and very sick landowner. Thereupon the itinerant and his girl conspire to get her married to the farmer and so inherit his wealth when he dies.

Malick saw the plot as almost secondary to his great visions of emptiness, a vast sweep of oil-painting cinematography set against the grain-country landscapes. He had also decided, somewhat to Paramount's concern, against using well-known actors, arguing that established Hollywood stars would overshadow his narrative by bringing their own personas to the film. He wanted exactly the right actor for each role.

John Travolta was among those being considered, but in the meantime he had filmed *Saturday Night Fever* and the word was that he would be a major star by the time *Days of Heaven* came out. It was at that point that Judy Lamb suggested to Malick that he should interview an unknown New York actor named Richard Gere who, she said, possessed the right qualities, was similar in looks to Travolta, and actually might be just the man for the role.

Back then, in 1976, mere association with Malick would have put Gere into the spotlight and given him far greater prominence than might otherwise have been the case. That Malick should consider him for the lead in *Days of Heaven* put a shine on Gere's persona that was virtually unmatchable at that particular moment in his career, and overnight his name was added to the lists of all the major casting directors. When he signed the contract, Malick told him: 'This film will change your life.' Indeed it did. From that moment on, Richard Gere never looked back.

Gere himself takes up the story: 'Terrence Malick got in touch. We talked a lot and we did a lot of things on tape. He tried to match up actors. There was no screen test, *per se*. Genevieve Bujold had been set for the female lead but backed out, for her own personal reasons. The preliminaries seemed endless. It took months, during which time I had endless conversations with him before he finally offered me the role. It was as much to do with the selection of the other leading actors. He wanted to see the chemistry before it had begun, and in that I think he was quite remarkable.'

Malick on Gere: 'I couldn't be sure. He had not spoken more than a page of movie dialogue to that point which was OK by me. He was very quiet, very restrained, and I had to push to get a glimpse of the characterisation, the menace that I had been told he was entirely capable of and indeed had ably demonstrated in his theatre work. I had to be sure . . . and I had to be sure the actors matched my preconception of the characters.'

There was one more surprise for Gere. It was at this point that he discovered that the second male lead, the sick farmer whom he and his screen girlfriend conspire against, was to be played by Malick's friend and one of Gere's personal heroes, the playwright Sam Shepard, who had longed to be in the movies ever since he took a part in the 1969 film *Zabriske Point*, which he co-wrote with its director Michaelangelo Antonioni.

Later, after *Days of Heaven*, he went on to appear in many more films, including *The Right Stuff*, for which he received an Oscar nomination, and *Steel Magnolias* with, among others, Julia Roberts, the future co-star with Gere in the blockbuster *Pretty Woman*. But that was all in the future.

There and then, in the mid-seventies, Richard Gere and Sam Shepard, totally untried as film actors, were lined up by Terrence Malick to co-star with another unknown, Brooke Adams, whose only other credited role around that time was in Philip Kaufman's remake of the horror classic *Invasion of the Body Snatchers*, in which she starred with Donald Sutherland, Leonard Nimoy and Jeff Goldblum.

If there was a star in Malick's line-up of players and technicians, it was Nestor Almendros, the award-winning Spanish-American cinematographer, best known at that point for his work with the French director, François Truffaut. Malick felt strongly that the filming of the vast open plains where the story is set was as important to the movie as the acting in expressing the emotions of the characters.

Having selected his team, Malick moved them all to location filming in Canada, which apart from providing suitable landscapes also had the advantage of tax breaks for film-makers. For Gere and his fellow actors, it was a baptism of fire.

As with so many artistically based movies, with directors who have also written the script, it proved to be an arduous task getting Malick's mind's-eye visions and words on to film. The cast spent most of the time on remote Canadian prairies around Calgary, cooped up in cabins, while the director set up his shots and worked endlessly on the script. 'By the time we left, we were all crazed. Everyone was manic,' Gere recalled. 'Terry seemed to despise his own writing. We would be shooting a major scene, say in a wheatfield, and he'd stop us and say, "This is bullshit. Do something else." And so we would just improvise our lines. The script kept changing because Terry's a poet, often vague about what he wanted. We'd do take after take, and a three-page scene might finally end up slashed to two or three lines. What he wanted was a moment of truth, and you can't tell anyone what truth is and how to get it . . . he's a very cerebral and sensitive director and wanted a very special thing, a breath of life, something very difficult to communicate.'

The storyline of the film, in its edited form, always seemed to be subordinate to Malick's vision of the land, and he paid great attention to setting up some truly magnificent shots and images – a train crossing a wheatfield, workers huddled at their tasks, a spectacular fire, set up and filmed at night, a plague of locusts, tight close-ups of grasshoppers and even of the wheat seedlings pushing through the earth. These are interspersed with stark shots of the actors as the plot unfolds with minimal dialogue.

Gere, in the role of the immigrant worker Bill, is first seen in a mill in Chicago before he makes his way south to escape police after attacking his boss, taking with him his eleven-year-old sister and his girlfriend Abby. They end up in the Texas panhandle looking for work in the wheat harvest and there discover that the wide open prairies harbour their own dark secrets among the sparse community, with workers and animals alike becoming the victims of brutal foremen and landowners.

As outlined earlier, Bill is employed by a dying farm owner, played by Sam Shepard, and he and Abby devise a plan to make them all rich. However, once she has accepted the farmer's proposal of marriage, the plan begins to go awry. The farmer's health begins to improve, and then unexpectedly a real affection develops between the couple. Bill resolves to rescue his plan by violence, and both men end up dead. As in *Badlands*, Malick used the device of voice-over narration, in this case by Bill's sister, played by the young Linda Manz.

Gere was already on the very edge of his nerves when filming was completed and would then have a long, long wait to discover the critical reaction. This was one of the few occasions that he would become close to his leading lady, Brooke Adams, with whom he had both a personal and a professional relationship, doubtless because they were newcomers thrown together by the intensity of the work. 'I'd heard he was a serious actor,' said Adams, 'and I was afraid I'd make a terrible mess of it all. But it all turned out great from our point of view, because Richard was great to work with.' As it happened, Brooke was also Penelope Milford's best friend, and soon both actresses would audition for *Coming Home*. Adams remembers she was furious when Gere told her that Penny would be better for the part – 'and he was right, of course, but I didn't like to hear it at the time'.

Malick meanwhile went off into Paramount's editing rooms

for a marathon, almost epic, stitching together of the miles of beautiful footage that he could hardly bear to cut. It was almost eighteen months before he emerged, and by then Gere had made two more films.

Malick's movie was a stunning enterprise, though critical reaction for such a venture was always unlikely to be unanimous. An interesting aspect of the reviews was that many concentrated purely on the atmospherics and the cinematography – born out by the fact that Nestor Almendros won an Oscar for his work – and paid little attention to the acting performances. 'Can any description of Terrence Malick's *Days of Heaven* quite evoke the sense of wonder this film inspires,' wrote the influential critic Roger Ebert. 'It is a unique achievement – I can't think of another film anything like it.'

Ebert's words were overshadowed by others who described it as pretentious and overblown, claiming that the story was too slight and the characters overwhelmed by the landscape. But it is impossible to dismiss this film. It possesses a magnificence of its own that has to be viewed again and again like a masterpiece of art, and thus the star of it was the artistry of Malick himself. That much was evident from the reaction of the actors themselves when they saw it.

They were apparently astounded. It was not the film they thought they had made and they were, to say the least, surprised and agitated that some of their most dramatic scenes had been hacked down to a few sentences of dialogue, while others had even been cut completely in favour of Malick's scenic shots. Gere himself said, 'There were some major, dramatic passionate scenes, because it's a fucking incredible story, like something by Thomas Hardy. The way scenes are normally constructed, you sort of do elliptical dances until you get into the meat of a scene. But Terry he left in the elliptical dancing and cut out the meat.' Having said that, he went on to praise the film. *Days of Heaven*, in Gere's view, took its audience into 'primal territories' and he was full of admiration for the finished work.

It was left to his agent, Ed Limato, to answer the critics, who were mixed in their reception of Gere's performance. One welcomed this new screen actor as an interesting cross between Gregory Peck and Montgomery Clift, but *New York* magazine reckoned that 'Gere's anxious street-hustler intensity, modelled after De Niro's manner in *Taxi Driver*, doesn't seem to fit the period at all.' Several of the major critics did not even mention him.

Limato countered with the news that some of 'Richard's best scenes, his most dramatic takes, were edited out, never to be seen by film audiences.' But actually, though it was perhaps important at the time, it did not matter that much what the critics felt. From a personal standpoint, Gere was being spoon-fed by directors who could teach him much; it was certainly a most interesting start to his movie career and his next film was similarly instructive.

Long before *Days of Heaven* was released, word was about in Hollywood that Richard Gere was a new talent worth watching, and regardless of the controversy and heartache surrounding the Malick film, it gave him the kind of opening to his movie career that few actors have achieved. Gere himself described this period in his career in somewhat precious terms: 'I knew what was going to happen . . . the buzz was already in the air. I became what they call an industry star. People knew about me or heard about me and wanted to work with me, even though I was still totally unknown. The bloodsuckers are quick . . . always looking for the next guy to make a buck on . . .'

Not a nice way to talk about future employers, but near enough true, and he displayed a certain amount of courage in letting them know his feelings. In effect, he went from nowhere to stardom in one move and though the critics were lukewarm about the three films he had so far appeared in, he was already consolidating his position. His performance was, as is often the case with artistic movies, better received in Europe, where he won the Italian film industry's David Donatello award for Best Actor of 1978.

The fact that it took Malick so long to bring the film to public view had a beneficial side effect for Gere. Although he was nervous and apprehensive about the outcome, he did not have to concern himself with the prospect that his future depended upon it. Even as he was filming *Days of Heaven*, his most ardent supporter in Hollywood, Judy Lamb, had been promoting his talents to no lesser figure than Richard Brooks, one of Hollywood's most prolific directors.

Brooks was reaching the closing stages of a spectacular, if varied and occasionally patchy, career. Of high reputation as a star-maker in old Hollywood – albeit with a number of failures, too – the three dozen films which he had written or directed included a number of classics, and his list of credits ranged through a diversity of output starring some of Hollywood's finest: Humphrey Bogart in *Key Largo*, Glenn Ford in *Blackboard Jungle*, Elizabeth Taylor and Paul Newman in *Cat on a Hot Tin Roof*, Paul Newman again in *Sweet Bird of Youth* and Burt Lancaster in both *Elmer Gantry* and *The Professionals*.

Conversely, he was also accused of reducing Joseph Conrad's novel *Lord Jim* and Dostoevsky's *The Brothers Karamazov* to pulp, but regardless of his several catastrophes, Brooks was the kind of director every budding actor wanted to work with, simply for the experience of it.

As Gere concluded his work on *Days of Heaven*, Brooks had already started another project for Paramount, a screen adaptation of Judith Rossner's best-selling chilling novel, *Looking for Mr Goodbar*, a sex drama based upon a respectable teacher's quest for male companionship in singles bars. Brooks had cast Diane Keaton in the lead, and though he had tested a number of actors he had still not found someone for the role of Tony Lopanto, one of the lesser but more important roles in the picture, and which required a characterisation of considerable menace.

Judy Lamb suggested that Brooks might look at Richard Gere, and she produced a print of *Baby Blue Marine*, in which Gere was especially menacing, and managed to arrange a viewing of some of the rushes from *Days of Heaven*. On the strength of this recommendation, the director summoned Gere for a chat and introduced him to Diane Keaton, whose agreement was important to the chemistry of the movie. Gere was edgy and nervous when he met them, and having come straight from Canada, he knew nothing about the book, but thought it sounded like 'some crap novel'. He was a bolshie kid, even in front of greats like Brooks, whom he described as 'mad, crazy'. The director was certainly eccentric but it was hardly the place of a young whippersnapper like Gere to start doing a Freudian analysis on him – well, not publicly at least. The comments really did show his bad side – fast mouth and no respect for age and experience – although many of those he worked with would say that he wasn't really like that, and that his brash, rude manner was merely a cover for his shyness.

It was certainly true that Brooks had a quirky reputation. He had a particular obsession for secrecy over his scripts, especially those he had written himself. When he first contacted Gere, he gave him instructions that he should go to the nearest public telephone and call him. He did not want to risk being overheard or listened in to. When the meeting was arranged between them, Brooks would not give Gere a copy of the script, but merely tore out the lines that he would speak. He always did this, so that actors could not get a full appreciation of the work until he was ready to cast and go into rehearsals.

Gere discussed the role with Ed Limato in several late-night telephone conversations, his agent reassuring him that the sexual implications of the part and the image Gere might derive from it were of lesser importance than the boost his career would achieve by working with Brooks. Thus, when the director finally made up his mind and offered him the part, Gere accepted and reported to Paramount, where the filming of the early scenes had already begun.

In terms of experience, it was another episode that regardless of the eventual outcome was of considerable value to Gere's emergence as a Hollywood name. The story surrounding the film and the personalities involved also provides the ingredients of a fascinating scenario that could easily have been turned into a screenplay itself. Brooks, then sixty-six years old, was a very self-centred director who would not be moved from his own interpretations, and certainly not on this film, in which he had tampered considerably with the themes of the novel. He could at times be sensitive and understanding, and yet could explode into violent rages to achieve what he wanted from a particular scene.

The opportunity of playing opposite Diane Keaton, fresh from her Oscar-winning role in *Annie Hall*, was also important to Gere. She was a deep and interesting character actress, discovered, manipulated and made into a star by her erstwhile lover Woody Allen. She had been a struggling actress in New York around the turn of the decade until she landed a role in the stage version of *Hair*, when she was spotted by Allen and awarded a part in the theatrical staging of his *Play It Again Sam*. In the same year, she won the role of Al Pacino's second wife in *The Godfather* and then went on to star in four of Allen's 1970s movies, *Play It Again Sam*, *Sleeper*, *Love and Death* and *Annie Hall*. Only in the last did Allen allow her to diversify from the comic–straightman syndrome, a progression further aided by her dramatic role in *The Godfather Part II*.

It was Keaton's underlying and unexplored sexuality that apparently attracted Brooks into casting her as Theresa in *Looking for Mr Goodbar*. Her character was a teacher of deaf children who by night turned towards dangerous sexual experiences. In selecting her for the starring role, Brooks took a risk in that audiences had come to accept Keaton with a certain warmth. It might even be possible that neither he nor she herself could have imagined the audience reaction to her being cast in this film.

In Rossner's novel, her character was portrayed as a masochist, with deep childhood scars in her psyche. Brooks changed the emphasis and turned her into a carefree woman who drinks, takes drugs and falls into the wrong kind of company in the singles bars for the sheer pleasure of it. Thus his version became a message for the promiscuous women who go home with men picked up under seedy circumstances. In due course this would have rather unpleasant repercussions for both himself and Richard Gere, one of the fictional perpetrators of sexual excess with Theresa.

Gere's role of Tony, the animalistic hustler, was by no means a central character, but was again one of the most memorable. He swaggers on to the screen, rough-hewn and darkly handsome, oozing a sex appeal that barely camouflages his latent psychotic tendencies. He is high on drugs and is in a constant state of animation, with darting eyes and tapping fingers. Above all he has a thoroughly sexual presence in every movement of his body, something that Brooks exploits in the film's sex scenes.

Both Gere and Keaton, neither of whom had ever performed overt sexual activity on screen, were nervous about the sex scenes. Gere said that Keaton was shy about the nudity, while he was nervous about everything. He had walked into a film that was already shooting and he didn't know anyone. He was very uptight on the first day and because of it, Keaton, who had heard about him, thought he was playing games and did not like her. 'I was not responding to her as an actress because of it,' said Gere. 'But at the end of the first day, we talked it out; it was a very creative experience. In the sex scenes, we asked for a closed set and we improvised a lot.'

The troublesome scenes involving Gere explode on to the screen after Theresa riskily accepts this young man into her life on the simple promise that he will give her an experience in bed the like of which she has never experienced before. The scene had audiences on the edge of their seats as Gere performed an erotic pre-sex dance wearing just a G-string and swishing the air with the glinting blade of a lethal knife. To aficionados of the movie, it became known as The Jockstrap Scene.

Then, in a typical Brooks change of pace at the climactic moment of menace, Tony switches to intense lovemaking which takes Theresa into a sexual frenzy, with orgasm after orgasm that, truly, she had never previously enjoyed. The scene created an image for Gere – because in such situations the audience naturally transfers its thoughts about the character to the actor, and in this case they were thinking that he had incredible animal magnetism, the 'he' being Richard Gere, not the character he was playing. Director Brooks, when challenged on this aspect, admitted: 'That's exactly why I chose him.'

Looking for Mr Goodbar was premiered in New York towards the end of 1977, long before *Days of Heaven* was released and thus providing the critics with their first real look at Gere – in every respect! Their response was as fascinating as the build-up. Brooks himself was criticised for tampering with the direction of Rossner's novel and accused of attempting to make a movie with a message. Keaton was rightly applauded for a beautifully paced performance. But some critics displayed a certain hostility to the fact that the nice Ms Keaton found herself in such a movie, as if she herself – not the character – was being violated.

Her skilled performance, sharp and carefully choreographed, dominated the reviews and Gere found himself relegated to mentions which were generally briefer than his attire in The Jockstrap Scene. His appearances on screen totalled, after all, less than twenty minutes. Even so, those who could not pass up the arrival of a newcomer without comparing him with an established star made reference to Gere as being in the Pacino and De Niro mould, though more handsome than either.

It actually took time for the impact of his performance to

sink in. He did nothing to promote the idea that this was the dêbut performance of a new Hollywood sex stud. In fact, the reverse. He refused press interviews on the subject and would only talk generally about his experiences in making the film and how he owed Richard Brooks an absolute debt of gratitude for 'changing my whole perception about film-making'.

The recognition of his sensational attractiveness to women was one of several reactions which followed in the wake of the film's general release, a development aided by the fact that there were angry protests from the burgeoning 1970s feminist groups that the film was exploitative. Brooks received a torrent of hate mail, serious threats to his life, and his home was vandalised. Gere began to receive telephone calls and letters from 'every kind of nut' offering every kind of sexual diversion if he would care to call. Fans who discovered where he lived hung around hoping to get a glimpse of him, and some even turned up at the gates of his family's home in Syracuse, asking for photographs of him. Gere had suddenly become a sex symbol, but the alarming fact was that he was perceived as a symbol of somewhat perverted sex. He decided to clam up and refused point blank to do publicity interviews.

The other main effect of the film was the increased demand for Gere's services. Offers flooded in, mostly for similar sexy roles. 'I had enough offers to play Italian crazies for the next fifteen years,' said Gere. 'The bastards want to put you in a box with a label on it and crush it. If you have any hope of growing, of being taken seriously, you have to control the vultures.' He turned down the Italians, and he also turned down *Midnight Express*, the big Alan Parker movie for 1978 which earned an Oscar nomination for best picture and for which Oliver Stone won an Oscar for best adapted screenplay.

Gere concluded that *Midnight Express*, a tale of American students arrested in Turkey for carrying hashish, had too much gratuitous violence and 'lacked significance'. To turn such an opportunity down and to make such a statement had the ring of both youthful arrogance – a word that seems unavoidable in the description of some of Gere's remarkable decisions and sayings in those days – and foolhardy disregard for two of the most talented filmmakers of modern times. It would make him a number of enemies.

When the dust had settled, Ed Limato assessed the situation, studied the reviews and analysed the comments of the critics, all in his usual businesslike manner. Almost every reference focused upon his client's handsome features and, above all, his lithe, slender body that would undoubtedly send women into raptures. Limato identified the trend for the future. Gere might well be a very capable actor but his externals – as that renowned Method tutor Stella Adler used to describe physical attributes – were as good as any in the business. The critics were right. He was in the style of De Niro, and though he did not match him in the depth of his acting, he had the potential for greater box office appeal and bankability which, as even the studio mail delivery boys know, is what Hollywood is all about.

Gere, somewhat reluctantly it is said, accepted that it was his body people were after. It soon became popular folklore down Sunset Boulevard that he demanded a nude or near-naked scene in every one of his early movies. It wasn't true, but it made a few good headlines.

Chapter Four

No Publicity, Please

Even before Richard Gere hit the screens in *Looking for Mr Goodbar*, the remarkable undercurrent of interest emerging from producers and directors anxious to sign him put him in direct competition for parts with his friend John Travolta, whom he had met a few years earlier when they were both scouring the casting calls of New York for work. The two were similar in looks, both tall, dark and handsome, and for a time they were running neck and neck in their progress.

Travolta, who was four years younger, began to overtake Gere after director Brian de Palma chose him as the high school roughneck who doused Sissy Spacek with pig's blood in *Carrie*. It was a competent performance but gave no hint that he was on the brink of the stratospheric take-off that came with *Saturday Night Fever*, a film which sent young girls and even older women into delirium. This was quickly followed by the movie version of *Grease*, and then by his starring role in *Moment by Moment*, already in production.

Direct confrontation between Gere and Travolta was already in the offing as a series of roles came to the boil together. The two actors made an interesting comparison. Gere was being written up as the hot new kid on the block, while Travolta had already, and somewhat prematurely as things turned out, been elevated to superstar status. Gere's fame, such as it was, had been largely generated by word of mouth and occasional mentions in *Variety*. The fact was that working with Terrence Malick on *Days of Heaven* had given him an incredible boost, but there was still nothing tangible to show. The movie had yet to be released.

While Travolta's publicity machine was in danger of overheating, Gere remained remarkably quiet and almost reluctant to involve himself in the razzmatazz of the film world. He kept well out of sight, seldom went to the power parties and certainly did not go out of his way to promote himself as the latest hotshot to arrive in Tinseltown. When in Hollywood he stayed in that popular but discreet lodging house so familiar to visiting New York actors, the Château Marmont, where he occasionally ran into Robert De Niro, who also used the place as his Los Angeles domicile after splitting from his wife in 1977.

He wandered around in torn jeans and an old T-shirt, and was already becoming noted for his reticence to the chroniclers of Hollywood trade talk – another reason for him to be categorised in the Pacino/De Niro school of non-communication. 'Frankly, I couldn't take the hassle,' he admitted. 'So I talked to nobody.'

The critic Rex Reed, who was once refused an interview by Gere, complained: 'Interviewers ask . . . Who is Richard Gere? The public is asking the same question . . . his determination to do quality work is admirable. But what does his name mean at the box office? Not much. Not yet, anyway.' To those who unsuccessfully attempted to get him to open up on his feelings about his imminent rise to acclaim, he was a strange mix of contradictions and not at all like the flamboyant Travolta, who travelled everywhere with an entourage of people.

Some, including Reed, castigated Gere for being an arrogant punk. He was seen as a would-be star who did not much care to have his photograph taken or talk about his personal life. He was classed as a bit of a snob, a highbrow character who played lowbrow roles and whose handsome, stud-like appearance bore no resemblance in real life to the spicy image that the studio publicists would be seeking to feed to the gossip columnists and profile-writers.

All of this – and the fact that Gere and Travolta kept bumping into each other – was due in some measure to the state of Hollywood itself at the time. Sexy male stars were in short supply, and that in turn was reflected in the media pursuit of Gere – the glossy magazines which relied upon famous faces for their covers and their editorial were truly desperate for some younger blood.

British producer Trevor Wallace, who had moved to Los Angeles as the movie business in his homeland declined to the point of virtual nonexistence, recalled for me the scenario that existed in the late 1970s and early 1980s: 'Everyone in the business was searching for new male talent at that time. You only had to look around at the options and you could virtually count the younger stars on one hand. Paul Newman was well past fifty. Robert Redford was over forty and hankering to make his own films. So was Burt Reynolds. Dustin Hoffman had passed forty and anyway was never in the sex symbol stakes. Clint Eastwood, almost fifty, was betwixt and between his ambitions to direct. De Niro and Pacino were highly selective and into heavy and serious drama and were very fussy who they worked with. Christopher Reeve was tied up with Superman and Nick Nolte hadn't really broken through. That left Nicholson, who could do anything, but was also over forty. And so if you imagine that at any given moment there might be a dozen major movies in production in Hollywood, there was invariably a call for a sexy, young actor. There weren't that many to go around. Travolta and Gere were there and available at exactly the right moment in movie history, which is why for about three or four years they were being considered for virtually everything that was going. That is not to say that they weren't good. They were, but the competition was less then than at any time in recent history. Remember, the Brat Pack hadn't been invented yet.'

New stars had to have a build-up, a long process of informing the public of their whole persona. Gere may have assessed that he was doing quite well without great media exposure. It was a deliberate strategy to let his films do the talking and the publicity take care of itself. So a certain antagonism was building on various fronts. Penelope Milford, one of the few people close enough to observe his inner feelings, said he anguished about his work constantly, especially when he had made a decision about something and then had to wait around while Hollywood made up its mind.

Two projects that caused Gere a good deal of grief were hanging in the balance at this time. The first concerned the production of *American Gigolo*, the movie that would confirm his arrival as a star. He was first approached with the script for the movie by its author Paul Schrader, best known for writing the screenplay of Martin Scorsese's *Taxi Driver*, which brought raves for Robert De Niro.

Schrader, who had just completed the movie *Hardcore*, starring George C. Scott, which delved into the sleazy world of pornography and prostitution, had decided that his next sizzler was to be about a male prostitute. He personally wanted Gere for the lead. He went so far as to tell the actor, and then had to backtrack when Freddie Fields, the veteran producer who was calling the shots financially for Paramount – and who incidentally also produced *Looking for Mr Goodbar* – said that Gere was still too unknown to carry such an expensive and controversial movie.

Paramount wanted Travolta, and so talks about *American Gigolo* were inconclusive as far as Gere was concerned, although it looked at that point as if it would go to Travolta, who was anxious for a dramatic role after the froth of disco-dancing.

Weeks of negotiations passed without decision. At the same time, the British director John Schlesinger approached Gere about the British-based production of *Yanks*, for which Travolta had also been a possible candidate. But Schlesinger had problems in trying to raise the finance for his picture, and for the time being Gere's involvement in both projects hung in the balance.

Meanwhile he had been sought out just as he was completing *Looking for Mr Goodbar* for a project whose preparation pedigree looked encouraging but which, in hindsight, he perhaps ought to have rejected. Director Robert Mulligan, who had a long list of credits of which the best known were *To Kill a Mocking Bird*, with Gregory Peck, and the well-received exploration of new permissiveness and sexual initiation, *Summer of '42*, was searching for a young actor to co-star in his movie *Bloodbrothers*, under production at Warner Bros.

In this instance, 'young' was the operative word. The role was of a sensitive eighteen-year-old youth at the crossroads of his life, but Mulligan had been unable to find a boy of that age whose acting was strong enough for the demanding characterisation. He scanned the pages of the actors' directories, tested numerous young men around Hollywood, and also scoured New York. He looked at Gere and decided he was too old – ten years older, in fact, than the age of his screen character. Gere also ruled himself out when he was first approached, for the same reason.

Weeks passed and still Mulligan hadn't filled the vacancy and once more considered Gere. They met and talked. Like others before him, Mulligan found Gere an intense person, wrapped up in his work and who talked about the need for 'creative artists' to be at one with the parts they undertook, something which certainly posed some problems in this particular film. He worried too about his own position and how it was essential for him to try to chart a progression in his career, a fact already borne out by the endless telephone calls to his agent Ed Limato about what he should do next. Playing an eighteen-year-old kid almost seemed like a backward step.

Finally, after much discussion about the role's dramatic potential, Mulligan decided to make an offer. Gere joined a strong trio of character actors – Paul Sorvino, Tony Lo Bianco and Leslie Goldoni – to complete the Italian family at the centre of the story, and they all moved to location filming in the Bronx.

Gere, however, would find it difficult to come to terms with playing a much younger character, a fact that undoubtedly brought confusion to an audience which was still largely unaware of him. His role as Stony De Coco portrayed him as a boy on the edge of manhood torn between his own hopes and dreams and those of his father (Lo Bianco) and uncle (Sorvino), both heavy-drinking, brawling and whoring construction workers. The two older men expect him to follow them in the family traditions of the tough male line, while Stony himself has an altogether more sensitive approach to life and plans a career working with children as a hospital therapist.

Director Mulligan, well known for his meticulous preparation and insistence on rehearsal and adherence to the script, kept a very tight rein on the scenes, and unusually for a film of this nature, in which a natural situation is being set up and filmed, there was very little improvisation. The film became bogged down in its portrayal of life among a noisy Italian/American working-class family, crowded round the dinner table shouting at each other, with Gere's character wincing as if he does not really belong.

The story is riddled with problem people: the whoring father with a penchant for Oriental ladies, following his army service in Vietnam; the uncle whose only child was accidentally suffocated as a baby; the local neighbourhood barman who is a paraplegic with a difficult homosexual son. Gere himself, in trying to escape, finds solace and sexual experience in the arms of a girl who has a local reputation.

There were actually some very decent scenes, and the writer, Walter Newman, received an Academy Award nomination for his script. But overall, the film's attempts to explore the simple emotions of a very ordinary family did not hang together, and at times it turned into a parody. The film was an unhappy choice for Gere at what turned out to be an important stage in his career – the first time he would receive serious attention from the critics and a host of mentions in high places. It is interesting to look back on these contemporary reviews to gain an idea of first impressions, of both the actor and the movie. In this case, the movie was panned. Inevitably, the difference between Gere's age and that of his character was questioned – and rightly so, because there were few occasions when he could be believably passed off as a teenager, in spite of the almost perpetual presence of his unshirted torso, which, as one reviewer put it, looked as if it had stepped out of an advert for a health club.

Harold Schonberg, in the *New York Times*, said that Gere was the victim of a notable error of miscasting: 'By no freak of genetics could he have come from the lines of his parents . . . Gere is a fine young actor with immense charm, but he is not believable . . . not even he can overcome the stylistic, contrived qualities of the role and the picture.' *Time* magazine was not convinced about Gere. The jury was still out, the magazine reported. 'He is a powerful sexual presence but he affects too many Brando pauses, De Niro stutterings, and Travolta grins. He may yet become a Somebody in the movies, but not until he stops acting like everybody else.' Pauline Kael, of the *New Yorker*, complained that Mulligan was 'trying for something crude, powerful, volatile . . . but it goes terribly wrong'.

When the film was premiered in California, however, Gere received a standing ovation, a kind response from a friendly local crowd recognising the arrival of a new talent. He would say that members of his family who saw it had been 'in tears'. When Gere allowed his own opinions to go into print, he perhaps not unnaturally praised Mulligan's direction and assessed the final outcome to be a very worthwhile film, 'a simple, straight-ahead emotional opera.

I liked that. I went with it.' His enthusiasm was not shared by potential audiences, and the film took less than $1 million at the US box office, a flop in any language.

Gere's upward mobility remained undamaged, however, because by the time the reviews came out he had already signed for two more movies. John Schlesinger had finally raised the money to go into production with *Yanks* – and he offered it to Richard Gere. After concluding location work in the Bronx and studio filming on the Paramount lot for *Bloodbrothers*, Gere flew straight to England to begin work on what had now become a much-publicised project.

For Gere, the film represented another opportunity not to be missed. Schlesinger, whose string of superb British-based movies in the 1960s won him international acclaim, was, like Brooks, Malick and Mulligan, a director any intelligent actor would love to work with, almost regardless of the success or failure of the project. Even his failures, which so far had been few, had very considerable merit, with his particular forte lying in illuminating complex human relationships.

He was also famed for his handling of sensitive actors, and notably for bringing to stardom one of the most sensitive of all, Julie Christie – later to co-star with Gere – whom he directed in *Billy Liar*, *Darling* and *Far from the Madding Crowd*. The American Academy recognised his work in 1969 when he was awarded an Oscar for his direction of the brilliant *Midnight Cowboy*, which he followed with another career milestone, *Sunday Bloody Sunday*.

Yanks was Schlesinger's very own project. He had personally outlined the story, set in 1943 in a northern British town which was a wartime base for American servicemen. It centred around a group of Americans waiting to be sent abroad and, eventually, for the invasion of Normandy with the focus, of course, upon their affairs with British women.

As usual, the British film industry was on the floor when Schlesinger went in to bat with his project, and there was little money around, so he headed west to Hollywood. He began trawling the studios but discovered unexpected resistance to his idea. 'It was hell,' Schlesinger admitted. 'For a time, it looked as if I would have to drop it.' However, he finally managed to put together a three-party financing deal between two independent producers and United Artists as distributors. They gave him a budget of $7.5 million, which allowed him to go ahead.

He commissioned two writers, Briton Colin Welland (later to win an Oscar for his screenplay of *Chariots of Fire*) and the American Walter Bernstein (whose previous work included *Fail Safe*, *The Molly Maguires* and *The Betsy*), in order to meet the demands of the backers that the views of both countries be properly represented.

Schlesinger then spent a great deal of time casting his film, which focused on three separate romantic relationships. He had cast Vanessa Redgrave and actor William Devane, then a popular choice among directors in America, for the upper-crust affair. Of the lesser roles, central to the run of the film is the affair involving a US Army cook, a principled home-town boy from Arizona who falls for a naive English girl but refuses to consummate their love in case he is sent abroad and never returns.

For this role, Schlesinger said that his idea was to create a 'reincarnation of Gary Cooper in the forties', and it was suggested to him that he consider Gere, whose only major film on release at that time was *Looking for Mr Goodbar*. 'I did not care for the film, but I found Gere's performance arresting. I arranged to meet Richard, and we talked on several occasions,' said Schlesinger. At that point, the financial backing was still under discussion, and with the producers looking for 'bankability' among the cast, the director was tempted to hire a major name whose presence would help the movie.

'I talked to everyone,' said Schlesinger. 'Al Pacino and Dustin Hoffman were high up on my list and it was argued that they would have been a better draw. But I still felt Gere was the freshest, most interesting actor for the part. There was a complexity in him that hadn't been tapped in his previous films, a sensitivity and beauty which to my mind gave him qualities similar to Montgomery Clift.'

And so the deal was done, and Gere just had time for some research before going to London. In this, there were shades of De Niro's well-known preparatory work for his roles. He flew down to Arizona, home state of the character he was to play, with his tape recorder to take an insight into local accents and get the feel of the communities there.

Next he went to the US Army base at Fort Dix, New Jersey, and obtained permission for temporary assignment to the kitchen as a mess sergeant – the rank of his man in the movie. Finally, he went home for some long discussions with his father, who had been in the navy around the time the film is set. He researched the archives, studied old photographs, by which time he was due to fly to London, where pre-production work was already under way.

He was billeted at a small flat near Hyde Park, temporarily sublet from the actress Jan Sterling, and with great media interest being shown in the film, he had to employ a publicist for the first time in his life – not with the intention of getting him interviews, but to ward off visiting reporters and feature writers.

He explained that he had to try to stay in character by 'wiping the last twenty years of history out of my head'. He said that to have to give interviews about his work in the present would distract him from the 'innocence of the times'. He also demanded a closed set when he was working, which was virtually unheard-of in Britain. So began the gradual build-up of an enmity with the news media which would soon explode into hostility on both sides.

Nothing changed when the cast moved on to location filming in the north of England, where Schlesinger had meticulously recreated a US base with all the hardware and wartime authenticity he could muster. The film took on epic proportions in the making and it was an arduous shoot, lasting almost eight months and with Gere heavily involved in many of the major scenes.

As in the past, he kept himself pretty much to himself, travelling back and forth daily from his lodgings. Critic Rex Reed turned up from New York looking to write a preview piece on the film, but got no joy from the new star. He moaned: 'Gere virtually slinks home from the set each weekday evening, falls into a deep coma, is awakened by the alarm the following morning, only to be driven by limousine to a location site where the process is repeated ad infinitum.'

Gere admitted that he kept himself isolated, partly intentionally, to keep a clear focus on his character, and partly through exhaustion during a difficult shoot. In off-duty hours, he would take off alone on his motorbike, riding around the Yorkshire countryside. For a time, he arranged to stay in the village of Kildwick, not far from Ilkley Moor. 'No one knew who I was and they didn't care,' said Gere. 'They just treated me like one of the lads. I felt really comfortable there, having a drink at the local pub and playing darts.'

He found the film his most demanding role to date and had little inclination towards socialising with the rest of the cast, who found him aloof and largely unapproachable. His mother and father flew to England to visit him on set. His mother cried when she saw him in uniform because it reminded her of her husband when he was in the services, and when the movie was finally completed the family would note that Gere had drawn heavily on his father's image in his portrayal of the role.

As media interest in the movie heightened, there were rumours that Schlesinger and Gere had fallen out on a number of occasions over interpretation. The actor was cast in the mould of an 'upstart', fighting against the great Schlesinger, who had complained that Gere was too restrained in his performance. Later, Gere cheekily went on record to dismiss the whole thing as a case of 'creative artists not seeing eye to eye. John has strong ideas, I have strong ideas.' He considered his views equally as important as the director's; perhaps they were, but the way it came out, he seemed to give no recognition to the fact that he was a snotty nosed kid compared with Schlesinger's mastery of movie-making.

He pressed on with his appraisal of the working relationship in a manner which gave a rather extravagant view of his own importance: 'John is very precise about what he wants and devotes so much care and time to detail. If he has to fight for his position . . . he may come up with something better and that's what happened on *Yanks*. I fought certain things, and improved it.'

Schlesinger politely confirmed 'differences of opinion' but maintained that it was a healthy aspect of making movies. By the time *Yanks* was released in the autumn of 1979, the hype and the publicity surrounding it all augured well, and the trade commentators were heralding the arrival of a masterpiece and a smash hit for Schlesinger. Unfortunately, it did not turn out that way.

Yanks was a highly regarded film, with some fine individual performances, and was especially noteworthy for its authenticity, skilled and compelling dramatic construction and cinematic narrative. But it received a poor response at the box office, and though well reviewed, there was invariably a sting in the tale among the American critics. Somehow, the film just did not appeal to US audiences, although it did much better in Europe.

Gere became a target for critics on both sides of the Atlantic. Though his character was quite endearing and his acting accomplished, it was felt, perhaps rightly, that he had underplayed the role and given a performance that was so controlled and meticulous as to leave the viewer with the impression that he was always on the brink of making it more interesting but never quite managed it. As someone said at the time, Schlesinger lit the fuse, but Gere did not explode.

In *Bloodbrothers*, his mentions in reviews had become lost in the confusion over the movie; in *Yanks* he was a central figure in a movie which had aroused great expectations. The accusation of underplaying would occur time and time again, and was generally disregarded by the subject himself because it genuinely was his style. He had argued with Schlesinger over it and he would repeat down the years that he, Richard Gere, was not a naturally loud and forceful character either in private or on stage.

That was the way he was and that was the way he would stay. The challenge to his acting abilities would always focus on this aspect of quiet, restrained presentation and it began back then, in the autumn of 1979, when the critics were reviewing his performance in *Yanks*.

If he were going to change his style, he would have done it then, because the welter of press comment that arose during that period might have forced him to reconsider his views on a number of issues – not least his lack of co-operation with the media, which was now attracting almost as much comment as his work itself. But he did not budge, and suffered a very bad press as a result. It would remain another open sore in his life, continuing through the years as he became more famous and his star rating in Hollywood increased.

A new round of confrontational situations emerged with the news that he had literally been praying for – that he was a definite contender for the starring role in Paul Schrader's high-profile movie, *American Gigolo*, about which much was being written in both the trade and the general press. All the speculation about the movie's sexual content put Gere right back in the front line of media interest, even though, with the release of *Yanks* months away, he was still caught in the no man's land between completing work on a film and seeing it in the cinemas. So the hype was being propagated by publicists on two fronts – for *Yanks* and for the upcoming *American Gigolo* – and was made more focused because Gere was fortunate enough to be associated with directors whose movies always created a stir for anyone involved with them.

As Rex Reed pointed out on several occasions, it was

largely to do with the directors he worked with that Gere was being labelled a star before anyone had seen any substantial examples of his work and while the moviegoing public generally still did not recognise his name. Refusing media interviews had added to the intrigue surrounding him, and famous glossy-magazine writers whose courtship had been rejected began to talk impatiently of him in terms of the latest puffed-up actor who thought his middle name was Garbo.

So the war with the media went on. Nothing attracts attention more than the seemingly unapproachable or the mysterious, and the word went around that Gere had something to hide. He was followed and spied upon by fans and media alike, and after returning from England, he never went back to the shopfront rooms which had been his home for four years. He moved into a hotel, and for the time being lived out of a suitcase and ate in restaurants.

The interest in him, quite overdone and rather undeserved in terms of his CV at that time, came about so quickly that Gere was uncertain how to handle it. He hated the studio PR people, who were only interested in promoting a movie, regardless of what invasions of the star's privacy might follow. The PR people would counter that it was all part of the game – but Gere wasn't playing. 'Once the word spreads that you're hot,' he complained, 'everyone wants you, and I wasn't prepared for it. They all want you, but they don't even know who you are. It's easy to understand why the experience leaves so many performers feeling exploited and angry, or why they so quickly become cynical and hostile in return.'

The latter was one of Gere's best-known reactions at that particular period in his life. He laid it on the line then, just as he did again much later in life, complaining: 'You people in media have control. You can solidify concepts and personas so they can be marketed. It's false.' He fought back by ignoring requests for interviews and would only allow himself to be photographed by his own approved photographer, usually his friend and former flatmate Herb Ritts.

It all seemed a bit like the big-star syndrome before he had even got there, but there was no doubt that at the time he was being pursued with a certain relentless fervour. It became an interesting pastime, for those who knew him or were on the periphery of his life, to observe his reactions when he was out in the crowd, or at a restaurant where he might be recognised, or when he had to go to a party.

Author Richard Price, who wrote the novel on which Gere's movie *Bloodbrothers* was based, recalled such a moment: 'It seemed that at least half the people standing around us were staring at him out of the corners of their eyes with what seemed to be a mixture of anger and awe. Gere has always had the power to demand that you watch him. He was incapable of looking unaware of the people around him, incapable of projecting stay-away vibes. And now, in this room, it was as if he were holding everyone's neck in a noose at the end of a pole. They couldn't get too close and they couldn't walk away. But neither could he. Gere tried to come off as though he were oblivious to all this tension, but the unsmiling tightness of his mouth betrayed him. I couldn't imagine he had come to the party in anticipation of a good time. The night seemed like some blind foray into the combat zone. If Gere had exploded at that party, I don't know if he would have screamed, "I hate you all" or "Why don't you love me?" '

He was faced with a dilemma which has confronted many like him in the past and will undoubtedly do so in the future. Should he flow with the tide and accept that he was a celebrity, or duck out of sight? What was more important: sanity . . . or ensuring that his image was abundantly displayed through the bestselling magazines? Should he stay visible to his fans and co-operate with the journalists who wanted to record the minutiae of his life, or should he tell them all, using his favourite phrase of the moment, to 'fuck off'?

He decided upon a route that did not even approach the middle ground. He refused all television offers and chat shows, and even declined the highly coveted opportunity to co-host the top-rated show *Saturday Night Live*. Journalists of every persuasion were ready to stand in line for the opportunity of an hour with him – even at this stage of his career.

He had decided, however, to give only a limited number of interviews, and made it clear that personal questions would not be answered. He would only discuss films or the making of them. He showed cynical contempt for bad interviewers and for the process of star interviews itself. One writer noted Gere's reluctance: 'He would dearly rather be somewhere else, perhaps at his dentist's undergoing a little root canal work.' He also fuelled the media's displeasure of this limited co-operation with some unfortunate off-the-cuff acts, as when the interviewer for the *Ladies' Home Journal* asked him, 'How does it feel to be a sex object?' – a question which seemed to be the first one everyone asked.

On this occasion Gere sat for a moment, then raised his eyes to the ceiling and stood up, unzipping his trousers and dropping them to reveal his most private parts: 'This is what I call a sex object.'

The writer was unfazed by this act of indecent exposure. She looked down and in a matter-of-fact way said bluntly: 'I've seen better.'

It was not long, of course, before the writers themselves were reacting in print, and bellowing headlines asked: 'Who does he think he is?' The *Village Voice*'s Arthur Bell, who had been an early supporter of Gere, now turned on him. He remembers: 'I know dealing with the media becomes a bit of a pain and the *Voice* never pesters. But Gere's Greta Garbo act was verging on the ridiculous. He was a new name and there was a good deal of interest in him. On the one hand, you had the publicists trying to get you interested in the movie and on the other, you had Gere himself saying "I want to be left alone". There was simply no attempt at a common ground and the whole thing developed into an unseemly situation in which journalists *en masse* became resentful of Gere, and that's bad news for anyone in showbusiness.'

Gere, convinced he was merely being exploited, began to seek the solace of meditation and showed early inclinations towards the spiritual, the esoteric and contemplative religions when he said, in a moment of distress about the pressures of his new-found fame: 'I feel I could walk away from this, and I would be so happy. I could go to a Zen monastery.' The thought may have been fleeting at the time but he would gradually spend more and more time on the contemplation of his soul, especially as the media explosion around *American Gigolo* hit the streets.

And to ram home the message of what lay in store, Earl Wilson, gossip columnist for the *New York Post*, ran with great gusto an item hinting at what was coming: 'Richard Gere, the shy, sensitive boy from Syracuse . . . doesn't know he's a star and he's going to be thoroughly shocked and shaken . . . he does not want to become a new John Travolta who has to stay home or go and run for his life. No torrents of publicity, no hype. He's refusing interviews and TV spots. He wants privacy.

'WELL, HE WON'T GET ANY!'

Chapter Five

Sylvia the Stalker

Richard Gere had a bad time in between the completion of the filming of *Yanks* and its actual release into the cinemas – one of the worst periods of his life, he reckoned. When he got back to New York, he had to hire a public relations firm to stave off the media blitz, and his personal life was in disarray: not only had he been forced to abandon his home, but during his eight-month absence in England, he and Penelope Milford had drifted apart.

Milford had completed *Coming Home*, her movie with Jane Fonda, and been nominated for best supporting actress. She was now looking for advancement, though well aware that the situation with actresses in Hollywood was the reverse of that with actors: there were plenty.

When Gere came back from England, he told her it was all over, and she left. She would try to figure out the nature of the man but could hardly cover her true feelings of being hurt and dumped: 'I know about Richard. If somebody he loves doesn't relate to him he just lets go. Well, that's all right. Richard was dealing with stuff that was very important to him. It takes a lot to accomplish what he'd accomplished. In any relationship, it seems unequal if one takes and the other gives but it's not. I had as great a need to give as he had to take. I don't mind talking about it. For a time, I did feel hurt but so did he. The difference is, I'll be the one to admit it because it's not manly to admit your weaknesses.'

The ending of this long-running affair, which had anchored Gere through difficult times, left a void which was filled by a succession of fleeting dates and romances, including a brief liaison with Barbara Carrera, the smouldering Nicaraguan actress. Unknown to the pursuing media, by the early months of 1979 there was already a new woman in his life, who arrived there by rather devious means. It was a relationship which had developed quietly from strange beginnings – with a Brazilian beauty who trailed him like a stalker until she finally got to meet him.

She had been writing to him for some time but her missives went unanswered. His mail had been heavy. The deluge began after his appearance in *Looking for Mr Goodbar*, with dozens of letters from admiring fans of all ages, some quite explicit in their rapturous fantasies. Marlon Brando used to get the same kind of attention when he was appearing on Broadway in the late forties, and it soon became common knowledge that if the admirer left a hotel bedroom key in an envelope backstage, Brando was quite likely to pay a call.

Gere, according to a friend who had known him since the early days, avoided all contact with fans and never took up any of the many sexual offers he received. Sylvia Martins, an artist from a wealthy Brazilian family, who was living and studying in New York, was different. She wrote to him repeatedly to explain that she was not just a star-struck fan but an intelligent woman who was seriously interested in meeting him.

He ignored the letters, but she managed to get his telephone number at the Sherry-Netherland Hotel, an elegant European-style establishment on Fifth Avenue where he was living at the time.

It was in his hotel suite that the calls from 'Sylvia' were witnessed by visiting *Playboy* contributing editor Bruce Williamson in February 1979 – only he did not know then of their significance and nor, for that matter, did Gere himself. After weeks of trying, Williamson had finally persuaded Gere to see him for a brief talk, although he never managed to get him to open up in the manner normally achieved for the renowned *Playboy* celebrity interviews: while Jack Nicholson's, for example, ran to ten riveting pages, Gere answered only five questions, giving a page and a quarter of copy.

While Williamson was in Gere's hotel suite, the phone was ringing incessantly. Williamson recalled, 'Gere's interest was piqued by a series of calls he received from a girl named Sylvia. In Rio de Janeiro.'

Gere confided to him: 'This chick I've never met keeps calling me up from Brazil. I don't know how they find you but they do. A lot of fruitcakes started coming on to me after *Mr Goodbar*. All kinds. They want to drop over for a drink. Or they want you to come over for a drink. They assure you you'll enjoy yourself.'

Williamson thought no more about the incident and went away, while Gere himself eventually began to hang up on Sylvia, then refused to speak to her at all and instructed the hotel switchboard to monitor all incoming calls. Sylvia did not give up. She discovered his social movements and found out that he regularly went to Elaine's, a smart, snug and expensive little Italian restaurant on Second Avenue which Diane Keaton had introduced him to. It was the kind of eatery where people on the way up liked to be seen and to be greeted by name by Elaine, the voluptuous hostess.

Sylvia began to stake out the place, until one night she saw Gere arrive. He had not been at his table long, and had ordered a Chardonnay and pasta when he looked up to see an exceedingly attractive brunette standing before him. He was quite used by now to being approached in restaurants but by all accounts, from the surprised look on his face, he sensed that this lady was rather different.

'Hi,' she said. 'I'm Sylvia. Sylvia Martins.' She held out her hand, which he shook rather meekly, and apologised for barging in on him. It was only then that he realised exactly who she was. Gere was not amused or placated by her apologies and blew up, causing a major scene in the restaurant. He chased Sylvia outside, shouting that she should get the hell out before he called the police.

At this point Sylvia began to get emotional. She explained that she was interested in him as a fellow artist and was not some nut, as he had described her. Soon she was recounting her life story. She came from a well-to-do Rio de Janeiro family. In her late teens and early twenties she had been a model and had had her picture on the cover of the Brazilian edition of *Vogue*. She had also studied art and had come to New York in the hope of establishing herself as a painter, although she regularly returned to Brazil for long visits, especially during the cold New York winters.

Gere was intrigued and agreed to meet her the following weekend. It was the beginning of an exotic, tempestuous relationship that would last more than seven years. Before long, she was visiting his new apartment in Greenwich Village. Within a couple of months, she was staying overnight, and then virtually living there. 'Their relationship developed rapidly,' said Molly Erlich, an actress who knew them both. 'It was an odd beginning because you hear so many stories about fans stalking their idols and some are quite dangerous. Most of the time, they never get near their subject. Sylvia was determined to meet him, come what may, and just kept on and on until he gave in. I think at that moment, Richard saw that she was not a loony trying to get him into bed. Well, the bed part was probably correct, but she was quite normal, if temperamental.

'In fact, she was very good for him. She was a very open and friendly person who enjoyed a number of Richard's own quirky pursuits, like his interest in all things mystical and spiritual – for a time at least, although, later, she did get a bit bored with the Dalai Lama. She had a very calming presence and with her Richard was a much nicer person. He needs a woman like her around him.'

Other friends describe how with Sylvia, Gere eventually became less manic about life and did not feel quite so threatened by public and media scrutiny, although he was still extremely wary of it. 'He was halfway up the learning curve,' said Erlich. 'He still would not major in a class on How to Win Friends and Influence People. He had this very disconcerting intense gaze at you, and he was very impatient, always anguishing over something or other, pacing about lighting one Marlboro after another. Inside that brain of his, he was always basically a very nervous, shy person and found person-to-person contact difficult. He covered it with this façade of arrogance, and eventually because of all the confrontations he had with the writers, especially those who came just to bait him, it became the public face. But, you know, truthfully he was a seriously nice guy to know – once you got to know him. Sylvia used to have a problem, early on, when he'd come back in a furious rage about something that had been written about him or a journalist who had just gotten too close. She would soothe his brow and work out the anger.'

There certainly would have been plenty of anger and confusion at the time, because for a while it looked as though Gere had lost the lead in *American Gigolo* to John Travolta.

The film's author and director Paul Schrader said he remained convinced that Gere was right for the part of Julian Kay, the classy, swaggering, $1,000-a-trick male prostitute who spoke five languages and would be seen in every mode of attire from birthday suit to Giorgio Armani's finest. 'As an actor, he had a wealth of riches,' said Schrader. 'He could be a traditional leading man, a tormented soul, a stage actor. Most actors around did not have all those options. The other important thing about Gere is that he takes risks – does the roles that others might not consider.'

Much as he wanted Gere, Schrader was overruled by the

studio. Paramount, who were financing the movie, still wanted a bigger name to carry what they knew would be a sensitive project from which critical backlash could be expected if the sexual content was not handled with a degree of decorum. Producer Freddie Fields thought Travolta would be a better bet to shoulder the $10 million budget, and entered protracted negotiations with his management. The original offer of $750,000 was eventually increased to $1 million, plus extras for the star's entourage.

Gere described it as 'murder, sheer murder' to be told the news, although the blow was softened a little when he heard that he was in the running for *Urban Cowboy*, a new movie which former Paramount boss Robert Evans was producing, and which would evidently have a plot vaguely similar to John Schlesinger's *Midnight Cowboy*.

Two months later, however, after new scenes were added beefing up the sex, Travolta dropped out of *American Gigolo* because he felt his reputation might suffer in the aftermath of a rather sordid and sexually explicit role. His explanation for withdrawing was that his mother had just died; the truth was that since he had first agreed to star in the movie, his superstar career had suffered a traumatic setback.

Having been on the crest of a wave since the box-office bonanza of *Saturday Night Fever*, he took a very severe hammering from the critics for his new movie, *Moment by Moment*, which producer Robert Stigwood, the former London pop group manager and impresario of the 1960s, had dashed out in double-quick time to cash in on Travolta's 'overnight sensation' syndrome. *Moment by Moment* was mercilessly panned, and rightly so. It was a dire film and proof, if ever it were needed, that a bright new name alone cannot compensate for a bad picture.

Schrader was well aware why Travolta pulled out of *American Gigolo*: 'John Travolta liked the title . . . liked the clothes, liked the poster, but after *Moment by Moment* he was just too damned scared that he would fall flat on his face again.'

Even so, the situation was not immediately resolved in

Gere's favour. There was a stark statistical fact that the money men could point to: the combined gross box-office receipts from the three movies in which Gere had appeared, and which had so far been released, were less than the gross of Travolta's single flop, *Moment by Moment*.

According to the Hollywood rumour mill, Paramount then offered the part to Christopher Reeve, who had also just zoomed to overnight fame and fortune in his first leading role, as Superman. The word was that Reeve was offered $1 million but turned it down because he had already signed for *Superman II* and did not want to damage the very clean image that this movie required. And so at last Schrader got his way and Gere was hired for $350,000 plus a percentage of the net profits. Schrader said with some satisfaction that he was 'now making the picture I originally envisaged'.

Coincidentally, Travolta then signed with Robert Evans to play the role that Gere would not now take – the all-macho star of *Urban Cowboy*, with Debra Winger – and ironically fell flat on his face in this dull and fatuous copycat tale, taking another beating from the critics in the process. Even the 1983 sequel to *Saturday Night Fever*, *Staying Alive*, also produced by Stigwood and clumsily written and directed by Sylvester Stallone, failed to rescue Travolta's downward spiral, which knocked him out of the movies for the rest of the decade.

So now it was Gere who was swaggering forth with a spring in his step to take full advantage of Travolta's misfortune, and whereas once it was Travolta who had the edge in their private battle for movie roles, now Gere was pushing back into the lead. He was also fortunate to have the confidence of Paul Schrader, who was himself firing on all cylinders with a succession of stories built around moral and social deviation which did not always meet with the critics' approval.

American Gigolo was no different, except that by necessity Schrader had to give a classy, stylish look to the seedy undertones – just as Gere did in *Pretty Woman* almost a decade later.

Schrader had actually written the screenplay for *American Gigolo* four years earlier. The idea had originated from a discussion with students at the University of California in Los Angeles, where he was lecturing on writing for the screen. He had asked them to consider subjects or occupations around which a film might be built, and one student called out the word 'gigolo'. The next day Schrader was in session with his psychotherapist and used the phrase again when talking about personal relationships and how it was more difficult to receive love than to give it. 'It was then that the notion of the gigolo as a metaphor for the man who can't receive pleasure hit me . . . after that it was just a matter of plotting it out.'

He made it sound simple, but of course it wasn't. The success of *American Gigolo*, and even its acceptance as a project by Paramount, rested upon painting a sophisticated gloss over a story that at times wallowed around in the murkiest regions of Hollywood Boulevard, that street of real shame in Los Angeles where every kind of sexual preference and deviance is dangerously accommodated.

The central character – and he is hardly ever off the screen – is Julian Kay, the high-class prostitute serving wealthy women. But the audience sense that he has not always been in that league and the movie occasionally harps back to less salubrious days and hints of bondage, transvestites and homosexual prostitution.

This was really the root cause of Travolta and Reeve both turning down the role. They refused to risk the reaction which would inevitably ensue from rights groups from both gay and straight quarters, not to mention the all-powerful Catholic and Christian Fundamentalist lobbies. And it was also why Schrader applauded Gere for being prepared to 'take risks'.

Gere himself claimed that he never gave the sexual implications of the part, or the way it might rebound upon him, a second thought, but there is little doubt that he desperately wanted a role that would put him in the A-list of young actors. Schrader was delighted with his enthusiasm.

'When Richard got involved,' he recalls, 'I got back to making a real movie again, a story about people, themes. In one day, Richard asked all the questions John hadn't asked in six months.'

Gere was given forty-eight hours to consider his answer after Travolta dropped out, and once his agent had agreed terms, he had just ten days to prepare for the role. A good deal of this time would be taken up with a stroll through the lavish sets, and fittings for the expensive costumes Schrader had ordered from Giorgio Armani. The fashions, especially Gere's clothes, became a noted feature of the movie.

In spite of his middle-class background, Gere had never wanted to own such a wardrobe himself – although he continued to wear much of it after filming was completed – and off duty he was more likely still to be found in jeans, T-shirt and leather jacket. 'In that respect, it wasn't particularly easy for me to get into the style aspect of a gigolo,' he admitted. 'I knew what it was all about emotionally but not stylistically. I did a lot of research and fairly quickly came to the point where I could make the same decisions Julian would about clothes, about books and so on.'

Schrader was also looking for top-drawer surroundings. Months earlier, he had gone to Rome to hire Bernardo Bertolucci's famous designer Ferdinando Scarfiotti to build the luxurious sets. Scarfiotti, who became a good friend of Gere's, described how he had to change many of the sets when Travolta pulled out. 'At that point,' he said, 'Travolta was like a myth, a legend, who had to have everything a certain way and in certain colours and backgrounds. His entourage wanted it that way. When I met Richard, I realised that he was nothing like that. He was a regular guy. So I rushed over to the set and changed the colour scheme of his apartment in the film to one that coincided with his more down-to-earth sophistication.'

And so, suddenly, the movie for which Gere was once rejected was being rebuilt around him.

Chapter Six

Gigolo

The occasional coincidences of life that occur in movie-making began with *American Gigolo* when Richard Gere was put in direct counterplay with one of America's best-known female bodies of that era. Lauren Hutton was a famous model of the 1960s who had gone on to win the coveted contract with the Revlon cosmetics company, and from her great fame as a cover girl had made the rare transition to films. Exactly a decade later, Gere would be involved with Cindy Crawford, another Revlon model whose career followed almost exactly the same pattern – though at the time this film was being made, she was not even old enough to see it.

Lauren Hutton brought to *American Gigolo* the touch of class that Schrader needed, in the role of the senator's wife with whom Julian Kay becomes involved. The basic level of the film's plot generally proved too vulgar for quite a number of Establishment critics to stoop to praising it. Viewed today, it looks considerably less sleazy than it did in 1980, probably because real-life stories not a million miles from this one are becoming fairly commonplace.

In a nutshell, Kay picks up the senator's wife, and as a consequence is framed in a kinky murder case. In the meantime, he makes the mistake of falling in love with her and so refuses to allow her to face the public humiliation of revealing that they were together on the night of the murder. In his attempts to find a defence, Julian tracks down the pimp who has framed him and then, to his horror, the pimp himself is killed. At last the senator's wife has to go public and confess to her association with the male prostitute.

The general scenes are played out in the stylish surroundings of the Polo Lounge sets and luxuriant bedroom silks, but as he backtracks through his past connections, Julian takes us on a kinky journey through the sexual deviancy of the Los Angeles low-life and gay scenes. Among the several flaws of this movie, however, is its vagueness about the past; it makes circles around its own implications but never quite gives the answers.

Originally, it was Schrader's idea to have virtually no sex in the movie but to rely on the sumptuous surroundings to provide the image of the gigolo. 'I wanted to set up the theme that this man was special,' said Schrader, 'and above all I wanted to get away from the beach-bum character with the suntan-oiled chest and that kind of sleazy appearance.'

As the script proceeded, however, Schrader knew he would have to include some hot sexuality to demonstrate to the audience Julian's prowess and technique so that they could assess him as part of the scenario in which he was set. Gere himself added to the rethink by confirming his willingness to appear in full-frontal nude scenes. Once again, his body would be amply displayed, especially during a vivid post-coital scene where Schrader allows his camera to explore his star's entire anatomy.

The love scenes made Lauren Hutton nervous. 'She was mortified at the thought of exposing herself,' Schrader remembers, 'and when we began filming a particular scene she covered up the parts of her body that were not going to be shown on camera. Richard wanted the sex to be far more graphic than it was and he worked the whole day in the nude. I'd say Richard is very comfortable with his body.'

Hutton said that Gere's decision to walk around the set nude gave her the confidence to go on. When it came to the intimate scenes where they were making love and she would have to disrobe, he insisted that all unnecessary personnel be cleared from the set. This was in addition to his prerequisite which had been in operation since filming started – regardless of the sex scenes, he wanted a closed set, with no strangers and absolutely no media people. Hutton was eternally grateful. 'There was a deep sensitivity beneath the tough, moody veneer Richard puts on in *Gigolo*,' she said. 'You could see it through his eyes. There was a real true sweetness and tenderness in Richard Gere the person, as opposed to the actor. The day I realised we were going to be friends was the day he had to stand naked in a room full of men and make a speech which, in fact, he had to do several times over. I was very touched. I was just lying there in that bed, listening and watching, and after a while, I found myself reacting to Richard not as Julian Kay but as himself and tears were streaming down my face, tears for all the pain an actor must go through.'

Although Schrader was meticulous over the sex scenes, he paid less attention to other areas, and there were wide gaps in establishing the general relationship between the Hutton and Gere characters, about which the audience was given insufficient information from the beginning. Otherwise, both performed their roles admirably, and Gere, posing in his Armani sports jackets, played it with the same kind of restrained technique that he had developed in *Days of Heaven* and *Yanks* – a fact which would certainly annoy the critics.

Gere admitted in a rare interview after filming was complete that he had visions that *American Gigolo* could really take off and that, 'Yeah, I give a shit . . . it would be fantastic for me personally as well if this movie did incredible business.' That comment alone highlighted the change that had occurred in his thinking in the eighteen months or so since he had said, 'Quite frankly, I could walk away from the whole thing.' Now he was talking about wanting to be 'up there, being watched and appreciated . . . the whole bit.'

But he was in trouble with the ambitions. He wasn't keen on the sex symbol prospect but there was no denying that that was the area in which *American Gigolo* gave him his biggest boost. As for his performance otherwise, and the movie overall, reactions were decidedly indifferent. Reviews were, as they say in the business, 'mixed' but erred towards the dissatisfied, some seriously so. The trouble was that the character of Julian was not a very likeable one, or one that the audience could readily identify with, partly because of Gere's tendency to keep a tight rein on his emotions.

He was narcissistic and shallow, and his only passion was shown when he had proved his ability to satisfy his clients. After that, his eyes were often deadpan, his movements precise and lacking in spontaneity. The only real tension came towards the end of the movie; in the intermediate stages the sex was what kept the audience amused.

So in portraying the character as written, there were bound to be accusations that Gere was underplaying again, the same criticism he faced on *Yanks*. In this case his performance was actually central to the effect Schrader was seeking. The audience, however, may have been overtaken by a sense of dullness. Movies which, in different ways, tackled the same kind of issues – *Midnight Cowboy* outstandingly and Warren Beatty's *Shampoo* in another way, and with a much lighter touch – hit the mark with more movement and reality.

Having said that, *American Gigolo* is a stylish, eminently watchable film, especially viewed today from a distance of a dozen years, when its subject matter no longer gets in the way of general considerations. At the time, there was a good deal of discussion about that aspect of the movie, and indeed there were some measured – and a few outright – attacks on both Gere and Schrader.

While the critics were, by and large, unhappy about Gere's performance, many of them seemed also to be settling a score for what they considered his ill-mannered reaction to the media. None, however, doubted that Gere had talent, even if it was, as Pauline Kael scowled, a 'soap opera' impersonation of Robert De Niro.

Invariably, the focus came down to his sex appeal, which would remain with him long after the discussion over *American Gigolo* had subsided. In this, he was his own promoter – aided by his struggling friend Herb Ritts, with whom he had lodged a couple of years earlier. Since then, Ritts had worked in a variety of jobs but had decided to concentrate on his photography and now used Gere as a model for a portfolio of stunning sexy snaps which would be sold to newspapers and magazines. He also produced glamour posters of Gere which were marketed commercially. It was, said the actor, the only way he could control the way his image was projected.

So Gere himself played a large role in the way his image was perceived as *American Gigolo* established him as one of the sex symbols of the 1980s. Perhaps not unexpectedly, because of the nature of the role and the admitted homoerotic subtext of Gere's performances, his appeal bridged the male–female divide with photographs that were clearly focused upon their sexual ambiguity.

The bold and frequent display of his naked body was an obvious and deliberate attraction to women. Heterosexual men also found him stylistically interesting, because of his Armani clothes, his stances and his moody, sullen glances, combined with his obvious ability to control his impulses and passions to the point of being the epitome of Mr Cool.

He also found himself a sudden hero and pin-up of the gay community, who were attracted firstly by the intriguing background nuances of *American Gigolo*, which were never fully explained, then by Gere's body, and finally by his off-duty attire of leathers and jeans, the former Dean/Brando uniform long ago adopted by many gays as their own. Suddenly, the posters that he had had printed of Herb Ritts's pictures of him were in terrific demand.

The character that Gere was creating and offering up as his own was full of dark corners, simply because he did not conform to the accepted pattern of emerging stars. And the homoerotic theme that caused so much impact was carefully choreographed.

Paul Schrader and Gere agreed between themselves how this multisexual appeal should be achieved. Schrader commented, 'It was a time when we were at the apex of the gay movement with all its manifestations, especially in the arts. The influence was everywhere, in fashion, disco, even the drug scene, and it affected the film's aesthetics too. All my friends at the time were gay. I didn't know what Richard's sexual orientation was, and I didn't care. I made him watch *Purple Moon*, with Alain Delon. I told him I wanted the same cocky arrogance from him and that's basically what he did. The result was quite incredible.'

The cocky image was not something he could just leave up there on the screen. It was taken pretty much as read that this characterisation was actually the real Richard Gere, the same Richard Gere who had been so elusive and touchy virtually since his name began to be mentioned in the critics' circles. The fanzines and gossip columns also began to show decidedly more determination in their attempts to uncover clues about his private life and personal relationships, which became the object of constant investigation by writers anxious to get him to commit himself.

Whenever they got the chance, they asked the questions they asked of all stars: How's your love life? When are you getting married? Gere responded enigmatically, and thus fuelled the mystique: 'I don't know what marriage is,' he once said. 'It's nothing I understand. I understand relationships with people but getting married and having a family is not a drive of mine.'

Sylvia Martins, who had joined him in Los Angeles during the filming of *American Gigolo*, recalled those early years of her association with him as sometimes traumatic, often embarrassing and occasionally hurtful. 'He was a real drama queen,' she recalled in 1990, after their relationship had ended. 'He was the most ambitious person I'd ever met. I could never understand why he would want such success and then act the way he did. He was Sean Penn before Sean Penn was. When people wanted his autograph, or girls would come up to him, he could be quite rough with them. Twice he even took his clothes off in public . . . you know, pulled down his pants. What is it you say, showed them his moon. I was mortified. But all of that is a cover . . . he is so afraid of being hurt.'

He continued as best he could in his efforts to keep his private life private, and gradually let it be known that his liberal views and personal assessment of the right of the individual to choose would not rule out association with gay causes, gay rights or gay topics, or with various other minority rights groups.

From these early stages of his rise to fame, beginning at the time of his involvement with *American Gigolo*, he showed none of the manic fear of gay association that was the nightmare of stars who truly were closet homosexuals, and so he became viewed as a media curiosity, a star devoid of the usual defining boundaries because he had himself refused to set them. His star appeal therefore broadened to include an unusually wide range of fans, and if his reticent, almost self-conscious performances on and off screen got up the noses of the critics, they also tantalised his followers, gays, straights, men, women and movie buffs alike.

By the time *American Gigolo* appeared, opening in 600 cinemas on 31 January 1980, Gere had also added a new dimension to his persona, plunging straight to the heart of theatrical controversy.

For all the great expectations that were held for *American Gigolo* when it opened, it might have been expected that Gere would have held himself in readiness for the flood of movie offers that were sure to result. In fact, far from courting a new screen role, he ducked out of sight almost as soon as the filming of *Gigolo* was complete, and flew off to Europe and the Far East to begin negotiating his return to the stage, in what promised to be a most outstanding proposition.

In May 1979, when he was released by Schrader, he went first to Cannes to attend the opening of *Days of Heaven* at the festival, where he was warmly applauded by an appreciative European audience. This was an important moment for him. He then flew to Rome for a meeting with Italian director Franco Zeffirelli, who wanted him for an all-star production of *Hamlet* which was to be staged in Los Angeles in the autumn. From there, Gere travelled eastwards for his first visit to India, to which he would return on many occasions in the future, and then on to Nepal, Thailand and Bali.

Although he considered New York to be his base, he still had no permanent home there, having been living out of a hotel room for months. His few possessions would have fitted into the back of a car, except that he did not own a car either. He intended to move to Los Angeles just as soon as Zeffirelli gave him a date for the start of *Hamlet* and was expecting to be taken up with it for a year, first in rehearsals and then in performance. So he had made no other plans and told his agent Ed Limato to hold all calls.

In fact, he made a lot of sacrifices for the Shakespeare project. He turned down two film offers and cleared his diary for months ahead, expecting a long run. He was fascinated by Shakespeare, and for an American actor it was a rare chance, an enticing experience: to be directed on stage by Zeffirelli in a four-hour adaptation of the play specially edited and shortened by Laurence Olivier, who had won an Oscar for best actor and best picture when he produced, directed and starred in his own film version in 1948.

Additionally, there were some fine actors already signed

to the project, including Roy Scheider, E. G. Marshall and Jean Simmons, who had co-starred in Olivier's film version. It represented an unmissable feast, and quite apart from the experience, there was a considerable prestige factor – playing Hamlet before an audience which could be guaranteed to include people with power and influence.

But less than a month after he returned to the US, the Zeffirelli project was cancelled. The Los Angeles theatre group which had been sponsoring the production pulled out, apparently alarmed at rising estimates of costs. Gere was naturally disappointed but his yearning to go back to the theatre was assuaged almost immediately by another remarkable opportunity negotiated for him by Ed Limato. He would take the lead in the Broadway production of the controversial play *Bent* which was running at the Royal Court Theatre, London.

The play had originated at the annual O'Neill Playwrights' Conference at Waterford, Connecticut, which was founded by locally raised funds in 1965 as a centre where new authors from all over America could have their work presented and discussed, and where young actors could gather in the hope of getting a role in one of the performances. Many famous plays have been first performed there and many famous actors have passed through the summer camp: Michael Douglas, for example, was a scenery hand there when he met his friend-to-be Danny DeVito in 1969.

In the summer of 1978, all the talk was about a play by Martin Sherman, a dramatic account of homosexuals in Nazi Germany and their battle for self-preservation in the concentration camps. It had aroused controversy even before its première at Waterford on 4 August 1978, with incredulous murmurings about the merging of these two most sensitive issues.

Like all plays at the conference, *Bent* was scheduled for three performances and then subjected to a critique and discussion, with the author expected to defend his position if so called upon. While the production was generally admired, the play itself was attacked and Sherman was accused of using it as a kind of clarion call to gay activists, a warning that the attacks upon pre-war gays in Germany could be repeated in modern society.

Sherman denied that this was his intention, and during the heated discussion about the play's content and structure, which, it was noted, was quite political, he declared that it had not been in his mind to equate modern isolated murders of homosexuals with an official government policy of extermination. However, there was outrage over the implication of there being competition in suffering between Jews and homosexuals.

The play was already set for a lively media reception when, after some rewriting, it opened in London on 3 May 1979, under the direction of Robert Chetwyn and starring Ian McKellen and Tom Bell. The producers, presumably to try to avoid the sort of row that had followed its presentation at Waterford, made a point of inserting a long note in the programme outlining the history of gay persecution in Germany from 1871 to 1936, and events leading up to the atrocities committed in concentration camps. The notes included a bibliography for anyone interested in pursuing the subject further.

The play, as might be expected, drew a wide mix of reviews and a considerable amount of criticism, especially from the Jewish community, whose leaders were outraged at the suggestion that the Jews were better treated by the Nazis than were homosexuals. There was wider controversy over the implication that the brutalising and murder of gays could somehow be equated with their treatment by modern society. The most ardent gay activists, then, as now, would insist that it was an entirely feasible notion; the actor who could portray that view would certainly be their hero.

Although the notices were not wholly encouraging, *Bent* did reasonable business and was transferred to a larger theatre, the Criterion, on 4 July 1979, settling in for a run of almost five months. The play needed the British run to get it on to Broadway, but the American producer, Jack Schlissel, who was planning to stage it in New York with a December 1979 opening, insisted: 'It is not a British import. I picked up the option first.'

Nevertheless, the Broadway director he had hired, Robert Allen Ackerman, flew to London in May to watch McKellen and Bell, and came back full of enthusiasm. It was another three months before the production was confirmed, along with the news that Richard Gere and David Dukes would take the starring roles. Gere was ecstatic and accepted as soon as the offer was formalised, in spite of warnings by some of his friends that it could destroy his movie career in homophobic Hollywood. He saw the play as an important cornerstone of his career, giving weight to his own personal claim that he was not just a pretty face and a sexy body, suited only to Hollywood froth.

In September 1979 Gere was back in Europe to attend the Rome film festival, where he won the Golden David award for his performance in *Days of Heaven* – an example of how the Europeans steadfastly make their own judgements; they have given awards to many actors who have been knocked sideways by US critics.

From Rome, he went straight to Germany to study the postwar social history of homosexuals, and then on to Dachau itself. Returning to the US, he arranged to meet novellist Christopher Isherwood, whose best-known pre-war works include *Mr Norris Changes Trains* and *Goodbye to Berlin*, based upon his own experiences in the decadence of pre-Hitler Berlin.

Bent opens in Berlin in the mid-1930s. Max, the character played by McKellen and Gere, and his lover Rudy are identified as homosexuals sent to Dachau. Max, however, denies his sexual proclivity, and to prove his claims takes part in the killing of his lover and has intercourse with a dead thirteen-year-old girl.

This behaviour enables him to wear the yellow Star of David rather than the pink triangle emblazoned upon the clothes of homosexuals. Eventually, however, he falls in love with a fellow prisoner, Horst (David Dukes), and they consummate their feelings by talking to one another, fully dressed, three feet apart. The scene climaxes with a remarkable mutual orgasm. When Horst is murdered by guards, Max rips the pink triangle off the body of his lover and puts it on his own uniform.

Bent opened at the New Apollo Theatre on 2 December 1979, two months before *American Gigolo* was released. So, quite apart from the controversy of the play itself, there was great attention paid to its leading actor. It was a physically demanding work and he was on stage virtually throughout. But it was not the mere physical demands of the play that were draining. As McKellen himself had confirmed, it was also hugely demanding both mentally and emotionally. Gere commented: 'I've never had a part like it. I had never imagined what it's like to be shattered every night. When I break through my own selfish defence and gently make love to Horst when he's so sick, because I need him, too. That's a beautiful moment. Then the guards say, "Watch. Watch." Then they kill him. Eight times a week I'm destroyed.'

Bob Ackerman, the director, praised Gere's very 'thorough' performance. 'There was nothing he would not reveal to the audience . . . he never showed any temperament and worked extremely hard with quite extraordinary dedication.' He won similar applause from the critics, and even those who took issue with the play's message heaped praise upon him, most specifically for having the courage to take on the role at all, considering the risks it entailed for his career.

As Cynthia Heimel, who was at the opening night for the *SoHo Weekly News*, wrote: 'Richard does his final curtain call, his performance was uneven with flashes of pure brilliance. Now he looks scared and small as the audience cheers for him. I have tears in my eyes for that arrogant son of a bitch.'

To those who knew him off stage and off screen, Gere *was*

an arrogant son of a bitch. Tennessee Williams went to see what all the excitement was about at the New Apollo. His friend Dotson Rader, author and Lincoln Center committee member, recalls in his memoir *Cry From the Heart*: 'In Hollywood and on Broadway an entire new generation of actors had reached stardom . . . Tennessee went to see *Bent* [and] after the performance he and his good friend Maria St Just went backstage to congratulate the actors on their performance. When Maria and he entered Gere's dressing room, they found the actor lounging in a chair wearing only a pair of Jockey shorts. Gere stared at them. Tennessee shyly introduced himself and Maria, and proceeded to compliment Gere on his performance. Richard Gere said nothing, simply sat there staring at Tennessee with a look of smug boredom, Maria losing patience with what she knew was insulting behaviour, that he did not have the courtesy to at least stand when the nation's greatest playwright came backstage to compliment him on his acting. Gere said nothing and Tennessee left in confusion having once again suffered loss of face.'

The play ran on Broadway for eight months. Gere's physical appearance altered dramatically, quite apart from the need for a shaven head. His weight dropped almost visibly week by week, until he had lost nearly a stone from his already slim form. In the weeks and months he performed the play, he received well over 2,000 letters, many from gay people applauding his willingness to take the role. There were letters from people in all walks of life, from lawyers to priests, from teachers to housewives. Although some were cranky and suggestive, and some were critical of the play itself, most were supportive.

Together, *American Gigolo* and the Broadway run of *Bent* finally launched Gere into the star bracket, due as much to the controversy of both actor and material as to anything else. He had also proved that he could take risks and win; he didn't have to be nice to people, and generally speaking he wasn't at this particular stage of his life. Paul Schrader noticed evidence of this when he visited Gere backstage during the run of *Bent*. 'The demographics of the stage door have changed since the opening of *Gigolo*,' he said. 'There was an extraordinarily hardy contingent of young people of both sexes who weren't there previously. They did not seem to mind in the least when Gere came marching out of the theatre each night looking like a Dachau victim instead of the "luscious fruit of Hollywood", the glamorous Southern California fantasy they'd come to see.'

Chapter Seven

Hello, Dalai

So what does it take to be a star? The most remarkable thing was that there should be a debate at all on the strength of one sexy but otherwise moderate movie, and three others that similarly did not constitute a major sensation. But it was like the opening of a floodgate; the water had been building up and suddenly it was let loose. Gere was totally encircled by hype and media. Everyone had been talking about him for months, clutching at slender straws because he would not tell them anything, and now at last there was something concrete to focus on and take issue with.

For example: there was an argument going on in a well-known newspaper watering hole named Costello's on New York's East 44th Street that I happened to run into early in 1980. The chat was loud and lively by happy hour and that night Richard Gere was the subject of the conversation. Gere had apparently just been barracked by the press corps in Washington for being 'rude and uncooperative' when he attended a White House tribute to James Cagney. That in itself spoke volumes: why would a powerful group of journalists in the nation's capital, more used to dealing with the Tricky Dickies of this world, feel it necessary to turn on a relatively unimportant New

York actor? It did not make sense.

One of our number had been to see Gere in *Bent* the previous night and thought he was brilliant. Another who had already seen him in a press preview of *American Gigolo* said the movie proved only one thing, that Gere's greatest asset was his body, and it was the talk of his sex appeal, not his talent as an actor, that was drawing the audiences in large numbers to the movie.

But, claimed the opposite view, it was impossible to say that about his performance in *Bent*, because with his hair shorn and his clothes at the opposite extreme to the Armani togs he wore in *Gigolo*, Gere had to rely solely on his strength as an actor to keep the punters happy. That discussion among largely cynical newsmen more or less mirrored the media comment, with most journalists agreeing that it was Gere's blithe willingness to bare the body beautiful and his rather sensuous oral and facial qualities that had brought him this far.

The debate was also about money. The talk was that Gere would be a millionaire from the proceeds of the film and would certainly get $1 million or more, plus a percentage, for his next movie. And so from nowhere, he was promoted into the lower regions of the A-list, a substar, although as producer Trevor Wallace has pointed out, this was in part due to the dearth of young male stars who were considered 'bankable' at the time.

A glance at that year's Oscar nominations, for example, shows no real sign of more youthful aspiring stars coming through. The list for the best actor award comprised: Dustin Hoffman (who won it for *Kramer v. Kramer*), Jack Lemmon (*The China Syndrome*), Al Pacino (*And Justice For All*), Peter Sellers (*Being There*) and Roy Scheider (*All That Jazz*). Pacino, at forty-one the youngest of the group, was himself only just edging towards the $1 million-plus pay scale. The fact was that Hollywood was on the brink of a new era of blockbusters, with the mainstream studios, now in the hands of multimedia conglomerates, revising their marketing strategy and development programmes towards the mythical $100 million grossers that would soon become commonplace.

The strategy was in its infancy and after the huge success of movies like *Superman*, *Saturday Night Fever* and, later, *ET* was being tailored to aim at the younger end of the market – the fifteen to twenty-five bracket. It was also linked for the first time in history to the emerging video boom which followed the Walt Disney organisation's unsuccessful litigation to stop Sony selling video recorders because of potential copyright violations. Though widely supported in Hollywood, Disney's action was seen as just as much a head-in-the-sand attitude as that of the old Golden Age moguls who refused to have anything to do with television in the 1950s. In time, of course, Disney slammed into reverse and became one of the biggest beneficiaries of the video boom.

The movie industry was in 1980 in a state of upheaval and redirection on a scale only comparable with the arrival of mass ownership of televisions. The business plans being drawn and redrawn by the studio executives would direct Hollywood's output to more sex, more violence and ultimately the explosion of the art of the spectacular. Within three or four years, a whole new generation of movie actors in their early twenties would be tearing up and down the Los Angeles boulevards in their Porsches or on their Harley Davidsons, and fees for the lead stars would go through the roof.

Gere was there as it all began to take off, and because of the lack of young stars, the arc lights of media attention beamed down upon him as the millions were being racked up in the box offices for *American Gigolo*. In spite of the largely indifferent reviews, the film took more at the cinemas in its first week of release than the rest of Gere's movies put together.

More importantly for those casting their net for new stars in Hollywood, *American Gigolo* took more than three times the grosses notched up for Robert De Niro's masterpiece of metamorphosis in *Raging Bull*, released the same year. In the emerging age of all-powerful agents and deal-makers, that was always the bottom line. As Ed Limato would say, as a matter of policy for the giant agencies which managed the stars: 'You have to get into the position of being the hunted, not the hunter. Then we can really talk money.'

That was another bone of contention among critics like the *New Yorker*'s Pauline Kael, who, it will be recalled, acidly described Gere's performance as a soapy impersonation of De Niro. In other words, the critics were saying: Is there no justice? On the other side of the journalistic fence, however, Gere was being plastered all over the feature pages. This undoubtedly helped the movie no end. For a brief moment after *American Gigolo* was released and the reviews were being read, it had looked as if Gere would remain in Limato's category of the hunter, looking for parts.

Then the box office tills began to jingle and there were queues around the block for the movie. Overnight it all changed. As Gere himself admitted: 'Paul [Schrader] and I were just saying we must find some other way to make a living, running guns to Afghanistan, maybe. Then suddenly, people who wouldn't take our phone calls a week ago are calling us.' Schrader had experienced the high and lows of public and critical reaction as an author and director, and recognised that for an actor – especially one in Gere's position on the precipice of fame – success at the box office was crucial.

In those early months of 1980, with the success of *Gigolo* being compounded by the actor's performance in *Bent* several career options opened up to Gere. Perhaps the asset that most swung him towards the Hollywood star syndrome was his appeal to the younger audience. This, however, clashed with his personal aim to be seen as a serious actor, not as an icon of the teenyboppers and attractive young things of both sexes who crowded around the stage door of the New Apollo every night. That appeal was the subject of much discussion.

Author Richard Price, who had known Gere since 1977, said that although directors' raves seemed unanimous, the response of the ticket-buyers had always been mixed. 'Young women and young gay men seemed to be turned on to Gere almost straight across the board. But when you talked to others, he ran into trouble; they found his sexuality diluted by his inability to reach out and make them feel needed,' he said.

Paul Schrader recognised the same trouble and thought it was to do with Gere's personal struggle about using his sexuality. 'The limit to his success as an actor,' said Schrader, 'was the degree he played to his looks or played against them. I'm not sure that he knew which way to jump. He was apprehensive about the sex symbol tag but he was not even sure that he should deny it, either.'

With Gere on public view nightly on Broadway, the producers and directors who were interested in hiring him had ample opportunity to watch him work, a major plus for any actor in his position. Being seen working is very different from being called in for an audition reading or an interview, as several other actors around at the time well knew. It was also easy to see why he became a media personality: there were few in his generation of stars who were anywhere near as appealing for photographic spreads in the glossies.

Michael Douglas, for example, six years older than Gere, was still struggling to hit the big time. He had already won an Oscar, for *One Flew Over the Cuckoo's Nest*, but as a co-producer not an actor. He had just appeared with Jane Fonda and Jack Lemmon in *The China Syndrome*, a movie that he initiated and nurtured, but high-profile roles still evaded him. As he himself said, apart from the period of his television series *The Streets of San Francisco*, rejection had become a way of life.

Nick Nolte was also finding it hard to break through. Though he had appeared in a couple of movies that foretold the arrival of a distinctive new face, it was well into the

1980s before he was widely recognised. Other contemporaries like Kurt Russell, Jeff Bridges, Kevin Costner and Robin Williams were all at the 'struggling actor' stage. Mel Gibson had made the first *Mad Max* film in Australia but it was not until *Mad Max II* in 1981 that his career took off. Bruce Willis, meanwhile, was still a wannabe serving cocktails in a New York bar.

One of the traditional Hollywood traits is the need to compare new actors with others, living or dead. It is something that is done not only in the fan magazines but among the studio executives too. Gere's screen presence was commonly summed up thus: 'Well, he's a moody mix of Dean, Brando and Gable', or 'He's Gary Cooper with De Niro's mystique . . .' Considerable attention was paid to his looks: 'Gere has the angular face and masculine wistfulness of the traditional sentimental tough guys – from Bogart to Garfield to Dean . . . he has high cheekbones, deep-set brown eyes and a street fighter's nose,' wrote one critic.

It was true that he would have few rivals in a beefcake parade of current male actors, and now he was a strong contender on the 'Who's Hot' list, bolstered by an apparent willingness to expose his body, and to take risks with parts like Max in *Bent* that few other budding stars would have touched. The telephone never stopped ringing. At the same time Gere's bristling, Garbo-esque attitude to the media clamour for interviews and photographs became self-feeding, although he mellowed somewhat as the need to keep the customers coming through the doors of the New Apollo became a matter that he could not neglect. Even so, he tried to control the interviews around safe subjects without letting journalists inside his head. *Rolling Stone*, *Cosmopolitan*, *People* magazine, *Newsweek* and others all came knocking on his door and usually went away to write a piece which highlighted the enigma of the man. Michael Segell in *Rolling Stone* described him as 'The Heartbreaker' because of his new status as a bankable star, but remembered meeting him some months earlier: 'It occurs to me five minutes into our first conversation that it wouldn't bother me a bit if he strangled himself. He seems to reserve for interviews the sentiments a dog has for flea baths.'

And lest anyone should not get the message, Gere would emphasise, as he did to Segell after an enquiry about his love life: 'It's nobody's business but mine who I'm fucking and who I'm not fucking.'

Guy Flatley of *Cosmopolitan*, despatched to discover the inner man on behalf of his eager readers, decided that it was 'the perfect time to probe the motives and methods, the private dreams that initially propelled Richard Gere into the public spotlight. Yet sitting opposite this emotionally and physically spent actor after a taxing matinée, I hesitate to pry into the possible parallels between him and the tormented homosexual he plays in *Bent* or the sublimely proficient hustler in *American Gigolo*. And for a very sound reason – namely Gere's celebrated contempt for baring his psyche (if not his body) in front of strangers.' Flatley hardly managed to prise any great revelations from Gere, though he did get an interesting, sensible and unusually frank response to his question about the problems of playing a gay man, a question which could easily have been dismissed with a meaningless answer.

'I don't think the problem is getting into the head of a homosexual,' Gere replied. 'We are all capable of being stimulated by members of both sexes, of taking pleasure in the sexuality of both men and women. In its purest and most innocent sense, sexuality has no bounds. What isn't so easy is experiencing the precise guilt and fear that homosexuals have been forced to live with in this society . . . but an actor doesn't work from direct experience alone. He deals in metaphor and analogy also. My sexual preferences aside – which should be of concern to no one – there are things in my life that I've been made to feel guilty about, things I feel I must hide. Although society isn't telling me I have to love a woman, I certainly have some impediments in loving fully.'

Such references simply made everyone more anxious to get to him, with the interest focused more on the man himself than on his acting proficiency. Writers everywhere enjoy the prospect of a verbal duel that can be transcribed into a readable piece that has, as they say in the trade, a bit of balls, rather than the usual kind of pap that the publicists prefer to be proffered by the interviewer. In that respect, when he did agree to be interviewed, Gere clearly had deeper thoughts than most would give him credit for, and in the end he made good copy.

It was also interesting that those who were successful in breaking through the barriers he set up around himself usually did so on neutral territory. Few managed to glimpse the accoutrements of his newly enriched state which had enabled him to throw out an anchor and dispense with his nomadic existence of the past year. He did not actually rush out and buy a Porsche, but he did equip himself with a yellow Alfa Romeo Spyder which he kept in Los Angeles, while in New York he settled himself in a half-a-million-dollar penthouse apartment in Greenwich Village and established an identity that his friends reckoned had been seriously absent from his life. House and home tells much about personal tastes, and that was why he kept the 'vultures' away.

His apartment had an expansive living area, with polished timber floors covered with a scattering of Persian rugs. A grand piano took central position, and he played it often. The rooms were carefully if sparsely furnished with a mixture of American antiques and contemporary pieces placed around a steamer-trunk coffee table. He was noted among his friends as a considerate host, with camomile tea always on hand.

His closest companions, of whom there were in fact few, might be invited to join him in a work-out of t'ai chi ch'uan exercises, which he practised daily and which were credited with having a calming effect on his media-invaded soul. And to help keep his body in shape, he had equipped himself with a mini-gymnasium of barbells and weights.

His attention to his physical and mental well-being had been a preoccupation since his student days when, it will be recalled, he had intended to major in philosophy. He had continued his interests in that direction, acquiring dozens of books on associated spiritual subjects.

Gere's appearance in *American Gigolo* coincided with the onset of a new era of social madness and sexual disarray. No one could have recognised it at the time, but the undercurrents in this movie had implications that would rebound down the years, for Gere himself and society in general.

With hindsight it can be seen that the film was coincidentally positioned between the end of the raging freedoms of the 1970s and the beginning of a new set of social parameters that arrived with the 1980s, with the explosion of cocaine usage and the AIDS panic. Gere's reactions to this change were curiously at odds. On the one hand, he went through a period when his use of cocaine took him way beyond the description of flirtation or experimentation with the drug. There were few movie sets around at the time where cocaine was not being freely pushed, and for two or three years he was a heavy social user.

At the same time, he had begun to expand his interest and research into Buddhism. The search for the roots of this spiritual force had captured the interest of many artists and writers and other prominent people in the West. It had already taken Gere on his tour of Asia, and in 1981 he had his first meeting with the Dalai Lama, the spiritual leader of the Tibetan nation who had lived in exile in the mountain retreat of Dharmsala, India, since the Chinese invaded his country in 1950.

The meeting was arranged through the writer John Avendon, by way of Gere's good friend Jann Wenner, the editor and publisher of *Rolling Stone* magazine, whom he had got to know well in the late 1970s. Wenner counted many actors and directors among his friends, and through these contacts ran many revealing interviews with personalities – although Gere was not one of them. The two men were close enough for Gere, a couple of years later, to stand as godfather to Wenner's first son.

The meeting with the Dalai Lama came at a time when Gere's mind was filled with worries and troubles about the direction of his career and personal life, and it had a profound effect on him, leading him, in due course, towards a dedication to the Tibetan cause and to wholehearted devotion to Buddhism and the spiritual leader himself. At that time, in 1981, it was a developing situation. Within a couple of years, it would engulf his thoughts and help shape his future.

What remained a positive determination in his life was to keep himself to himself, and let no uninvited intruders into his world. If there was a similarity between Gere and De Niro, as some had tried to suggest, it was in this resolve to keep his private life completely watertight. There had been virtually no mentions in the gossip columns of his girlfriends, he was seldom caught by the paparazzi out on the town and his relationship with Sylvia Martins remained, for the time being, unreported.

The offers of work coming in, meantime, had failed to give him the kind of material that he wanted. After his appearances in *American Gigolo* and *Bent*, another flood of sexually explicit scripts arrived from producers from various independent companies trying to tempt him back to the screen after he concluded his run at the New Apollo.

He was in no hurry, and for months rejected offers from all quarters – including one for a new project at Paramount which was being sold as having been tailor-made for Gere. He had a good relationship with the studio, which was desperate to get him back on its lot to pursue a follow-up to the success of *American Gigolo*. He had, in the studio's view, already been away too long, and the commercial impact of *Gigolo* would be fading the time he was back on the screen.

The new project was entitled *An Officer and a Gentleman*, and would in time prove to be Gere's most outstanding film to date, in prestige way above anything he had tackled before – but he would have to be persuaded of that. At the time, he did not want to know. The film began life as an outline for an original screenplay by Douglas Day Stewart, who had just finished work on the 1980 remake of *Blue Lagoon*. Its theme was very much in the mould of both *Gigolo* and *Bent*, dealing as it did with a love story that did not accord with the normal Hollywood concept of romantic love. There *was* romance, and a good deal of energetic, erotic sex and steamy scenes with the female co-star, Debra Winger, but it was presented in the manner of two people learning about themselves and accepting others for who they were.

Gere was very much into that kind of discussion both personally and in his characterisations. In this case he could see the thematic similarities with the roles of Julian Kay and Max. The character's emotional dramas were given the added depth of being set against a gruelling thirteen-week training course at the Naval Aviation Officer Candidate School in Washington state.

It therefore seemed a logical move for him to accept the role quickly and willingly. But surprisingly, he turned it down flat. Jeffrey Katzenberg, production head of Paramount, was astounded. He had not believed for one moment that the upcoming star – or any young actor in Gere's position, for that matter – would have a single doubt about the part.

But Gere did. And he went on refusing, in spite of being implored by Ed Limato to accept.

Katzenberg realised at that point that Gere was not motivated by money, which was being offered in larger quantities than he had ever received before. He seemed more concerned with the art of the film than how much it would make at the box office. Katzenberg actually pleaded with him to take the part, and still Gere was reluctant. Finally, Katzenberg met him one night at an opening and went down on his knees to get Gere to say yes. Gere called him the next day and agreed.

His character, Zack Mayo, the standard military academy hero with a chip on his shoulder, is a wild youth with tattoos on his arms. A fearless rider of his motorcycle, he arrives at the academy ready to take on the world. He is a complex character, the son of an alcoholic sailor and a mother who committed suicide after her husband deserted her.

Zack has spent his formative years living in the squalor of his whoremongering father's house and is determined to rise above the mess of his parents' life. He decides he is going to turn himself into 'an officer and a gentleman' and finds himself pitted against the man charged with that task, the ruthlessly tough drill sergeant, played admirably by Lou Gossett. The training programme provides the core of the picture. Off base are the love stories and characters which populate the surrounds of the academy, notably the local girls who dream of meeting men who will whisk them away to a more glamorous life.

There are various couplings, such as the girl who tries to trick a trainee into marriage with a false pregnancy, but the Gere–Winger love story is the central romance. She is the illegitimate daughter of a similar encounter twenty years earlier, when an officer candidate loved and left her mother. Now, history is repeating itself. She meets Zack, falls in love and wants to marry him, but he is afraid of the commitment, unable to admit that he cares for her.

Meanwhile, in parallel to these off-base emotions, Zack's training as an officer and a gentleman is transforming his character and his view of life, until he has to admit to himself the truths he has tried to hide. The plot is familiar and the characters are a trifle clichéd, but the performances of the actors raise the film above what could easily have been a rather standard picture.

The sharp direction of Taylor Hackford also made it work. Hackford was a virtually untried director who had made only one movie, *The Idolmaker*, a very in-house look at the pop industry with Ray Sharkey. He had never handled screen emotions or temperamental actors and was quietly nervous about dealing with Gere, who he knew had come through the schooling of five highly starred directors. 'Richard had this immense, complex stuff inside,' said Hackford, 'and I felt I had to deal with that and reveal some of it on screen. I had always felt Richard had a terrific presence on screen, but I'd often felt he was putting up a kind of veneer there, that shut you out. When I talked with him, we had to be very honest with one another, and I said what I would hope to do was try to get past that.'

Hackford actually went straight to the heart of one of the most often-repeated criticisms of Gere's acting – that he created a gulf between himself and the audience. Hackford spent a lot of time with Gere on that very topic and the result was a total transformation. For the first time, he gave a performance which was aimed directly at the audience rather than at laying his own inner demons about acting and life in general. The discussions were not always calm and rational, and Gere, knowing that he had come into this movie in a position of strength following Katzenberg's pleadings, stood his ground. The word 'arrogant' would be used by several members of the cast in their descriptions of him.

The movie provided Gere with the opportunity to dispose of his angst, centring as it did on the rigorous demands of the officers' training course. The anger and aloofness of his screen character are swept away by the repetition of scenes which hurt him physically – 'virtual torture' under the cruel supervision of Lou Gossett's training sergeant. The result was an entirely believable performance, and one that would take his audiences with him. Hackford reckoned he had dispelled the awkward narcissism of Gere's Julian Kay so that he grabbed the emotions as well as the sexual feelings of the viewers.

The latter aspect, however, remained well to the fore to satisfy those attracted by Gere's physical presence. There was abundant exposure of what had become his most famous attributes, scenes in which he was more than adequately joined by Debra Winger. In her role of Paula, the factory worker in love with Zack, her natural and honest screen presence certainly encouraged Gere's emotional exposure as well.

Winger has co-starred with John Travolta in *Urban Cowboy*, and had also played a prostitute in the screen adaptation of John Steinbeck's *Cannery Row* with Nick Nolte. So, in the space of little more than a year, she had been cast opposite three of Hollywood's leading male attractions. But it was her appearance with Gere that moved her into the 'star' bracket. She did not particularly enjoy the experience.

Word from the set was that Gere and Winger simply did not hit it off, and director Hackford was worried that the personal anger between them was disturbing the romance of their most crucial scenes.

Winger has generally remained tight-lipped about the experience, but did confess: 'Oh dear, I am always trying to find diplomatic ways to talk about Richard and that film. The truth was that the experience I had making it was horrendous. To me, Richard was like a brick wall.' In the beginning, she found him pleasant and helpful, but during the three-month shoot, the relationship between them developed into a situation where she hardly wanted to know him, let alone get into bed with him. She described him as a cold fish who got his way by shouting at people on the set.

Gere admitted there was 'tension' between them, but dismissed it as one of those things that happens making movies, and claimed that in the end tension wasn't always a bad thing. Even so, his treatment of Winger was at complete variance with the way he took to actress Lisa Blount, who played a lesser role. 'I was a bit overawed playing opposite him, but he was a very kind man. He looked out for me because I was so keyed up,' said Lisa.

Lou Gossett, who shared a house with Gere, put his stand-offishness down to his shyness. 'We shared our pain on set because it was truly a hard film physically,' said Gossett, 'but voluntarily we stayed apart. We were in the same house, shared the same swimming pool, but he had his lady [Sylvia Martins] there and she kept him working. We'd just nod at each other on our way to work.'

Hackford put the disunity down to the demands of filming, admitting that he was a hard taskmaster. 'Richard was exhausted. I was beating him up every day. If I got to a point where I wanted a scene to look authentic and it didn't, I'd naturally do it over, again and again. Sometimes he could barely stand but he'd do it. You also have to remember that the aggression that fired Gere for much of the picture was very necessary to the story.'

Observers of these tense working relationships were worried that one of the most important love scenes in the movie would be affected. It wasn't, and Winger's performance, lying astride Gere with her face puffed with emotion and her damp hair falling over her face, was one of the most erotic exhibitions of bodily contact ever seen in a mainstream movie, long before Sharon Stone and Michael Douglas's coupling in *Basic Instinct*.

The scene caused ructions among the censors and among the studio executives, who were adamant that for commercial reasons a movie had to stay well clear of restricted ratings. The film had ignored an archaic rule in the censors' handbook which said that a woman on top wasn't allowed. The scene was, however, eventually approved, indicating the trend in Hollywood towards more explicit sex.

To the accompaniment of Winger, the love interest, and the menacing figure of Lou Gossett as the torturing drill sergeant, Gere had turned into the All-American Hero, and the critics generally responded by applauding a passionate acting performance which, as one pointed out, represented the rebirth of 'American Gigolo into American actor', implying that Gere himself had changed his approach too.

Excellent notices certainly helped to push Gere into the next level of his progression, but from the Hollywood standpoint of bankability the proof would come from the till receipts – and they were surprisingly good. Paramount Studios, by giving the movie to a relatively unknown director and placing the burden of its success on two actors who at the time were still in the waiting room of the big league, were clearly not expecting a blockbuster. But that's exactly what the film became.

After a slow-burn release in the late summer of 1982, *An Officer and a Gentleman* caught fire. The box-office grosses rocketed and it became the second biggest film of the year, beaten only by *ET* and eventually taking $125 million on the American circuit alone and $250 million worldwide. With the television rights pre-sold, the film was virtually in profit from the off. Gere had made it to the A-list.

Chapter Eight

More Heavy Breathing

The reflected glory of *An Officer and a Gentleman* helped Richard Gere to overcome his erratic, hustling image, and for a time it looked as if he would take his place at the helm of the new generation of stars bidding to replace the Robert Redfords and Paul Newmans. There were predictions that he would step up into higher things, progressing from the mediocre to the good and on to the great. Gere, however, had other ideas, and didn't stay in that comfortable-looking niche for long.

Almost as soon as he had finished *An Officer and a Gentleman*, he took a U-turn back into controversy partly as a key figure in what became something of a national debate in America in the early 1980s, the phenomenon of women ogling men. He was not a willing participant in this situation, but found himself involved because of his screen roles, which had, one after the other, involved disrobement and full-frontal nudity. In fact, he walked straight into the debate when he rejected more conventional Hollywood offers to take up another racy, sexual role in which his body would again be on full view.

Although he denied it, the new film looked like a deliberate career move to keep his 'moon', as Sylvia Martins described it, amply displayed. Sex and bodily exposure clearly remained important parts of his act. Aptly entitled *Breathless*, it was a remake of Jean-Luc Godard's new-wave classic, *A Bout de Souffle*, which made a star of Jean-Paul Belmondo in 1959. And it was to France that Gere, who was involved in the project almost from its inception, would turn to choose his own co-star.

He and director James McBride had repaired to the French capital almost as soon as he was released from *An Officer and a Gentleman*, and there they auditioned more than sixty potential leading ladies. It was important that Gere and his co-star were able to arouse in each other the required levels of passion, and so the selection procedure for the eleven short-listed young women was based upon acting out a love scene from the film. In order to achieve realism, according to one account, Gere spent three days in a hotel room, half-naked, putting the succession of passionate women through their paces, and afterwards apparently joked to McBride: 'I don't care if I never see a woman again.'

Having selected Valerie Kaprisky, an unknown eighteen-year-old, from the initial round of testing, a repeat performance was necessary to convince executives of Orion Pictures, because this movie, put up by independent producer Marty Erlichman, had been 'iffy' from the word go. Marty was the man who had discovered Barbra Streisand twenty years earlier in a Greenwich Village nightclub. He was involved in managing her until they split in the 1970s, and had been around for the most prolific period of her movie career.

Now he was out on his own, attempting to negotiate the hazardous terrain that is the lot of independent producers, trying to package and promote their wares to the Hollywood commissioning committees. And so a screen test had to sell the film, and confirm the choice of a totally unknown Parisian actress to star with Hollywood's hottest male lead of the moment.

The date was 18 July 1982, and the scene was a small sound stage rented by the hour on Francis Ford Coppola's

Zoetrope studio lot in Hollywood. Screen tests had originally been designed as a simple tryout of the acting abilities and photogenic qualities of the aspirant. Once, you could walk in off the streets and buy a screen test for $25. On it, they used to say, depended on Hollywood career.

On this one depended a Hollywood movie, and to produce an excerpt that confirmed not only the abilities of the actors, but also the tenor and style of the movie, they made it a top-shelf sample – with both Gere and Kaprisky in the nude. The five-minute piece of film would cost $35,000.

The young French actress was a touch apprehensive. She had appeared in only one movie to date, and suddenly she was being thrust on to the Hollywood casting couch with a high-profile actor. This was one of the reasons why the screen test was held in the utmost secrecy, and with a tidy measure of security. There was also the matter of the test's sexual content; it was still the early 1980s, and nudity and explicit sex in mainstream movies remained a sensationalist topic in the popular press.

Gere tried his best to put Valerie at her ease as he explained that she would have to go naked for the test. He stripped off without hesitation to help her get past the embarrassment factor. Actually, she wasn't that nervous about the nudity. She had also stripped off for her one and only previous film, *Aphrodite*, made in France the previous year, and had also featured in a spread of pictures in the French men's magazine, *Lui*.

Even so, strict precautions had been taken and the set was cleared. 'Richard and Valerie did not demand it,' said Erlichman, 'but I just wanted to reassure her it wasn't *that* kind of movie.' The sound men holding the boom stood behind a partition and the only people watching the two actors were director McBride and cinematographer Richard Kline, for whom such matters had become rather *passé* – the previous year he had filmed the steamy *Body Heat*, starring William Hurt and Kathleen Turner.

In the scene selected, Kaprisky is discovered lying on a

bed in her one-room apartment, with Gere resting his head across her thighs while she strokes his hair. As they speak, Gere slowly and noisily starts kissing his way up her body, beginning at her pubic hair, and it develops into an intense lovemaking session, with their bodies 'glistening with sweat'.

It was important, said Erlichman, to see how Kaprisky moved and to ensure that there was a chemistry between her and Gere. The actress herself was obviously impressed by the experience, especially as it was all new to her. 'I didn't want it to end,' she said. 'I can't act without feelings and I felt something very special for Richard during that scene. In life, when you feel something for someone, you spend some time with them, not just ten minutes, some laughs and some tears, and then goodbye.'

A long goodbye was still a possibility, because at the time the movie had not even reached approval stage. In fact, getting it to the point of acceptance by a studio had been a nightmare in itself. It had been to the brink several times, but at one point it seemed that the remake of *Breathless* would never get made. It had taken almost five years of battling by Erlichman to get to this stage, and it was only Gere's personal enthusiasm for the project that had seen it rise from the smouldering ashes of past rejection. Ed Limato explained, 'He was looking for something special and I was trying to steer him on a course between art and blatant commercialism.' Achieving it was another matter.

The script for *Breathless* seemed to have all that Gere wanted, especially since the French original had been an arty creation from the pen of François Truffaut, filmed under the direction of Godard. The revamped version was originally the brainchild of director McBride and his partner Kit Carson, who first delivered a ten-page outline to Erlichman in 1978. At the time, Erlichman had a production deal with Paramount, who expressed an interest, and McBride and Carson went ahead with writing the screenplay. Paramount gave the outline to Gere, who was interested in the film, but when the script was finally delivered the studio executives were unhappy and wanted new writers.

Erlichman then went to Universal, who likewise did not want McBride and Carson's version. They would only be interested if the pair dropped out – and so exit McBride and Carson. The studio commissioned a new script, which they offered to Robert De Niro. He procrastinated and then turned it down, and Universal backed out. A year later, Erlichman stirred some interest at Orion Pictures.

Orion in turn sent the script to John Travolta and then to Al Pacino. Both said no because of the nude scenes. After another year, Paramount were showing interest again, but at a rather low-key level. They gave the script to British director/writer Franc Roddam, whose only movie to date had been *Quadrophenia*, a quirky tale about mods and rockers in Brighton. Roddam also wanted Gere for the lead. It had reached budget stage when Paramount finally decided it did not want to make the movie after all. And so it was back to square one, except that now Gere was sufficiently interested to take a personal involvement.

He went back to Orion, who hired screenwriter/director Michael Mann to write a new script, which no one liked. Once again the project was foundering when a production executive at Orion had the idea of inviting the two men who had originated the project to return to the fray. McBride had done nothing of particular note to date, and Gere was unhappy about having him as director but nonetheless agreed to meet him. After talking for an hour, Gere said, 'You're the first guy I've talked to who really understands this movie.'

McBride replied: 'I ought to. It was my idea.' They agreed to join forces and produce a new script. Gere said he would like to be involved in the writing, because he could help develop the character he would be playing. Kit Carson was located and they all set to work. Carson recalled: 'It had been three years since McBride and I had worked together. He arranged to come to my place. Gere was a stranger with squinty Roy Rogers eyes and a certain cocky loneliness, but we have no time for personal considerations and we get down to the writing. Gere jumps in, playing both the joker and the judge. An ironic, mocking ease develops among us.'

The script was completed by the late spring of 1982, but even with Kaprisky's screen test delivered, Orion were still half-hearted. However, on 27 July, *An Officer and a Gentleman* was premièred to excellent reviews and within a week was clocking up the biggest box-office receipts of the year.

Now Orion became seriously interested. When their executives saw the Gere–Kaprisky screen test, the mood heightened to drooling enthusiasm and the movie that no one had wanted suddenly took on the appearance of a very significant project. The PR faction at the studio began a hastily arranged promotional effort. On 19 August 1982, when the publicity for *An Officer and a Gentleman* was peaking, Orion decided to strike while the iron was hot.

The studio's chief publicity executive, Lloyd Leipzig, took command, and organised a press party in the plush upstairs room of the Bistro, one of the smartest restaurants in Beverly Hills, to announce the news of their sensational new movie starring Richard Gere, and to launch their brand-new discovery, Valerie Kaprisky, who coincidentally also just happened to be celebrating her nineteenth birthday.

By the time Gere and Kaprisky were ushered in, the place was jam-packed, and they had to fight their way through the scrum to pose for photographs. Kaprisky was overwhelmed, especially as word of her sensational screen test leaked out. Lloyd Leipzig could be heard confiding to groups of reporters: 'Truthfully, I've never seen a test like it. You need a cold shower after you've watched it.'

Meanwhile, Marty Erlichman, who was only too willing to recall how this was just like the early days with Barbra Streisand, was predicting the arrival of a new star. 'We wanted an actress with a child-woman look,' said Erlichman, sounding dangerously like Roman Polanski. 'There were older actresses who could have played it, but they did not have her vulnerability or innocence. We knew Valerie had a nice body and she read well but it's how the camera sees her that is important. And I can tell you the camera is in love with her. She really lights up on the screen. Richard was in on the casting all the way . . . and the chemistry between them is really something very special.'

Erlichman went on to reveal that Gere was unflinchingly prepared to expose his body for the sake of his art. 'He's an organic actor,' he declared, and it was said later that one journalist misheard the quote and wrote down 'orgasmic', because Erlichman went on, 'Richard said that for him to be making love to a woman in front of the camera, it has to be someone he'd personally want to jump.'

So filming finally began on the McBride/Carson umpteenth rewrite of the Truffaut story about a petty gangster in love with a rebellious American girl, only now the nationalities are reversed and the boy is American and the girl French, and they act out the drama not in France but in Los Angeles. The other great difference, of course, was in the filming.

Godard's version was his first feature film and it established him as the most stylistic of the French new-wave directors, noted for his elliptical narrative and original use of a whole range of techniques, such as jump cuts and freeze frames, which gained him much critical appraisal though by no means universal approval.

The fact that Godard's version was an original made it a hard act to follow. Hollywood once had a similar idea of remaking Roman Polanski's first major movie, *Knife in the Water*, with Elizabeth Taylor, Richard Burton and Warren Beatty in the roles originally played by unknown Polish actors. When Paramount called Polanski and told him they wanted to do the remake, he simply asked, 'Why?'

Even so, the possibility of putting a modern overlay on the original version of *Breathless* was part of the project's appeal to Gere. He and his writers agreed from the outset that times had changed and cinema audiences were no longer surprised by the techniques that had made Godard famous. Carson explained: 'We felt that the present generation of kids had the sort of feelings that youth had when Godard made his film; the feeling of the future being very unclear . . . a generation that has no way to communicate with society. We were looking at extremes and there was no place that better typified extremes in everything than Los Angeles itself, where we set our version of the story.'

Their screenplay tells the story of Jesse Lujack, a petty car thief who kills a policeman who is pursuing him. He has only recently met French graduate student Monica but he dashes to her apartment and asks her to hide him. At first she rejects him, but eventually they fall in love and she agrees to go with him to Mexico. As they begin the journey out of Los Angeles, however, she comes to her senses and realises that she will spend her life on the run. She tries to make him leave without her, eventually by calling the police, but he refuses to go and tries to get her to commit herself to him. The film's ending is a tribute to Godard: a freeze-frame showing Lujack reaching for his gun as Monica shouts the words he wants to hear – 'I love you' – as the police start firing.

A lot of work had obviously gone into the characterisations, especially in achieving the complexity of Gere's Jesse, who is quite different from the Belmondo creation in Godard's movie. 'We had been talking about nothing else for two months,' Kit Carson remembers. '[Then one] afternoon it seems to hit him in mid-sentence. We were reworking a scene, Gere's running Jesse's lines; and the words start going faster and faster, no pauses for breath, in a new erratic rhythm. I look over and he's standing up sweat-soaked behind the desk reading, laughing, snapping his shoulders, raving on, wide open. Sounds strange, but I watch Gere change himself: loosen the outline of his body, shake up his dimensions inside. Right then he gets it, or somehow Jesse Lujack taps into Richard Gere.'

In fact, it was probably because Gere virtually created the

role for himself that his performance was interesting. It also had an effect on his relationship with Valerie Kaprisky, who was experiencing her first onscreen romance and finding that the intensity was such that the role overlapped into her private feelings. She admitted that in the end it was difficult to differentiate the actor from the character he was playing. 'Richard's character makes me, in my role, so much more sensual. The problem for me, the difficulty if you like, was that Richard was not far from the character and so it became a confusing situation. Richard was wonderful to work with. He gives you everything to react to.'

The film was shot in eight weeks in locations around Los Angeles, and everyone seemed satisfied. On the day after they completed filming, McBride and his technicians moved into the editing suite at Zoetrope and began the task of slicing their film into a presentable print, while Gere and Sylvia packed their bags and flew to Mexico. He was already behind schedule for his next movie, and was going into his films one after the other with barely a break between them.

It was a journey that started with great hope and promise and ended in fiasco and near-disaster – even though he had chosen his new film with care. Bits of his world were already falling apart.

For his next role, Gere had opted for a less spectacular part but one which he seriously wanted to do, in a film adaptation of Graham Greene's novel *The Honorary Consul* which had been initiated by the British producer Norma Heyman. The project was a largely British operation and Heyman had assembled a strong team. The film was based on a screenplay by Christopher Hampton (later an Oscar-winner for *Dangerous Liaisons*) and a good company included Michael Caine and Bob Hoskins, and Scottish director John MacKenzie, who had made a name for himself – and for Hoskins – with his brutal 1980 movie, *The Long Good Friday*.

Heyman's search for financial backing and an American distribution deal took her to Hollywood. She negotiated the sale of the US rights to Paramount, who sought the usual provisos about maintaining control of the American version of the movie. Of course, they would also like a hot American star in the lead, and they put forward the name of Richard Gere, with whom the studio had had a friendly and profitable relationship. Gere needed no persuading, and indeed even accepted a substantially lower fee than his current asking price of $1.5 million.

This was surprising to some, because his role in the film was once again an unsympathetic and unlovable character who would hardly win audience approval, Gere's most troublesome area in the past. But again, it had more to do with the prestige of the work than the commercial possibilities it might or might not hold. He loved the script. It also contained some love scenes, upgraded for the film version, in which his handsome physique would once again be amply displayed.

From the initial publicity sound-bites from Paramount executives, it seemed unclear whether they actually knew of Greene's book, or even what kind of a movie they would be getting. It appeared to be sufficient for them that the film contained several bouts of explicit sex in which Gere would be featured.

It must also be said that, like F. Scott Fitzgerald's work (notably *The Great Gatsby* and *The Last Tycoon* – both of which were filmed by Paramount), Graham Greene's novels are not easily transcribed to the big screen. The subtleties are often lost in the 110 minutes or so of film-making and the author himself was known to have disliked, sometimes hated, many of the previous efforts to film his books. Hampton had made a very passable attempt at this one, a political thriller with the usual Greene complexities of human behaviour which provide meaty roles for tortured actors.

Michael Caine was cast as the warm-hearted, heavy-drinking British consul based in northern Argentina who is kidnapped by rebel activists. Gere plays the central role of the consul's best friend, a doctor who betrays him to the rebels and then seduces his wife. Bob Hoskins is the ruthless police chief of the Argentinian town where most of the action is centred.

When Gere and Sylvia arrived for location filming in Veracruz, Mexico, Caine and Hoskins were already *in situ*. Although Hoskins was a newcomer and slightly in awe of his colleagues on what was his first major overseas location shoot with Hollywood involvement, he never let his nervousness show, and to Gere, he and Caine must have looked like long-time Cockney buddies. 'Hoskins is very much a "what you see is what you get" man,' Caine recalled. 'On screen he looks as though he might be a wonderful guy if you ever met him, and that is exactly what he is, besides being a brilliant actor. Not a bad combination if you are going to work with someone in a tough place for a long while – and Mexico is a tough place to work.'

Richard Gere, on the other hand, was the opposite of the two hearty Londoners and came into the situation in his usual quiet, aloof manner. 'What you can see of him [in person] is very little, and not necessarily what you are going to get,' said Caine. 'He is a very shy, inward-looking man until he gets to know and trust you and then, as I very quickly found, he is as charming as Bob and almost as funny. He was also, unlike Bob and myself, a very spiritual sort of a man and a devout Buddhist. As an actor he was also the opposite of us, for we are very similar in style, relaxed but forceful. He was very intense, both as an actor and a person.'

The film shoot was based upon a series of locations, starting at a small town outside Veracruz on the coast of the Gulf of Mexico. The heat lay over the area like a heavy electric blanket, interrupted only by a swirling wind that blew sand and dust everywhere. Living conditions were not good either and Caine recalled that 'every location we went to seemed to be filthier than the last one'. Before very long, cast and crew began to fall victim to dysentery and other local bugs; they became ill one after the other – except for Michael Caine, who had devised his own preventative medicine: one large straight vodka before meals, all food consumed with wine, followed by one (sometimes two or three) large brandy after meals.

About halfway through filming, Gere was taken seriously ill with suspected food poisoning, and in great pain and with a high temperature he was admitted to a local hospital, where he was hooked up to an intravenous drip to feed him vitamins and stop dehydration. 'He didn't want to cause trouble,' Norma Heyman remembers, 'but it was very debilitating. However, he insisted on carrying on and I would arrive ruthlessly early in the morning and whisk him off to work and return him to hospital in the evening.'

Michael Caine meanwhile did some investigating and asked Sylvia where they had eaten the night before Gere became ill. She told him it was a small restaurant near the hotel beach – which Caine described as a 'rubbish-strewn stretch of sand lapped by waves from a toxic nightmare'. He clapped his hand over his mouth in horror. A couple of nights earlier, he had been walking along the beach and passed by the back of the same restaurant. 'As I approached, I saw a sight I had never thought to see again after I left Korea, but there they were – thousands of rats who, when they saw me, ran under the café where Sylvia and Richard had eaten that night,' said Caine.

Filming in Mexico carried on regardless, and lasted a gruelling three months, during which time an already slim Richard Gere lost another half-stone in weight. There was to be yet one more dangerous incident. Gere and Caine had clubbed together to hire a small plane to fly them to Mexico City for a break. Caine's wife Shakira was flying in from Los Angeles to join him there.

They all spent a long weekend wining and dining and sightseeing, and on Monday morning Caine and Gere returned in their little plane to a location somewhere out in the wilds where the only landing facility was a grassy runway. As they came in to land, the plane was surrounded by a troop of machine-gun-wielding Mexican soldiers who accused the two actors of being drug smugglers; and they weren't joking. Eventually, it was all sorted out and Caine and Gere were allowed to travel on their way. 'It was the last of anything remotely interesting on this film and after an eternity we all flew quickly back to our loved ones,' said Caine.

But for Gere, the troubles on the making of *The Honorary Consul* were nothing compared with what was zooming towards him next. Ahead lay the worst two years of his life, problem after problem, and at the end of it his career and Hollywood status were on the edge of oblivion.

Chapter Nine

Sex Object

The new year of 1983 saw Gere back in New York after a month of final sound-dubbing and post-production work on *The Honorary Consul* in London. The welcome was hardly what he had imagined. There were frantic telephone calls and meetings between the production team of *Breathless* and its backers, Orion, who were hoping to rush out the movie and pick up the momentum of the publicity surrounding Gere after *An Officer and a Gentleman*, which was still doing the rounds and being released in Europe around that time.

With Gere attracting so much publicity, Paramount also climbed aboard the bandwagon by rereleasing *American Gigolo*, which began a second life on the American circuit and so intensified still further the focus on his new movie.

Orion executives, however, were not happy with *Breathless*. 'We felt it had great potential but needed a lot of work,' said one. 'We had planned for a March release but put it back two months and told them they had better deliver.' Director McBride found himself faced with having to reshoot several scenes and perform a totally new editing job. The whole team was reassembled at the end of January and they began a remake in double-quick time. Gere explained: 'Orion wanted to put the film out very quickly, which had forced the director and editor into making choices which weren't necessarily the right choices. So, when I came back, we sort of forced the situation and we didn't release the film, which allowed us to go back and do a good job with the editing and do some new scenes.'

They worked day and night for six weeks, taking the film apart, rewriting, reshooting and composing a new musical score which had also been heavily criticised by the powers that be. Orion insisted that it had to be ready for release in the middle of May because they had booked it into 700 cinemas across America, followed by its release in Europe later in the year. When the remake had been completed to everyone's satisfaction, or as near as it could be, the Orion publicity machine went into overdrive. The whole promotional effort was virtually slung around Gere himself and the media responded with alacrity.

Steamy stills of Gere and Kaprisky were released ahead of the première. Producer and director were wheeled into interview after interview and almost without exception they talked about Gere's sexual attraction. 'Richard's character is the kind of man every woman is attracted to in her fantasies,' said Marty Erlichman. 'He represents danger and passion.'

Valerie Kaprisky was put in front of a press conference and continued the theme: 'It's not difficult to fall in love with a guy like Jesse [the Gere character] because he's so alive. There are so many people who think about eating and surviving but he's always running, moving, laughing, crying, shouting, screaming, doing something. And he makes her very sensual.' And then she added the final touch: 'Richard's not far from Jesse. We are not acting the love scenes. They were half real. People told me [beforehand] that friendships made when making a movie end when it is completed. I am afraid I opened my heart too much and when I tried to close it, it wouldn't. I truly fell in love with Richard, but then it was all over.'

Orion's PR people basked in the glow of a mass of

magazine features and newspaper headlines which told their own story, inspired by the lavish adjectives the promoters had used in their hype: 'A sexual grenade: Gere exudes lust and a sense of danger' . . . 'Instant Ignition: Perfect Chemistry for Gere and French actress' . . . 'Gere would be a perfect date for an orgy' . . . And so on.

By the time the movie was released into the cinemas, there were few people in America who did not know that Richard Gere was back with a stunner. There was, however, a built-in flaw to the movie that may or may not have been anticipated – and that was the comparison with the original Godard film. The New York critics could not and would not let such a moment pass: that a studio should commission a virtually unknown underground American director who had previously directed movies that no one had ever heard of – like *A Hard Day for Archie* or *My Girlfriend's Wedding* – to remake a Godard masterpiece. 'It's a little like trying to reinvent the light bulb to pay homage to Thomas Alva Edison,' trumpeted the *New York Times*.

These sort of comments were fairly widespread, and probably deservedly so, although inspired by the usual touch of critical snobbery. Actually, it didn't matter. Was there really anyone in the audience, anywhere outside of France, who had seen or even knew of *A Bout de Souffle*, apart from the ardent film buffs? So perhaps that aspect could be disregarded. Viewed simply as a new movie, it worked very well. Gere's performance would, in the fullness of time, be seen in a better light than it was at the time. Several critics acknowledged that his lively, lunatic interpretation of Jesse represented a very real advance in his level of performance, although not all agreed.

The reviews in this instance did not really matter. They soon took second place to the comment about the lively sex scenes. *Variety* took issue with the trend and noted in a tone of muted admonishment that Gere's 'status as a sex star is certainly reaffirmed here, and not only does he appear with his shirt off through much of the pic, but he does some full-frontal scenes which is highly unusual for a major actor.' Another writer complained: 'His physical beauty and his self-destructive desire for the girl make him the sexual hero-outlaw that he's supposed to be . . . but you see too much of Richard Gere in *Breathless*, and I don't mean physically. His soul is immodest.'

The discussion, prodded and fuelled by the publicists, served to create interest in the movie and more especially in Gere himself. The box-office returns were quite respectable and *Breathless* stayed among the top ten US films for twelve weeks, thus increasing Gere's $1 million fee since he also had some percentage points of the profits.

More interestingly, Gere became the focus of another stirring movement, mentioned earlier, whose upsurge, if that is the correct word, was being noted by social study groups, university tutors and serious writers in heavy magazines and newspapers – the emerging trend of women openly ogling men, a subject which suddenly flared into a heated national debate.

The controversy focused upon the female inclination towards being pleasured, visually and otherwise, by hunky men, as evidenced by a growing number of women-only nightspots which in turn spawned all-male exhibition groups whose attractions were overtly sexual.

It wasn't just in the movies that the sexual turnabout was evident. Advertisements in Times Square, New York City, in the month of the release of Gere's new flick, displayed a muscular athlete reclining seductively in his white briefs promoting Calvin Klein underwear on a forty-eight-foot-high billboard. Elsewhere, books on beefcake were outselling the cheesecake variety. The studies recorded, an interesting trend, that the gallery of tanned, slick-haired male pin-ups appeared to have been selected to appeal as much to gay men as to straight women.

Newsweek magazine, which put a glamour shot of Gere on its front cover, recorded in a piece discussing this new phenomenon: 'Homosexuality always openly celebrated male beauty, and there's little doubt that the general acceptance of a gay subculture has encouraged an outspoken appreciation of masculine sexuality in the mainstream culture. Turn on the radio and there's no missing the innuendo of Olivia Newton-John singing "Let's get physical" or the Pointer Sisters crooning "I want a man with a slow hand". Turn on the tube and watch yesterday's *Gentlemen's Quarterly* cover boy transformed into the tele-hunk of the month, often with as little acting talent as all those starlet/models turned actresses who have dotted the media for decades: the "dumb blonde" reborn as a male. Open a magazine and see how Madison Avenue has eroticised athletes, turning Baltimore Orioles pitching ace Jim Palmer in his Jockey briefs into one of the pre-eminent poster boys of his day.'

As *Newsweek* pointed out, the fantasy figures who had dominated old Hollywood were coming back in new, hunkier forms, and women who at the height of the feminist movement in the 1970s would not have discussed such matters were now demanding sexy screen idols. 'And if there is a reigning new sex symbol of the eighties,' declared *Newsweek*, 'it is Richard Gere, riding on the wave of romantic excitement created by *An Officer and a Gentleman* or as a desperately romantic hood in *Breathless*.'

Gere was not the sole attraction, of course. Tom Selleck became a pin-up hunk on the strength of his TV series *Magnum PI*, Mel Gibson had just sent hearts a-fluttering in *A Year of Living Dangerously*, Harrison Ford was exuding old-fashioned masculine bravado in *Raiders of the Lost Ark*, and square-jawed Christopher Reeve's sexuality remained at all times completely covered by his Superman togs.

Once, the term sex symbol had been more usually and openly associated with women stars, because it was never considered improper to expose and exaggerate their sexual allure. The male stars were more precisely defined by their often distinctive personal qualities: Gary Cooper, strong and silent; Cary Grant, suave and smiling; Clark Gable, strong, reliable and incredibly handsome; Marlon Brando, rebellious and offhand; James Dean, sensitive and vulnerable. But they were all sexual icons and that sexuality was pushed up a notch further by the succeeding generation of Paul Newman, Robert Redford, Clint Eastwood, Warren Beatty and Burt Reynolds, who reigned for almost twenty years.

Then, with the burgeoning feminist movement of the 1970s, sexuality took a back seat. Hunks became joke figures. No one wanted a new Victor Mature. Stars like Jack Nicholson, Dustin Hoffman, Al Pacino and Robert De Niro rose to fame as actors, not sex objects. If they took their shirts off, it was usually to chop wood. It was at that point that love stories featuring major Hollywood stars virtually disappeared from the movie schedules and did not begin to return until the 1980s.

In the meantime, a subtle change had occurred in audience perception. Films could no longer be sold on sexuality alone; the male body beautiful or a bountiful display of tits and bums could not guarantee a movie's success or create a star who would remain in demand after the novelty of baring all had vanished, as Bo Derek discovered. Hollywood chewed up and spat out dozens, hundreds, of attractive young things, male and female.

The trick was to create and sustain a kind of composite, all-embracing persona, as Redford and Newman had done, which was where Gere, Selleck and Gibson came in, layering their acting talents with a carefully defined individual sexual attraction. 'We are looking at the new generation of actors,' said Mike Medavoy, executive vice-president of Orion Pictures, as he collected the rewards from *Breathless*. 'Until recently, there was a stigma against good-looking actors. Now the pendulum has moved back to the middle.' For one thing, there had been a big increase in the number of female executives in the studios, and like the trend towards ogling of males in the clubs, it was not considered sexist for a woman to ask:

'Yes, but . . . would you go to bed with him?'

In that respect, just as the dearth of young actors had aided his initial toehold on the success ladder a couple of years earlier, the new female-led sexual revolution came as a timely boost to Gere's appeal. He and Ed Limato had been aiming in that direction long before the sociologists discovered that women were becoming openly specific in their demands for beefcake. But as Gere's deliberate move towards that tendency began to develop and become established among audiences, he also continued to take risks that few other actors in his league would have dared to consider.

He began to radiate a kind of sexual energy that might be considered a turn-off for men but which clearly aroused women. The line-up told its own story: the unstable figure cavorting around Diane Keaton's bedroom wearing a jock-strap and clutching a phallic knife in *Looking for Mr Goodbar*; the male prostitute in *American Gigolo*; the chip-on-his-shoulder, no-commitment-please lover in *An Officer and a Gentleman*; and now the killer-hero with dangerous sex appeal and a tendency to be rough on women in *Breathless*.

If, as Limato said on record many times, Gere 'anguished' over which roles to accept and which to reject, he had brought himself to the point of being something of a master of the art of American sex appeal, based upon a beautiful male body sandwiched between undercurrents of carefree anarchy and overtones of sadism and violence, with a touch of the homoerotic thrown in for good measure.

The characters he played were almost exclusively unsympathetic, at best chauvinist to their women and at worst heavy-handed. Yet at the same time, Gere had introduced a second element into his sex scenes which was almost exclusive to him as an actor – he never maintained total dominance as a lover and often allows his female partner to take the lead, especially in *An Officer and a Gentleman*.

Furthermore, there was one other theme which had been ever-present in his movies to date: that while sex is fun and exciting, love is harder to achieve and is not necessarily a prerequisite to the sex – a theme which certain strident 1980s women interpreted as something of a clarion call: take a few risks and enjoy yourself while you can. This tendency, of course, would be curtailed, though by no means eliminated. Rock Hudson was already dying from AIDS.

Gere in his own way was showing both the light and the dark sides of the sexual revolution. He confirmed it as a deliberate policy when author Richard Price, who became a good friend of his, asked him if there was anything in particular that accounted for his success. Price said he answered without hesitation: 'Focus. I knew people who were as talented as I was who didn't have it. I think I've always felt that it was focus and commitment and concentration that made things happen. When things fuck up . . . you just keep going. You've got to outlast the fuck-ups . . . just keep going . . . keep going . . . keep going.'

And that, as it turned out, was to be a very prophetic statement, because the 'fuck-ups' kept coming in what was turning out to be the most disastrous period of his career. Walking home to his apartment late one night in August 1983, he had reached the corner of Broadway and 10th Street when, overtaken by an urgent call of nature, he stopped to urinate in the gutter.

Unfortunately, an angry woman who witnessed his display of public pollution flagged down a passing police patrol car. Gere was stopped and questioned. The officers were apparently slightly dubious of his claim to be Richard Gere, the well-known film actor, and took him to the station at Manhattan's Ninth Precinct where his identity was verified. He apologised to the desk sergeant but was, nonetheless, handed a summons for an environmental violation, answerable with a small fine which he subsequently paid without more ado.

Other more serious matters were bearing down. No sooner had the problem with the initial print of *Breathless* been resolved than he hit trouble with *The Honorary*

Consul, which was set for release in the autumn of 1983. When the British producers delivered their print of the film to Paramount in Hollywood, there were ructions. Paramount, it seems, had been expecting something more sexy to go along with their American star's current image. There was plenty of explicit sex, and the Gere rear was amply on view once again. But studio executives who had coughed up most of the modest budget for the film were not happy with the emphasis.

They announced their intention to make cuts to the director's final print, and wanted to alter the dialogue in several scenes to make the Gere character appear more sympathetic. Clearly, his role was not in accord with the sexy posters and trailers that Paramount intended to launch to publicise the film, thus taking advantage of his current high-profile 'sex appeal' on which the movie was to be sold.

The marketing people were concerned that Gere's character was likely to alienate the audience, and that could damage their perception of the movie. Director John MacKenzie, backed up by producer Norma Heyman, maintained that he was not prepared to make the changes Paramount were asking for, and Gere fell in behind him. Paramount, who had total control over the film's release in America, prompted hired another actor to dub in the altered lines.

Gere unleashed his wrath. 'My role . . . Dr Plarr was a very passive character,' he said. 'He's a "maybe" person – that was his character in the book. When Michael [Caine] asks me "Do you believe in anything?" Plarr says "No, I don't think so". The studio took out the "no", which is the guts of the character. It was just stupid.'

Gere angrily accused Paramount of tampering with the artistic integrity of the film. But worse was to come. The studio's marketing department was also worried about the title and conducted a survey to see if anyone understood the term 'honorary consul'.

No one did, and regardless of the fact that it was the title of an international best-selling novel by one of the world's most famous authors, the studio decided to change it. At a conference at the Paramount lot, they unilaterally decided to give the film a new title for the American market – one which was in fact even more unfathomable than the original – *Beyond the Limit.*

Gere complained that he found the whole business humiliating and blamed the studio for not understanding what the movie was about in the first place. They had tried to make it into something it wasn't – another sexy vehicle for a hot star. 'I don't know what they thought it was but they never approached the material on the level we were approaching it. I think they had some vague idea that there were elements they could market in a commercial way. They did their best to try and find them and what they couldn't find they invented,' said Gere.

Paramount denied that they did not understand what the movie was about and claimed that they were merely attempting to protect their commercial interests. The title had been changed so that it would be easier for the public to relate to. All along, however, it seemed that the studio's overriding fear was that in its existing form, *The Honorary Consul* would not do well. And it didn't, not even with the changes Paramount inflicted upon it.

The movie vanished quickly from the US circuit after a batch of mixed reviews. It fared better in England, where the original version was screened, but by then it was history, and Michael Caine had already put it down to experience. 'It didn't do very well anywhere,' said Caine. 'I saw Graham Greene not long afterwards, and he didn't like it either – although he said he enjoyed my performance.'

And therein lay the difference between an actor whose position was somewhat tenuous, like Gere's, and an established journeyman like Caine who all his life had wandered in and out of movies, some good, some indifferent and, as he admits, some 'bloody awful'. Whatever happened, his standing in the business, like Sean Connery's, remained unaffected: he was a true star. The offers just kept on coming, and Caine hardly ever refused anything.

For all the build-up he had been given, Gere had little power and even less control. His attraction to the producers at the time was his high media profile which they hoped would translate into box-office success. Although for a time it looked as though Gere would become an automatic box-office draw for mass audiences, his appeal in fact quickly levelled out, rather in the manner of that of Robert De Niro, whose body of work included some startling, critically acclaimed movies but also a high percentage of films that were never commercially successful.

To De Niro, it didn't matter, because he was one of America's finest acting talents, and the bottom line, the profit-and-loss account, somehow never seemed important. For Richard Gere, who obviously aspired to follow the same artistic guidelines that De Niro and Pacino used for their careers, it was not quite the same, because he did not have the acting strength as a back-up. If there was ever a moment when Gere seemed to be heading towards the status of one of those Hollywood icons whose work automatically attracted large audiences, it may well already have passed, almost unnoticed.

True enough, that summer of 1983 saw him heavily featured in the media around the world as *Breathless* went on its merry way. Spurred on by the acres of publicity in America about the way women now perceived sexuality in male stars, the learned scribes dissecting his surge in popularity concluded that it was founded upon primeval and unintellectual instincts which had very little to do with acting ability.

That was quite evident later that year, when he was contractually bound to embark on a promotional tour of Europe for *Breathless*. By coincidence, when he checked into the Plaza Athenee Hotel in Paris a week before *Breathless* opened there, he found Al Pacino on a similar mission with his own latest movie. Much to the chagrin of true aficionados of the cinema, Gere was grabbing all the attention, and there were those journalists ready to make the comparison and enquire of their readers: Is sizzling Gere just a pretty face?

By then Gere had had enough of it. He refused to answer the many questions about his life and times that Parisian journalists were eager to impart to his fans, and was clearly uneasy in making the comparison between the sexuality of his characters and his own. He had always professed his reluctance at being a sex symbol, and few knew of his fourfold rejection of *An Officer and a Gentleman* – but then on the other hand he had gone out and openly exploited his position.

At the time, he showed no compunction in accepting the financial benefits either. But he had become determined to call a halt to the sex theme that was engulfing him. He was shocked and exasperated by the way it had gathered momentum since *Breathless* was released. As one person close to him remarked: 'His anger boiled up over the *Newsweek* article and he just got angrier and angrier that his work was taking second place to debates about the size of his dick and where he was dipping it.'

Gere enjoyed the fame but hated the hassle. He took the money, and moaned about the consequences. Just like Brando, two decades earlier, he began slagging off the industry that had given him fame and fortune, complaining that his ambitions, born out of his successful and interesting work on the stage, had been overwhelmed by the nonstop demands of Hollywood. He was caught up in a whirl of Tinseltown hype that he found he could not begin to control. He talked openly about showbusiness being populated by leeches, vampires and hustlers and was even less polite about the media.

During this period of his life he retired into his apartment with Sylvia after work and, surrounded by his books on Buddhism, meditation and contemplation, began to dig deep into his soul and plan trips to India and other places of spiritual convalescence just as soon as his workload permitted it.

He might have discovered the route to inner peace, but the problems of movie-making continued to loom large and his next adventure took him on a roller-coaster ride the likes of which he had never experienced before.

Chapter Ten

Shooting Star

By the autumn of 1983, there were already two more back-to-back movies in the pipeline and it seemed that Gere's future growth as an actor and a star was assured. Then, having reached a certain pinnacle, having been acclaimed as the next best thing to sliced bread and having been placed on a pedestal by the power-brokers, it all began to go badly awry.

Within a matter of months, he found himself staring into an abyss of heart-searching and failure that had opened up before him after the massive publicity for *Breathless*. His next three releases hit the skids and knocked the stuffing out of the image he had been given by the media as the hottest property in Hollywood.

The change of direction in his career was partly of his own making. He faced up to the fact that he could not live by physiognomy alone and that he had to extend himself beyond the sex roles, if the studios would allow him to do so, and begin looking for material that would life him above the image. That in itself was not the cause of his troubles.

It was more fundamentally destructive than that, as all the build-up and hype of the past months melted away like snow in summer. The process was aided by the fact that he was out of the public eye as he went into demanding production schedules, one of which took him out of the country for four months.

No one knew it then, but Gere had peaked in his role as 'the sexiest actor in the world' – a title bestowed upon him by the pundits and Hollywood alike and which, as events would show, was no foundation on which to build for the future. Just as John Travolta had discovered when he was being heralded as the modern, sexy version of Fred Astaire after *Saturday Night Fever*, the clichéd labels counted for nothing.

Travolta had already virtually vanished from sight and would remain in the doldrums for the rest of the decade. Gere too was in for a bumpy ride, brought about by a combination of ill-fortune and Hollywood idiosyncrasies.

Not least among his troubles, however, was a media that had given him a lavish build-up and then proceeded to turn upon him in the most hostile way, encouraged, they would say, by his own attitude and lack of enthusiasm in giving journalists more than the time of day.

Some remarkably vitriolic headlines began to appear: 'Richard Gere, the man who fell in love with himself'; 'Officious and Not a Gentleman: The naked truth about the ghastly Mr Gere'. But the slide down the other side of the mountain really had its beginnings one summer's day in 1983, when 'the most famous producer in Hollywood', Robert Evans, ran a couple of Gere movies in the projection room of his $15 million Beverly Hills mansion and then decided to offer Gere the lead in his own new movie, *The Cotton Club*.

In due course, Gere was invited to the mansion for talks and accepted a $2 million offer to star in the movie, which to all the world sounded as if it couldn't fail. How was he to know he had just assigned himself to a glorious fiasco of mammoth proportions? It was a movie that would go down in history as one of Hollywood's modern calamities, with its underlying troubles stemming from the interpolation of real-life events – life imitating art and vice versa in no uncertain manner – which so often befalls the dream factories and turns wonderful hopes and aspirations into shattering disillusionment.

All of this lay ahead for Gere as he moved into what was being billed in the trade newspapers as his period of consolidation as a 'major player' in the romantic hero stakes – although that was before *The Honorary Consul* was released. At this time, Evans was in the process of setting up his massive project, which he believed would match his success with *The Godfather* more than a decade earlier.

Since this venture would detain Richard Gere for more than six months and involve him in one of the most traumatic episodes of his life, a saga so colourful that it would have been considered too far-fetched for a television soap opera, it is worth taking a slight diversion to look into its background. The fact was that *The Cotton Club* was the dream and then the obsession of Robert Evans, the movie that was intended to put his name into the history books alongside such luminaries as Irving Thalberg and David O. Selznick.

Evans had already done much to earn the comparison. He was the golden boy of a golden era of 1970s film-making who was Hollywood's modern and true-life Last Tycoon. His best friend, Jack Nicholson, who went to his mansion every weekend to play tennis on one of the best courts in Beverly Hills, used to call him 'Mogul' after they'd made *Chinatown* together. That was just one of a string of successful films produced at Paramount when Evans was in charge. There were many others: he selected *Love Story* from a pile of scripts, and made it his own by marrying its star, Ali McGraw, who later decamped with Steve McQueen. He gave Roman Polanski his first break in Hollywood by signing him to direct *Rosemary's Baby*, which was a runaway success, and then made Nicholson an international star with *Chinatown*.

He brought *The Godfather* to the screen, as well as *The*

Great Gatsby with Robert Redford, and jointly with Sam Spiegel funded Elia Kazan's direction of Robert De Niro as *The Last Tycoon.* Some of his less successful films included *Darling Lili, Finian's Rainbow, Paint Your Wagon* and *Urban Cowboy*, but even his failures had merit. His enemies, of whom there were plenty, said his successful movies were made in spite of him, because in fact when he took over as head of production at Paramount, Robert Evans had never produced a single picture.

He had just been lucky, in the right place at the right time, like the subjects of many Hollywood success stories, fictional and real-life. He was a struggling actor when discovered by Norma Shearer, who thought he was the image of her former husband, the legendary MGM producer Irving Thalberg – the 'boy wonder' on whom Fitzgerald based his unfinished novel, *The Last Tycoon.*

After being discovered by Shearer, Evans took the role of Thalberg in the 1957 James Cagney movie biopic of silent-screen star Lon Chaney, *The Man of a Thousand Faces.* He then won a part in *The Sun Also Rises*, but after these early successes, he struggled as an actor and was 'on his ass' when he returned penniless to his family home in New York to work in his brother's clothing company.

By a stroke of good fortune, the brothers sold the business for $2 million in 1964, and with his share, Evans set himself up as a producer. By another stroke of luck, Charles Bludhorn, the late creator of the Gulf Western conglomerate, had just bought a company which in turn owned the virtually bankrupt film studio, Paramount. Bludhorn knew nothing about the film business and he hired Evans after reading a profile of him one day in the local newspaper. Six months later, Bob Evans was made worldwide head of Paramount productions.

In the coming decade, which he later described – as he did every – as 'magic', he became the new miracle-worker of Hollywood, The Man with the Midas Touch, and he made sure that everyone knew it. He surrounded himself with all the trappings of great power and influence, including his vast reproduction French Regency mansion with its thirty-two telephones, countless rooms, a personal bathroom in sheer black marble, and a swimming pool with eighteen fountain jets that looked like something off a tropical island. Visitors could hardly fail to miss, either, his Etruscan artefacts, all with individual spotlights.

At dinner, the food was served on china, designed by himself, showing a naked girl riding on a centaur, and after Ali McGraw walked out, he decorated his arms with gold bangles and the latest fashion models. He hobnobbed with the rich and famous. In Hollywood his party guests were the élites of the profession. In higher circles, Henry Kissinger and Edward Kennedy were among his friends. His became the supreme success story, which he lived with the highest profile, modelling himself on his hero, David O. Selznick, even down to a flirtation with stimulants. In 1980, he pleaded guilty to possession of cocaine, and part of the condition of a probation order was that he should make at his own expense a $400,000 anti-drugs film, which starred Olivia Newton-John and Burt Reynolds.

Quite suddenly, Evans decided he needed a change, and he left Paramount. People asked, as they always do, 'Did he fall, or was he pushed?' It mattered not. The Mogul had followed the route of moguls past, through the door marked Exit. He wanted to produce his own highly individualistic movie – just as Selznick had done with *Gone with the Wind* – and for him, it was to be *The Cotton Club*, to be written especially by Mario Puzo, who had penned the marvellously successful *Godfather* screenplay from his own novel.

The Cotton Club too was to be a gangster story, involving a ruthless, bloody gang war set against the musical setting of a nightclub in Harlem in the 1920s. Evans hired Francis Ford Coppola to direct the movie, thus recreating the very same team that had produced *The Godfather*.

Evans said it was going to be a musical masterpiece, a light-hearted version of *The Godfather* set to the tunes of

Duke Ellington and Cab Calloway. But for once, the super-salesman was unable to convince the backers, and by the autumn of 1983 he had failed to find finance, largely because of a heavy budget, set at well in excess of $20 million. This lack of enthusiasm for his project can almost certainly be put down to sour grapes and revenge for disjointed noses from the past, but there was also an underlying flaw in his package.

Unlike *The Godfather*, the cast of dozens was being carried by only one well-known actor – Richard Gere (at the time Bob Hoskins, who had also been hired, was still an unknown in the US) – and it was widely considered that neither his role in the picture nor his status as an actor was strong enough to shoulder the burden of a $20 million budget single-handed. Evans, convinced that he would find the money, put the film into pre-production in the autumn of 1983 and funded the $140,000 a week costs himself. He sold the last of his Paramount stock to pay his debts and took out fresh mortgages on the mansion. Although he was still committed and confident about the success of his vast project, by then he had got a tiger by the tail and the problems surrounding him began to look serious.

First, there was a disagreement with Mario Puzo over the script, and Coppola himself began the task of rewriting. Evans did not like what he came up with and brought in another writer, William Kennedy. It was rumoured that in all, thirteen draft scripts were written, as well as several 'final' drafts. Meanwhile, the actors and actresses had assembled at the Astoria Studios in Queens, New York, where the movie was being filmed and where huge and expensive sets had been built.

Gere, along with Hoskins, doleful comic actor Fred Gwynne, plus hoofer extraordinaire Gregory Hines and his brother Maurice, were in place, practising for the vast extravaganza of music and song, murder and mayhem. There were dancers, chorus lines and big bands rehearsing material from the period, while Gere himself, cast as a corner player with slicked-back hair and moustache, was bringing his own playing up to date.

His role underpins the story. He witnesses a gangland killing, is drawn into working for one of the gangsters and finally escapes to Hollywood after Gloria Swanson, visiting the club, tells him he should take a screen test. The plot is thin and is held together by meandering sequences of colourful and beautifully staged and photographed scenes, but clearly there is something fundamentally missing.

The production began to attract very negative press comments. Scenes were being shot out of sequence, rewriting was going on almost to the point that daily shooting schedules were being delayed. Rows between Evans and Coppola were becoming heavy and there were even reports of fights on set, one involving a newspaper photographer when a production assistant tried to stop him taking pictures of Gere. Meanwhile, costs were mounting and Evans was desperate. The banks were closing in and the delays to the shoot had brought revised estimates of a $30 million spend.

Other more daunting problems were developing away from the studio, and a remarkable series of incidents began to unfold as Evans cast his net for backers. The next development resembled one of those unbelievable coincidental happenings from the movies. Evans's ex-wife Ali McGraw, still a good friend, had happened to mention to her limousine driver one day that Bob was having difficulty in raising the cash for *The Cotton Club*. The driver, a black actor doing the job while resting, in turn passed the news on to a woman from Florida whom he had been chauffeuring in Los Angeles.

She described herself as an importer of jewels and appeared to be exceedingly rich, which in reality she wasn't. There followed a long and complicated round of negotiations between Evans and the woman. She in turn drew in a whole mass of other people with connections which tailed back into the seedy drugs world of Florida and Colombia and about which Evans knew nothing at the time. The upshot of it all was that he went into partnership with a Puerto Rican banker and an unsavoury New York promoter. Things turned sour, and the promoter ended up murdered by contract killers in a row over a missing cocaine consignment. His body was found riddled with bullets in a remote canyon in California and Evans found himself in the middle of what became known as The Cotton Club Case – a trifle unfairly, because the shooting was to do with the cocaine and not the movie deal.

The village of Hollywood was agog. The name of Robert Evans was being mentioned in a sordid murder enquiry in which the protagonists had links to consignments of stolen cocaine and, ultimately, connections stretching to the Colombian drugs cartels. How could Evans have become involved with such a set of people? Before very long he was asking himself the same question. Suddenly life looked grim for the one-time studio supremo. It took the Los Angeles police force five years to investigate the murder, virtually putting Evans's career on hold and certainly dragging his reputation through the mire as rumours abounded that he would be charged with conspiracy to murder.

The District Attorney's office at first indicated that he might be implicated, then, failing to discover any evidence to prove it, listed him as a chief prosecution witness. Nevertheless, the Hollywood cold shoulder was applied with vigour and Evans was outcast by all but a few of his closest friends.

Meanwhile he had found other backers for *The Cotton Club*, principally two Lebanese casino owners from Las Vegas, but as costs escalated further, he lost control of the picture. The movie eventually cost $37 million to film and another $13 million in post-production expenses. Evans found himself on the wrong end of a nasty writ. The film flopped badly and he blamed Coppola, while Coppola in turn blamed him and Evans was drawn to financial ruin.

For Gere, and all the cast involved in this great movie fiasco, there were substantial financial benefits arising from Evans's problems. In addition to the $2 million salary Gere was being paid – in itself the highest upfront fee he had ever received – he would also get an extra $150,000 a week for each week's work after a certain date. The penalty became due for payment and Gere received a bonus of $1.5 million when the production stretched on for twenty-four weeks.

Much has been said and written about the picture, especially in view of the background involved. The critics generally gave it a hard time, focusing on the events in the wings rather than the film itself, and it turned out to be an exceedingly expensive flop.

As a movie, the problems with the script were never really resolved and it jumped edgily through its narrative, which annoyingly interrupted the superb musical spectaculars, especially from the Hines brothers. Overall, *The Cotton Club* deserved a much better fate. It could probably have been rescued before its release, but by then, with so much money expended, an air of panic was wafting over the entire operation.

The cinematography beautifully captured the dark and moody setting of the Harlem nightclub that featured the nation's most talented black entertainers playing on stage before an all-white audience. Coppola told the story through two developing love affairs which, at the same time, explored the racial undertones of the period. Gere's character, Dixie Dwyer, is a smart musician who saves the life of a gangster and is immediately recruited into the hood's inner circle, where he meets and falls in love with the gangster's teenage girlfriend (Diane Lane), and they conduct a secret affair. Meanwhile, black tap dancer, Sandman Williams, played by Gregory Hines, falls in love with a member of the chorus line, Lonette McKee, a mulatto whom people think is white.

The two stories are played to their conclusion against the foot-tapping entertainment going on at the club, where the gang bosses waft in and out of the action with machine guns and knives and bloody violence that is reminiscent of Coppola's *Godfather* trilogy. There are some powerful individual performances in the movie, especially from Hoskins, Nicholas Cage, playing Gere's brother, and the teenage newcomer Diane Lane.

Gere acquitted himself competently, but no more than that; once again he seemed restrained and it was unfortunate that some of the dullest moments of the picture were his scenes. The majority of reviewers gave *The Cotton Club* a severe mauling, but it remains a piece of cinematographic history – though a very costly one – that is worth bringing out and watching every now and again, if only to confirm that it could have been so much better.

By the time filming was completed, Gere had to get away. The whole thing had dragged on too long. Tensions were at breaking point and he was wanted for his next picture, whose production had already been put back by two months to accommodate his overrun on *The Cotton Club*. Paramount were making threatening noises about getting their star released to begin work on the project, a religious epic retelling the Biblical story of David.

That he had been selected for the Paramount picture at all was an indication of Gere's standing at that particular time in his career. He was moving from one film to the next without a break, and his services were being booked well ahead, so critical appraisal of his work took some time to catch up with his output. It was also a sign of Hollywood's desperation to discover new projects and make the best use of new stars.

Gere had been signed for the new Paramount movie on the strength of his performance in *An Officer and a Gentleman*, but before his row with the studio over *The Honorary Consul* and, of course, long before he had even begun work on *The Cotton Club*.

To Hollywood observers, a religious film about David was

a curious vehicle for an actor who had made his name in contemporary movies of a sexual nature and whose whole public persona was based upon his physical attractiveness, with echoes of Victor Mature. But as would soon become clear, the producers had in mind a more modern interpretation.

They had committed a budget of more than $20 million to the production of *King David*, and there would be considerable reference back to the studio's earlier efforts in the genre. Paramount was the home of Cecil B. De Mille's acclaimed Biblical epics: it was almost thirty years since Moses parted the Red Sea in *The Ten Commandments*, with a cast of thousands, including such names as Charlton Heston, Edward G. Robinson, Yul Brynner, Yvonne de Carlo and Cedric Hardwicke.

Against that line-up, the new production looked decidedly shallow: a cast list of British actors relatively unknown outside their own country, led by the 'hot' Richard Gere. It was the kind of strategy that a number of studios had reverted to in an attempt to keep costs at a manageable level, and it was also a risky prospect.

Paramount came out bullishly proclaiming that they had every faith that Gere would carry the $20 million load with aplomb. However, exactly what their intentions were with this movie may well have been questioned when the man chosen to direct, Bruce Beresford, announced: 'The Bible keeps reiterating how handsome David is. He is so attractive, he gets his own way. Not only is Richard handsome, he's a good enough actor that he won't sound like a 1983 male walking around dressed in a tea towel.'

Were they turning David into a sex object? It was not an unreasonable question at the time.

For Paramount, the arrival at the point of announcing the go-ahead for the film was the culmination of a six-year debate over whether or not to proceed. The idea had come to their executives at a brainstorming session. Jeffrey Katzenberg, then head of production, said that they had posed themselves the question: 'What kind of movies are we interested in making?' One of the more senior figures at the meeting, Michael Eisner, the studio's president, pondering past successes, noted that there had not been a Biblical picture produced for more than fifteen years. And so the upshot was that Katzenberg instructed his research department to trawl through the history of Christ and 'find out if there is any historical character we could build a motion picture around'. Those were his very words.

The research people reported back that the only story relatively untold was 'the story of David, the rebel who became a hero-king and united the tribes of Israel'. Of course, Gregory Peck had had a shot at it in 1951, in the Darryl F. Zanuck production of *David and Bathsheba*, but that David, they said, had been hopelessly whitewashed and romanticised. Everyone wandered around spouting proverbs in a kind of Old Testament Disneyland. Their project would give a modern, authentic interpretation of 'the real David'.

One year later, Paramount hired a scriptwriter to construct the story. Katzenberg recalled: 'When it came back, it was a typical oversized spectacle screenplay without human characters.' It would also have been ultra-expensive. The project was back-burnered for two further years and resurrected when studio executives were once again casting around for what to do next. Andrew Birkin, author of *James M. Barrie and the Lost Boys*, was hired to write a new script and this time it was approved.

Next Paramount hired Australian screenwriter and director Bruce Beresford, who had scored an unexpected hit with the Boer War story, *Breaker Morant*, which he made in Australia for $750,000 and which won him an Oscar nomination. He repeated the performance in America with the critically applauded *Tender Mercies*, starring Robert Duvall and Tess Harper, a small, quiet movie about a reformed alcoholic country and western singer. Duvall won an Oscar for best actor on the strength of his performance in the film, and Horton Foote, who wrote the screenplay, won the Oscar for best original script. Much later, Beresford's *Driving Miss Daisy* won Oscars for best picture, best make-up, best adapted screenplay and best actress (Jessica Tandy).

Paramount's *King David* represented Beresford's first big-budget movie and he admitted nervously to a press conference, 'If I don't pull it off, I'll have ruined the careers of a lot of people.' He said he intended to handle the story with modern realism – 'without the mumbo-jumbo of the DeMille Biblical epics. Archaeology has proven that the Biblical stories are real. There will be no heavenly choirs, no disembodied voices – in fact it's not at all religious in the strict sense. People aren't going around talking about God.'

While Beresford went off to scout locations, Gere still had the completion of *The Cotton Club* ahead of him, and with the latter's repeated delays and overruns, the start of *King David* was put back from January to April 1984. Sylvia already had their bags packed and as soon as Gere was free of *The Cotton Club* they set off for London, where initial filming was staged at Pinewood Studios. Beresford had a decent company, made up largely of British actors, the best known of whom were Edward Woodward (who had starred in *Breaker Morant*) and Denis Quilley. The rest were deliberately lesser known; the director wanted to avoid that popular pastime of days gone by of spotting familiar faces behind the beards in biblical epics.

The script called for Gere to age fifty years, encompassing the life of David from his anointment as King of Israel, through his marital and political struggles, to his fall from grace with God and his redemption. The movie thus provided him with a far greater range than he had so far experienced in film. It was also a completely different role from anything else he had ever tackled, although as Beresford had made clear from the outset, he did not want it played with pious preoccupation.

Beresford was careful to avoid the temptation to fall into Ye Olden Times. In Gere's portrayal David was a man with universal, timeless emotions. As well as dealing with

Goliath and slaying the Philistine, Gere had to deal with the David who loves Saul's son Jonathan. 'We decided not to get into this heavily,' said Gere, 'because the movie has a gentleness of spirit, an ease of touch. We felt it better to show it this way with a purity of expression devoid of any coy sexuality. But all the relationships among the male characters are extraordinarily strong and bizarre.'

Filming took them on location to Italy, and then on to North Africa, because Beresford had been unable to find suitable or safe locations in Israel. The weather and other mishaps were not kind to Beresford, and they ran behind schedule and over budget. Word filtering from the locations in northern Italy was picked up by the New York media with more than a touch of sarcasm – that Gere was cavorting about the place on imported sand and leaning against imported palm trees in a leather mini-skirt, chased by period groupies.

Gere was clearly worried about the way the movie was going. He spent a good deal of time alone. A member of the cast reported, as others have done in the past, that what free time they had he spent away from the set, and seldom mixed with anyone. He had also taken a detour to spend time in the Atlas Mountains with the Berber and Bedouin tribes, and he walked the river bed where David and Goliath had their encounter. He probably needed the time alone to draw up a new list of eye-catching techniques on screen. In this movie, the swaggering hips, the darting, piercing eyes, the animated bare buttocks were most definitely *out*.

He did well to rise above that, and was helped by Beresford's staging of the action and a screenplay that was populated with some marvellous characters, especially Edward Woodward's mad King Saul. It was to Gere's advantage that he also had to take on a totally new look from anything he had played in the past. He had to grow a mane of hair and a bushy beard. The physical accoutrements must surely have helped him. For the most part, he adopted his tortured spirituality mode, the shepherd who becomes the reluctant king, for which you could read the stage actor who becomes the reluctant sex symbol.

Gere carried the early scenes well, but later on in the ageing process, when David's life was filled with emotion and trauma, he was in difficulty. By then, however, so were the audience, who found themselves laughing when they shouldn't have been; Gere doing a sacred dance in his Biblical nappy, or smashing down a model temple, was not intended to be funny.

Well, perhaps Gere wasn't so terrific, but on this occasion the actors were not to blame. There were some good moments in *King David*, but generally confusion reigned in the telling of what were familiar stories. At the end of it, there remained very pertinent questions to be asked: Why was this film made at all? Why did Gere risk doing it, and even supporting it when Paramount at one stage seemed likely to pull the plug? Why did a supposedly intelligent group of high-powered studio executives imagine it was worth risking $22 million on a Biblical epic that had no relevance to 1980s movie-goers?

Audiences in search of the romantic, the spectacular and the nasty demonstrated just how out of touch those Hollywood mini-moguls were by staying away from the film in large numbers. The critics were cruel and merciless and *King David* was ridiculed from coast to coast. When asked to explain why he had chosen it, Gere explained that it appealed to him because of his personal interest in religions of the world: 'My motive was clear,' he said. 'I was interested in religious issues, the idea of one true religion fighting with other true religions fascinated me. So even though the reaction was unanimously disapproving, I'm not sorry I did it. At least I'm not afraid to take a chance.'

Chapter Eleven

Cold Shower

The turmoil in Gere's life and career was apparent in the months after he had completed his Biblical farce. The media view was clear – that the beefcake jerk was blown out and if there was any remaining value in his sex appeal, it had been laughed off the screen when he appeared in grown-up nappies in *King David.* Gere was stopped dead in his tracks as the trio of movies he had made in the previous eighteen months or so caught up with him: upon their release, *Beyond the Limit*, *The Cotton Club* and the disastrous *King David*, which he had filmed in quick-fire succession, created a domino effect on his standing, and the promise of a startling future, predicted even by the pundits who did not much care for him, evaporated into thin air.

The flesh was no longer the foundation of guaranteed success and the spirit was severely dented by a bout of crushing reviews. Richard Gere, who long ago had said he never wanted to be flavour of the month anyway, had finally achieved his ambition.

For the remainder of the decade, his star waned to the point of almost total eclipse but it was by no means entirely due to the failures of those films, or others he would make in the immediate future. He was about to change his life completely. His output fell back to virtual idleness and he was on the brink of ending his long relationship with Sylvia Martins, the real anchor in his life. Friends and Hollywood onlookers were left wondering what was going on in his mind. The young actor who was said to have the world at his feet at the age of thirty seemed to have lost it by the age of thirty-five.

But to judge him by his CV alone gives a false picture. The offers were still coming in. Hardly a month went by without the trade newspapers reporting that Gere was up for this movie or that, and then either the project or his interest in it was never heard of again. He was simply not accepting the material that landed on his doormat. 'What happened,' said David Stein, who was connected with his management, 'was that the stuff he was being offered did not seem to fit his own view of the way his career should go. He wanted to ditch the sex tag. He was furious at some of the things that were being said about him and he was looking for more meaty roles. I suppose it began when he came back from a trip to India at the end of 1984. He didn't seem at all interested in anything that was remotely fashioned after his early films. He had plenty of scripts sent in, but he just wasn't taking them. He had his own reasons for doing that at the time, but eventually people stopped asking.'

The change in his outlook had been brewing since the torrent of words written about his body at the beginning of the decade. Because of the failures that had come along afterwards, and the lack of current material, whenever the name Richard Gere was mentioned it still had the *Gigolo* tag or harked back to *An Officer and a Gentleman*. The news about him was stale and virtually obsolete. The story that he would not accept any movie unless he had a nude scene in it was repeated over and over again, and there was no doubt that in a sense it had been true, in that he had been actively looking for, and accepting, that kind of role. But those days were long gone, put behind him when he finished making *King*

David, as was confirmed by Jann Wenner, of *Rolling Stone*.

Wenner watched Gere go through the process of change from hot sex symbol to yesterday's hero. 'I think for a while he was afraid of his popularity. His choices *per se* were the opposite of popular. He began to choose obscure projects. He resented his success . . . because it had to do with a sexual heat he could generate on screen. He felt his worth as an artist was being subsumed by that power and it surprised him.'

After filming *King David*, Gere and Sylvia took off immediately for India, for another meeting with the Dalai Lama and a further period of spiritual convalescence. Those close to him had seen his interest in Buddhism grow since he first studied the Middle Way of Siddhartha Gotama Buddha as preached by a Japanese sect in 1973. A few years later, he switched to the Tibetan School, which combines the 2,500-year-old Buddhist religion with an ancient form of Himalayan worship. The basic teaching of Buddhism relies upon a simple phrase, 'withdraw and return', which, as will be seen, became a significant guide to Gere's own future plans.

On his visit to the Dalai Lama in 1984, he attended a high initiation ceremony conducted by the man who had become his spiritual mentor. 'Afterwards, I felt invulnerable,' he said. Emboldened with spiritual courage, Gere travelled on in search of Eastern mysticism that held the answers to life and death, with a semi-reluctant Sylvia Martins in tow. He had arranged to meet an explorer friend who had a house on the island of Bali, and from there they would travel on through the depths and wilds of North Borneo, into a region where, until quite recent times, head-hunters roamed the jungles and mountainsides to satisfy the ancient custom that required young males to present their prospective father-in-law with a severed head.

Gere and Martins, accompanied by their explorer friend, flew off across the Java Sea to Borneo and then continued their intrepid journey in a spluttering single-prop three-seater plane of World War II vintage, which took them to a Longnawan village, deep in the interior and close to the border with Sarawak. They arrived in the jungle clearing looking like cruising tourists, in shorts and sandals and carrying overnight bags, and were shown to their quarters, a mud hut.

Unfortunately, the monsoon came early and closed in around them almost as soon as they landed. The little plane that had brought them was disabled and they had to spend a week in the most primitive conditions, in torrid, sweating heat and with large leeches and mosquitoes the size of bumblebees discovering the delights of their white and tender skins.

Gere put the whole experience down to a unique lesson in the discovery of human frailties. Martins could not agree. Being subjected to such conditions – and dangers – was not her idea of pleasure and she just let rip. 'There is nothing like a Latin breakdown,' Gere recalled to a friend when they returned home. 'Total hysteria. It was not a polite breakdown.'

If a moment could be identified as the beginning of the end of their often tempestuous relationship, it was there in the jungle of Borneo. The trip also marked the beginning of Gere's own move towards a much deeper involvement with Buddhism, and the Dalai Lama in particular. He took back with him from that 'high initiation' the determination to bring the Tibetan cause to the attention of the Western world, along with plans to found the Tibet House, a cultural and information centre in New York, which he eventually pioneered along with other serious followers in America.

At the time, however, friends back home did not quite appreciate the extent of his commitment to the Tibetan people and their spiritual king. They thought it was more a case of a kind of spiritual psychotherapy sought by a man at a crossroads in his life, that he was more interested in seeking solutions to his personal needs and psychological explorations in the monastic, male-oriented traditions of the Dalai Lama's faith and beliefs.

It was something that clearly occupied a good deal of his thinking. He remarked on one occasion: 'I had an amazing vision one time. It had to do with seeing my whole male lineage behind my father, lined up through a field and over a hill. It went back hundreds of generations. I had this tremendous sense that I was the outcome of all that work and my connection to that was very emotional and very powerful . . . I felt I was one with all this love from all these men before me.'

Sylvia Martins, who had been at Gere's side throughout the growth of his career and was now witnessing it fading, remembers that period as fairly traumatic. 'He was always self-possessed – the most self-possessed person I knew, and I'm pretty self-possessed myself,' she said. 'But Richard takes himself very seriously. He couldn't relax. I think that's why he turned to his religion so much, though he'd been at it for a long time. When someone places so much importance on their career as he did then, not even pleasure is a diversion – then they have to find some escape, some solace. He finds it somehow in this Buddhist stuff. But he was no monk. He liked to go out. He liked to be seen. All actors like to be seen. Actors and actresses love to stare at each other. That's their real religion. He had to go on, looking deeper and deeper into his soul.'

Their return to the US marked the point at which Gere's changing attitudes took a dramatic turn, in part due to the arrival of another vital influence in his life – the British actress Julie Christie, whom he met on his next film. Within a year, everything in his life was different.

The meeting with Christie came soon after he got back from the East, when director Sidney Lumet sent him a script that Gere believed would take him on to more challenging and mature roles. Lumet was also a member of that select band of directors, like others Gere had come across, with whom most actors of note wanted to work at some point in their careers. He had been one of the new wave of directors who emerged in the 1950s, and went on to become one of the great survivors of the industry.

His list of credits was a diverse and bewildering mix of films that began with *Twelve Angry Men* in 1957 and included such movies as *The Pawnbroker*, with Rod Steiger, *The Hill*, which rescued Sean Connery from the James Bond syndrome, and *Dog Day Afternoon*, which did so much for Al Pacino. He also had a fair smattering of failures to his name and would say philosophically, 'We are just humble toilers in the vineyard. We've simply got to do the best we can . . . I never analyse why I say yes to a movie.'

In 1985, Lumet was hired by a trio of independent producers to direct a screenplay called *Power*, whose story focused on a hotshot media consultant involved in the 'preparation' of candidates selected to run for high office in government. Already booked for the film were Gene Hackman, who was to play Gere's PR mentor, and Julie Christie, in the role of a British journalist who is Gere's still-involved ex-wife. 'I chose Richard,' said Lumet, 'because the film was about a business in which appearance is substance. Richard had that appearance and also a wonderful technique which suited the role. I knew that when an actor is as beautiful as he is it is difficult to be taken seriously, especially early on in your career. But I felt he had come through that and was ready for a heavier role.'

Lumet was surprised at Gere's reaction in their first meeting. The actor enquired of the director: 'Why do you want me for this part?' Lumet said he had never heard the question posed before, and it was not said in an arrogant way, more out of a sense of vulnerability. 'Although he's utterly open about his work, I was amazed at his sense of privacy about himself,' Lumet recalled. 'Maybe he's using acting to be open when he can't be in real life.'

The film's story, with all its ramifications of political and media corruption, was especially appealing to Christie, and in her, Gere found a like-minded spirit, full of resentment and turmoil. After a wary start, the two established what was to be an enduring friendship. Julie, in her time, had been the female equivalent of Richard Gere, the sex object and wild child of the sixties, reckless, charming, shy, glamorous and relentlessly pursued by the paparazzi. One British writer's description of her in the sixties almost matched that of Gere in the eighties: 'She has become quite neurotic about being Julie Christie, to add to her existing neuroses . . . she wants to be talented, to be seen to be talented and special. But she does not want to be Julie Christie.'

Eventually, to escape her fame and the media, Christie went to ground, hiding herself away in a very private world. She spent her time on her political causes, which she interspersed with making the occasional movie and modelling little glass ornaments and figurines which she carefully wrapped and sent to all her friends. The similarities to her co-star in this movie, Richard Gere, were uncanny: in the way they had both become ultra-famous, and then hated what they had become and determined to avoid unwanted intrusions into their lives.

For professional advice in researching his role in *Power*, Gere turned to Roger Ailes, a PR consultant who spearheaded the Republican campaigns of the 1980s. Gere studied Ailes intently. He was invited to meetings and sat in on discussions, taking copious notes. And the PR men were just as interested in Gere, his attitudes and what made him tick.

Ailes said they were all struck firstly by Gere's perception and second by his sensitivity, which he assessed as 'quite unique' for an actor. When Gere sat in on their meetings, he didn't just take notes on conversations, but absorbed all the detail too, down to the kind of ashtrays they were using. 'But as a political candidate himself,' said Ailes, 'I'd say he'd make a great candidate, for about twenty minutes. Then, like me, he'd want to deck somebody.'

Sidney Lumet's film looked to have all the right ingredients and was certainly not underfunded in terms of hiring the best – Hackman, Christie and Gere, in their own ways, were among the most interesting actors around for that kind of power-play movie. The screenplay was sharp and punchy, full of the PR language and hype necessary to promote the image. It was a tough and intelligent film, with good character observation.

Gere plays the young, expensive, unprincipled and shrewd media man in total control of the politicians he works to put in office. 'My job is to get you in – once you're there, you do whatever your conscience tells you to do.' Lumet's direction was slick and he kept the narrative fast-moving. But the characters ended up looking a little plastic and the storyline certainly tested the audience's willingness to accept its credibility, especially in regard to the preponderance of media corruption. But it was never quite gripping enough for mass audience tastes and the critics did not go overboard either, except to applaud the strength of Gene Hackman, who stole every scene he came near. And so *Power* dropped away and Gere chalked up his fourth dud in a row.

If there was a positive outcome to the making of that movie, it derived from Gere's conversations with Julie Christie, a long-time campaigner for human rights who was at the time heavily engaged in efforts to help relieve the humanitarian problems in Nicaragua, Honduras and El Salvador. The Central American countries were caught up with in-fighting, with US aid being poured in for all the wrong reasons.

Christie, a former anti-war campaigner at the time of Vietnam, had been so outspoken against successive American administrations that she was watched by both the CIA and the FBI every time she set foot in the US. She had been to Nicaragua on numerous occasions, and especially since the World Court in the Hague outlawed American support against the Sandinista government – a ruling which the US said it would completely ignore.

While liberal in his outlook, Gere was not one to get quite

so highly strung politically as Christie. Until that point he had been steadfastly apolitical. But he admired Christie's dedication and devotion to her causes. They had long, intense philosophical discussions and Christie urged him to visit Central America to see what was going on. She told him in graphic terms of the human suffering being caused by the American support for the Contras, who were killing and injuring thousands of people, displacing whole villages and disturbing a thousand-year-old culture.

Gere remained sceptical about getting involved, but promised Christie he would go down and see for himself. Christie put him in touch with the right people and before long, Gere was ready for his mission, little realising that it would develop into a passion that mirrored his commitment to the human rights issues of Tibet. In 1986 both Central America and Tibet began to take up more and more of his time, partly because he wasn't making movies in the same frenetic, back-to-back way that had been the pattern for almost five years.

He became associated with an organisation called El Rescate, which was devoted to human rights issues in Latin America, and eventually became a well-known face among the political circles of the region. In July 1986 he joined an American delegation visiting refugee camps in Nicaragua, Honduras and El Salvador for what he later described as a 'life-changing event' – a three-week fact-finding mission.

He joined up with an American doctor, Charlie Clemens, a Vietnam veteran who, after that war, had worked with immigrant communities around Los Angeles and then walked from California to Latin America to bring attention to the plight of communities there. He had remained in the region as a community doctor, travelling into areas where medical aid was virtually nonexistent. He also made an award-winning documentary on the plight of the refugees.

Gere, who became close friends with Clemens, travelled with him from village to village, and Clemens took him as close as he dared to the danger zones. At first the doctor was deeply sceptical about Gere's motives, but was soon convinced that he was serious about wanting to help in whatever way he could. 'We flew to refugee camps in Honduras and heard statements from people who had fled the bombings,' said Clemens, 'and then a general who recognised Richard was so impressed he signed a safe-conduct pass which would take us into regions that were unreachable by foreigners and press – and also quite dangerous.'

Gere collected testimonies from families who had fled the reign of terror in El Salvador. 'I found an appalling situation existed that never got reported,' said Gere. 'I spoke to a mother who had her child taken from her arms and cut to pieces in front of her. I spoke to a child whose whole village had been wiped out, and who was alive only because he crawled under his grandmother's dead body. When I came back, I was in a state of total shock from what I had seen.'

On his return to the US, Gere would give evidence to Congressional hearings on his findings. He responded to requests to address America's back-yard rallies, and actively campaigned on door-to-door foot patrol for an anti-Contra Democratic election candidate in upstate New York. Neither was this a one-off. His involvement with El Rescate developed into a major interest. He kept his activity low-key and refused to allow the issues on which he campaigned to be aligned to his other world, that of the Hollywood star. He simply walked out on interviewers who did not respect his request.

He also made his first appearance on American television for more than ten years when he did a deal with talk-show host Dick Cavett, using his Hollywood fame as the lead-in for publicity about the efforts of aid workers. 'The deal was,' Gere explained, 'that I would talk about my movies for ten minutes, and then Charlie Clemens would feature in the rest of the hour to talk about our trips to Central America.'

For the time being, the major issue of Gere's life was not

where his next movie script was coming from, although his work had interjected one more time – for what would be his last movie for more than two years. At the end of 1985, he agreed to play the role of an undercover cop in a fairly small film called *No Mercy*. It had the appearance of being one for the money.

Although funded by the Hollywood studio Tristar, the movie was being produced locally by an independent company and brought to the screen by an unknown director named Richard Pearce. Gere's co-star was Kim Basinger, another fiery young rebel who, like Julie Christie, pretty well hated Hollywood and all it stood for. 'I don't have any friends in this business at all,' she once said. 'You have to be a little unreal to be in it . . . it's like the Mafia.'

Gere had been dubious about playing the role of a detective, which was a rather common if fashionable screen characterisation of the era. The plot is a familiar tale of cop out to avenge his murdered partner. There is a mysterious blonde involved who turns out to be the property of a local vice king. Gere tries to arrest her, they become handcuffed together and he loses the key just as they are about to escape from the henchmen who have orders to kill them. They flee into the bayou where Basinger, in torn, skimpy attire, attracts the local alligator population as well as the pursuing goons. The story had the footprints of other films and television dramas all over it.

Gere figured it was rather like *Beverly Hills Cop* without the Eddie Murphy jokes. In fact, when he first read the script for *No Mercy*, he turned it down because of the violence. It took several rewrites, to tone it down and beef up the romantic parts, before he would accept the role. Then it was further delayed because they could not find the right actress to co-star. They looked at dozens of names before finally settling on Basinger.

Gere set off for Chicago to research his role. There he negotiated inside assistance from the undercover unit of the Chicago police department, who took him along on their busts. After a couple of nights of action, he found himself starring in a dramatic, yet amusing, real-life scene. He was hovering in the background early one morning as gun-wielding police burst into an apartment with a warrant to search for drugs. There were two people in the place, a man and a woman. Gere recalled: 'They got the guy in handcuffs, and his girlfriend wailing at the top of her lungs, and then I walk in. All of a sudden, there's dead silence. Then the girl starts yelling again, only this time she's saying: "It's the gigolo!" And her boyfriend is going, "No it isn't!" We take them both out in cuffs, and they're fighting all the way to the station: "It is the gigolo." "No it isn't." I had to laugh.'

The making of the movie involved some additional excitement. Gere and Basinger had to spend night after night wading through a freezing North Carolina swamp known locally as the Alligator Pit. 'Kim supposedly is wearing this skimpy outfit, but really she had on like three wetsuits,' recalled Gere while trying to drum up some interest in the movie at the time of its release. 'Even so, she could only stand to film about ten minutes a night. And there were a few times I felt something wrap itself around my leg, but I thought I'd better not mention it.'

No Mercy was a better-than-average formula thriller, saved by its film noir style and some thrilling action sequences. Gere's performance turned out to be of particular interest because it marked quite significant changes in his style and approach. He now seemed determined to make his audience stop thinking about Richard Gere and accept him as the character he was playing, a complete reversal of his previous technique.

Coincidentally, the same situation applied to Basinger herself, who had often complained that producers chose her because of her appeal in a wet T-shirt rather than for her skills as an actress. If for no other reason, the film captured the attention because of two actors who were doing everything they could to avert the eye from their sexpot images by playing their roles with drama and pathos.

In the end, though, their personal determination to establish convincing and intelligent characterisations, to which they had both clearly devoted a great deal of thought and energy, was overshadowed by the clichés of the script and the obligatory final shoot-out that accompanies all such cop movies.

No Mercy was no blockbuster. Gere could be satisfied with his own contribution, and he received some decent notices, but the film did nothing at the box office and merely fuelled speculation over the decline of his career. That, added to developments in his personal life and attention to his causes, brought about a long period of hibernation.

After completing *Power* and *No Mercy* for their 1986 releases, Gere simply dropped out and began a re-evaluation of what was important to him. The decisions he made concerning the time he would devote to the Tibetan cause and the human rights issues in Central America caused tension between him and Sylvia Martins. It was apparent to all their friends that the more Sylvia tried to cling to what was left of their relationship, the more Gere pulled in the other direction, towards his new time-consuming causes.

In the end it was all too much for her, especially as Gere had shown no interest at all in getting married. Sylvia upped and left, and did not return, and though they continued to meet on occasions, it was only as friends. So ended Gere's second serious relationship of the last dozen or so years. The first, with Penelope Milford, had finished in much the same manner when his interest had lapsed while he was making *Yanks*.

The separation from Sylvia was the last piece in the jigsaw of change which had affected virtually every aspect of his life. He had effectively severed his contact with Hollywood beyond the professional commitments, and had positively avoided the glitz that most of his contemporaries were involved in. His face was missing from the parties and the social whirl, and he confined himself to a small circle of friends in New York consisting mainly of actors, painters and writers.

He put the changes down to the simple process of growing older, of maturing, and realising that there were other things in life than just making movies. He would make only one more film, a small one at that, in the remaining years of the decade. He had stayed in the limelight longer than John Travolta, with whom his career had for a time run parallel. The two smart kids who at the turn of the decade were being offered everything that was going in Hollywood were now nowhere to be seen. Travolta was gloomy and brooding and wondering if he would ever get back.

Gere, on the other hand, had acquired contentment and commitment to his various interests. Even the smouldering attitude that so many had taken for an awful arrogance – and they were probably right – had mellowed. One of his friends recalled how, in a restaurant one evening, some people on the next table were talking about Gere and running through his career. Gere obviously heard, but simply smiled. 'Five years ago, that person would have had a fork sticking out of his ear,' remarked his friend. 'That was the difference.'

Chapter Twelve

No Turning Back

So Richard Gere had jumped off the high pedestal of the sex god on which he had been placed at the beginning of the decade. It was a conscious decision. The talk now was that he had gone religious, after he admitted in public for the first time that these days he did not care much about acting. It might have been dismissed as the excuse of someone whose career was on the slide, but there were those among his circle who looked for a more serious, underlying reason.

Some spoke about him being brainwashed by the Dalai Lama into a cult-style acceptance of the teachings of the religious leader, to whom Gere always referred as 'His Holiness'. This, however, was the talk of people who did not know much about the history of the Tibetan race at the hands of its Chinese invaders, and who certainly did not understand the Dalai Lama's position as the exiled spiritual and temporal leader of Tibet.

What blurred the situation, and what people could not understand, was how Gere, who had been one of the notorious bad boys of the movie business for years, could suddenly turn his back on everything and be swayed by the plight and religious teachings of a far-off nation. Initially, few took him seriously; several spoke with tongue in cheek;

and most found it curious that the Dalai Lama himself should be interested in the attentions of a star famous for all the wrong reasons.

But Gere's spiritual affiliation was one he shared with a number of high-profile western figures of the 1980s, and to the cynics, it sounded like the all-too-familiar story of a showbusiness flirtation with fashionable causes, the bored star taking centre stage on behalf of some mystical figure or oppressed minority. There was good cause to be suspicious. In recent memory, there had been many similar excursions to India by a galaxy of stars, led by the Beatles and Mia Farrow in the early sixties. The Maharishi Mahesh Yogi and other Indian holy men and mystics became exceedingly fashionable around Hollywood and New York, and for a time, everyone had a pet guru.

More potently, Marlon Brando had walked out on the industry that made him famous, denounced everyone in it as a bunch of charlatans and frauds, and became the self-appointed spokesman and occasional financier of the American Indians. He famously delivered the final insult to the cinema establishment by sending an actress dressed up as an Indian squaw to collect his Academy Award for *The Godfather*. For a time, he was also deeply involved with the militant faction of the Black Power movement.

Jane Fonda became the infamous rebel with an abundance of left-wing causes, much to the annoyance of J. Edgar Hoover, Richard Nixon and the CIA. Warren Beatty chose politics, became a power behind the presidential election bid of George McGovern, and was virtual campaign manager for a similar venture by Gary Hart, until a sex scandal torpedoed his chances. Robert Redford went in to bat for the environment, and Jack Nicholson also got political, amassing large gatherings of his friends at expensive dinners to raise money for the Democrats. Then there was Sting, with his ill-fated venture to save the culture of the South American Indians and their rain forests; and Bob Geldof's Band Aid for the starving in

Africa. The list is endless and the results variable.

Gere's causes, however, were more enduring than some, and his interest, according to Sylvia Martins, who had seen it grow, eventually turned into virtual obsession. But those who claimed it was to blame for his career taking a nosedive had completely misread the situation.

What it had achieved was to get the intrusive media off his back, because he was no longer sexily interesting. A human rights campaign does not have the same potential for the front cover of the *National Enquirer* as does his naked body in yet another steamy love match. Even the demise of his relationship with Sylvia Martins went by with no more than a flutter in the same gossip columns that had been full of their exotic adventures in the social whirl of Manhattan a year or so earlier. And that was how it would remain for the time being, with only occasional mentions being made of his appearances with a number of eligible young women: social butterflies like British socialite Sabrina Guinness; the jewellery designer Tina Chow; or friends like Susan Sarandon from his closest circle which comprised, in the main, the Manhattan artistic set and well-heeled bohemians.

Among those who saw Gere around the time of his deepening involvement with Tibet was the author and writer Dotson Rader. He visited Gere at his apartment and surmised that the actor was clearing his mind, expanding his heart and exploring his soul.

One of the few writers to have been invited into Gere's home, Rader found that the apartment in Greenwich Village had become an austere place, with the walls lined with books on Tibet, Buddhism and philosophy. Gere, he said, still looked the same – 'dressed in blue workshirt, tight chinos and half-boots, he was tall, muscular and handsome. His mind was quick, complex, unsentimental and appreciative of irony. As I was to learn, central to his life has been a rebellion against received values and a search for new ones.'

Gere told Rader that at that moment in time he was not interested in his career. 'What matters is my faith . . . emptying the negative out of my heart. Discovering things. Knowing yourself. Growth. That's the real work of life.' Furthermore, his commitment to the Tibetan nation and to the Dalai Lama's teachings was something he had been involved with for a long time and would continue to be associated with in the future. It wasn't 'like the truck came by and I jumped on it'.

Gere always had a ready explanation for anyone who enquired about what had inspired his interest in Buddhism. 'I wanted to make sense out of a chaotic universe,' he said, 'and the easiest way of providing an explanation of that faith is to say that it's based on the belief that it's the quality of your mind which creates reality around you. That means you are totally responsible for everything that happens in your life – your perceptions, your feelings, your events, everything . . . it means that you are not buffeted about by external winds. There are no external winds.'

Dotson Rader had little doubt that Gere's process of self-discovery and his deepening involvement with the Dalai Lama was genuine. By then, the Greenwich Village apartment had become the temporary headquarters of Tibet House, the non-profit-making organisation which he had co-founded on behalf of the Dalai Lama to raise not only money, but also public awareness of the plight and the culture of the Tibetans.

He would quote chapter and verse the history of the nation and its suffering since the invasion by the Chinese in October 1950. The Dalai Lama had fled from the capital, Lhasa, ahead of the marauding hordes of Mao's armies as they began their conquest of the country, killing an estimated 1.2 million people and destroying more than 6,000 Tibetan monasteries during the next decade. Gere could recite off the top of his head statistics concerning deforestation, compulsory sterilisation and genocide that was the lot of the Tibetan people.

He could give anyone who asked an instant historical portrait of the Dalai Lama himself: born in Taktser in 1937 and discovered by monks who were convinced he was the reincarnation of the Compassionate Buddha, His Holiness was enthroned at Lhasa in 1940. His rights were exercised by regency until 1950, when he fled to Chumbi, in southern Tibet. He negotiated an autonomy agreement with the People's Republic of China the following year and served as nominal ruler until he was forced into permanent exile following the brutal suppression of the Tibetan uprising. He moved with other Tibetan refugees to Daramsala, in the Punjab, and refused repeated requests by the Chinese to return to his homeland until they returned national rule to its people.

Armed with his intense studies on the religious and historical aspects of the Dalai Lama's nation, Gere began in earnest his mission to aid the Tibetan people during the mid-eighties. His visits to India became more frequent and he paid less attention to the calls of his profession, while the profession, it must be said, along with the media, simultaneously paid less attention to him.

The materialistic trappings of fame that usually go hand in glove with Hollywood stars had never been an overly prominent factor in Gere's life. The apartment in Greenwich Village, as Dotson Rader reported, was relatively modest in terms of what he could afford. He had taken a small house in Los Angeles and his only other major property expenditure was a country retreat at Westchester, north of New York on the border with Connecticut.

The wealth he had derived from his films of the last half-decade, though not massive compared with the earnings of some A-list Hollywood actors – Sylvester Stallone and Jack Nicholson, for example, were raking in well in excess of $6 million a picture – could be counted in sufficient millions to keep him comfortable for the foreseeable future.

He determined to give the foundation of Tibet House two years of his life, and that was what he did, virtually launching it from scratch single-handed and working eight-hour days from his desk in the apartment, pushing the venture along towards the point where professionals could be hired to manage the organisation.

He was unafraid of being outspoken in public on the issue of human rights, and in September 1987 he sponsored a visit to America by the Dalai Lama to unveil plans for the permanent establishment of Tibet House. He arranged press facilities for photographers, who turned out in abundance to catch this rather unconventional movie-star photo-call. The Dalai Lama praised Gere's work, calling him Tibet's best friend in the US. He hoped that when Tibet House was fully operational it would give a complete history of Tibetan culture, showing exhibitions of art, photographs and artefacts as well as dispensing literature on the nation's heritage.

Gere meanwhile continued to lobby for his causes and took every opportunity to show his commitment. When, some time later, he attended a star-studded charity event organised by playwright Arthur Miller and addressed by Henry Kissinger, he loudly barracked President Nixon's former Secretary of State who, like Nixon, was a champion of the Chinese. 'What about China, Henry?' Gere shouted as Kissinger began his speech. A woman sitting beside him was similarly moved, and started to boo. 'What's that man doing here?' she cried. As others joined the protest, Gere's face beamed with satisfaction. He felt he had done something towards nullifying his narcissistic image and turning into what he described as 'aggressively human'.

Gere once talked about this period of professional inactivity as 'the best time of my life', although his friends began to fall away from his side, overtaken by a mixture of wonderment at the amount of time and energy he was devoting to his causes and embarrassment at their eyes closing as he pontificated on the subject.

One of his close buddies was quoted as saying that Gere's heady itinerary had done just that – gone to his head – and that although people used to joke about him playing King David, it was the only time he was truly typecast, because he 'really likes to play God. He'd like to be Buddha.'

Even so, the amount of attention the Tibetan cause received directly through his efforts was immense. He stirred up interest at a meeting with British peers in the House of Lords, and later organised a Buddhist celebration at the Cathedral of St John the Divine in New York which was attended by 5,000 people. *Vanity Fair* reported that Gere was 'sort of leading it all. The sense of power in his face that night . . . the guy never looked sexier.' Even in that role, he could not escape old judgements.

Although he devoted most of his time to being the Dalai Lama's 'best friend in the US', he also continued to work for the Central American aid projects, and later joined the celebrity campaign for AIDS research as the mounting toll of deaths cut a deep swathe through the performing arts. Gere was never afraid of showing his support for AIDS workers, specifically the AIDS relief groups in New York, or of speaking up for the gay community in what was a difficult period for them. He was one of a number of celebrities present at the 1988 unveiling of the 11,510 lb AIDS memorial quilt at Pier 92 in New York. The quilt contained the names of more than 1,700 victims of the illness, and he volunteered to read these out as the panels were unfolded.

These events and public appearances, however, were few and far between, and his fame was, for the time being at least, fading from the public consciousness. As a movie star, he was looking as popular as yesterday's milk. In that respect he took himself up to the wire and was in real danger of being assigned to Hollywood history.

In the autumn of 1987 he made a brief return to acting,

but it was not an excursion that seemed to have been designed to send him zooming back into the star arena. In fact, the movie, entitled *Miles From Home*, was made more as a favour to his friend, director Gary Sinise of the Chicago-based theatre group Steppenwolf, whose members also populated the film, along with the heavyweight character actor Brian Dennehy who appeared briefly at the beginning of the movie.

It was always going to be a small, low-cost production, with no one receiving much in the way of money. Gere himself was reported to have accepted little more than $100,000 to appear. It was one of those projects that with a fair wind could have taken off in box-office terms – rather like Warren Beatty's *Bonnie and Clyde* or Dennis Hopper's *Easy Rider* two decades earlier – but it would hurt no one if, as seemed more likely, it didn't. A combination of backers plus a distribution deal with Fox largely through the reputation and traditions of Steppenwolf put the movie into production and it was filmed over six weeks during the late summer.

It was an interesting little film, a modern and unconventional road movie that said almost as much about Gere himself as it did about the subject matter. He was still keeping out of the Hollywood game, sidelined partly through choice and partly through lack of interest in his particular talents as the movie industry itself went through great changes in the course of the 1980s.

The film industry was by then being firmly led by the marketing people in the wake of the video explosion. The studios changed hands almost daily; new chief executives came and went like the wind. Charts and graphs had appeared on the walls of every major studio as the finance and production executives studied the ever-growing lists of statistics, surveys and trends that accompanied every movie made in Hollywood, in order to discover what was selling, to whom and why. Sex, violence, pyrotechnics on a grand scale were all rolled up into an ear-shattering, nail-biting, sexually arousing package, and exaggerated into an astounding fantasy world by the new technology of film-making and its delivery into the cinemas.

A whole new breed of star had taken over, too: mostly young, brash, and noisy, and making movies that largely depended for their impact upon exciting, explosive visuals. Good acting and clarity of diction were not skills that were especially in demand. The era of the spectacular had arrived with the video explosion, and so had a new, unprecedented clamour for wealth and power, led by a powerful clique of agents and managers who were laying down unheard-of conditions for their stars, leapfrogging each other for huge pay cheques, percentages of grosses rather than net profits, percentages of marketing deals, and so on.

A star could make so much from one picture that, if he so desired, he need never work again. This remarkable turnaround had happened virtually while Gere wasn't looking, although he did have the opportunity to join in had he so desired. But he didn't. The age of the sensitive, brooding leading men had vanished, and though Gere's situation had been confused by his own desire to drop out, he was certainly not alone in discovering that demand for his style of acting, the mean pretty boy, had gone – and, of course, he had aged somewhat in the meantime, which further lessened the demand for his services. He was in a no man's land of age and style. Al Pacino's record told a similar story. He made only three movies between 1986 and 1990.

De Niro was still busy but his movies were seldom commercially successful and he had now diverted his attentions towards forming his own film-making centre in New York. John Travolta was still out of sight and two years away from his comeback in *Look Who's Talking*. Even Robert Redford had retired to his Sundance Film Center in Utah, to concentrate on making films rather than starring in them, and Michael Douglas, who had been best known for playing liberal characters in 1970s message pictures, was so fed up with waiting for someone to offer him a decent role that he changed his image to sexy swashbuckler and produced his own movies, *Romancing the Stone* and *The Jewel of the Nile*. Having established his presence as an A-list actor, he then made the blockbuster of 1987, *Fatal Attraction*. This trio of movies boosted his bank balance by around $25 million.

All around him, Gere saw people he had met on the way up who had suddenly hit the payload during the time he had been away. Hollywood had changed beyond recognition in the space of five years. There were the newer stars edging into the position once occupied by himself. The Brat Pack was growing up, and Tom Cruise was the new Mr Sex, after a scorching ascent via *Top Gun* and *The Color of Money*. Robin Williams, another New York actor, at last broke into the bigger time with *Good Morning, Vietnam*.

Sylvester Stallone and Arnold Schwarzenegger had the mass market covered with movies like *Rambo* and *Terminator*, from which they were earning $15 million a film, and Jack Nicholson was on the verge of recording Hollywood's biggest ever payday, an incredible percentage and marketing deal that earned him a reputed $60 million in fees and merchandising kickbacks as a supporting actor in *Batman*.

It was also a lucky time for Bruce Willis, who for years had struggled as an actor around New York and was serving cocktails to uptown yuppies until he finally secured a role as Cybill Shepherd's sidekick in the television success story of the decade, *Moonlighting*. In 1987 Willis moved to the big screen in *Blind Date* and had just been signed for a small fortune to make *Die Hard*.

Despite all the changes, Gere could have put himself right back in the frame at that point, had he wished to do so. It is not generally known that the screenplay of *Die Hard*, adapted from the novel *Nothing Lasts Forever*, was actually written with Gere in mind. Producers Joel Silver and

Lawrence Gordon did their best to persuade him to accept – with huge money on offer – but Gere turned it down. Willis got the part and put himself in line for his biggest ever payday and all that followed the film's massive success, including the two sequels from which he would earn more than $20 million.

That wasn't the only blockbuster Gere rejected at the time, either. Oliver Stone initially wanted him for *Wall Street*. Gere said no to that, too, and walked away from another of the big movies of the late 1980s, which starred Charlie Sheen and earned Michael Douglas his first Oscar as an actor.

Gere's manager could not believe that he would pass up such high-profile opportunities and yet give his commitment to a tiny little project like *Miles From Home*. The Steppenwolf group pressed on with the film in the hope that it might just break through the clouds. In view of the other material in the marketplace at the time, it is interesting to take a closer look at the movie Gere had chosen to interrupt his concentration on Tibet, in what did not even represent a half-hearted attempt at a comeback.

The film opens with what appears to be black and white newsreel footage from the year 1959, when the Russian leader Nikita Khrushchev paid his famous visit to an average American farm in Iowa. The footage shows him stepping across the threshold and shaking hands with the farmer, with two small boys standing nervously in the background. The film then moves into colour and comes up to date. It is almost thirty years later, the farmer is dead and the two sons, Frank and Terry Roberts, have inherited the land their father toiled upon. But theirs is a different world. The US farm crisis of the 1980s which put dozens of small farmers out of business hit them hard; that year huge rainstorms wiped out their crops and the banks are about to foreclose.

Gere plays the older of the two brothers, fiercely protective of his inheritance and now at boiling point as he sees it slipping away. After he is seen in the churchyard talking to his father's grave and apologising for the mess, he breaks down. He forces his brother to help him set fire to the farm and its fields rather than give it away, and against a backdrop of flames leaping into the sky they race away, leaving other farmers applauding their symbolic act.

Now, as the brothers go on the run, their adventures bring them into contact with a series of characters and events set against scenic and landscape cinematography that has echoes of Gere's film with Terry Malick, *Days of Heaven*. The influences of the Steppenwolf traditions are also clear, through the direction of Gary Sinise, and the emphasis lies heavily on emotional drama, in which the central figures are Kevin Anderson, who plays Gere's younger brother, and Penelope Ann Miller, his girlfriend.

The film was nicely done, but it could never be a contender against the Hollywood output of that year, when the lists included some vintage, pace-setting productions – like Bertolucci's *The Last Emperor*, Michael Douglas in *Fatal Attraction* and *Wall Street*, Jack Nicholson in *The Witches of Eastwick*, Mel Gibson in *Lethal Weapon* and Peter Weller in the bloody but marvellous piece of wham-bang sci-fi fun, *Robocop*.

In the spring, Gere went on a promotional trip to Europe with Kevin Anderson, and in May 1988 *Miles From Home* was given a screening at the Cannes Film Festival. It was a good year to be at the film jamboree and to watch the stars take part in the various meet-the-press luncheons and soirées laid on to secure maximum publicity. The lunchtime ritual is a pleasant and relaxed way for directors, producers and stars to be interviewed, spending a few minutes at each table of journalists and writers, all intent on trying to get their subject to open up on matters personal. Many do not, and will set definite parameters for questioning: by and large they will only discuss the work at hand or their personal interests – i.e. their causes. Long gone are the days when stars spoke frankly about their hopes, their fears and their relationships.

Surrounded by publicists employed to keep them out of the papers and ring-fenced by managers who try to control what is said about them, the stars today talk only about specific work-related topics – about the style of this director or that, or the hidden meanings and messages in the picture they have just made.

Robert Redford made the trip that year, too, and chatted about his latest movie, *The Milagro Beanfield War*, which he had directed but did not appear in. In fact, like Gere, he too had been off the screen since 1986, when he appeared in *Legal Eagles*. His project and Gere's also had similarities. Neither caught the box office, but both were visually effective and on similar subjects. Redford's was a charming comic tale of a Hispanic community fighting evil property developers. Thus, its subject matter was sufficiently close to his own interests for Redford to talk about his personal causes – which were minority rights and attempting to arouse a greater public awareness towards our fragile environment.

Most people were surprised to see Richard Gere undertaking the same round of table-by-table questioning, and some were quite obviously expecting a bit of knockabout fun with an old adversary, the Mr Nasty of yesteryear, but he still wasn't playing that game and set a very tight agenda for discussion. He was calm, cool and charming, and he said that he was very proud of his latest film. It would be nice, he said, if a lot of people came to see it.

It was a lead for some to question him about his personal attitudes and anxieties, bearing in mind that he hadn't had a major movie for several years. He replied that he did not really care too much about that and quickly moved on to talk about his faith and about Tibet. He spoke passionately if densely of his involvement with the Dalai Lama. 'Realism is a function of fluidity of the mind,' he said in response to a questioner who simply enquired what was important to him as a person, and then wished he hadn't. 'What I'm saying is that fluidity of mind is the reality, that all things come out of emptiness . . . I've devoted much of my time, probably ninety per cent, to the Tibetan thing during the past few years because there is no one else to do it. They have no protectors.' Then he thanked everyone for listening, smiled sweetly and went to the next table without having imparted any juicy piece of gossip that the writers could phone home with.

His film did not live up to his hopes. It was given a cool reception in Cannes and the producers recalled it before it went on general release, to have it recut, re-edited and re-scored. Even so, the critics did not give it a smooth ride, and on the whole used it as a cudgel with which to beat Mr Gere about the head, complaining that he was totally miscast. Even though he had been away for so long, they still put him in the category of a Hollywood star who needed to be taken to task. Actually, his performance was far better than he was given credit for.

Miles From Home was given only a limited release on the cinema circuit, taking little more than $1 million in US box-office receipts. It did not reach London until a year later and thereafter quickly vanished from view. It remained a curious if harmless event in an otherwise uneventful stage of Gere's career.

All around him on the publicity circuit, and in Hollywood itself, the stars of the moment were having a ball during this Hollywood renaissance, with the money flowing like water over the Niagara Falls. Gere, however, remained apparently content to stay out of it.

He admitted at Cannes that after turning down several major movies, he simply wasn't getting the offers any more, and he continued to insist that he wasn't looking very hard either. But one could not help feeling that there was a certain wistfulness in his eyes and his voice, that in reality he would dearly love to be back acting again in a decent film, or even on stage. In fact, it would be another two years before he was back on the screen, and he was coming dangerously close to becoming a forgotten man, certainly among the newer generation of cinema audiences. Unknown to him or anyone else at the time, however, events were unfolding elsewhere that would in due course rocket him back to the front pages – and in his view, for all the wrong reasons.

Chapter Thirteen

When Richard Met Cindy

Shirley Ritts was like a surrogate mother to Richard Gere, although his own was always in pretty close contact too. Shirley was worried. Richard seemed to be losing his way. Her own son, Herb Ritts, now a famous fashion and fine arts photographer, had come on in great leaps and bounds since he and Gere, his best friend from way back, shared an apartment in New York in the mid-1970s. Their careers had taken off at the same time, and both were based upon one thing – the sexy image of Gere that Ritts captured in a set of photographs he took of his pal in 1979 which appeared in virtually every major glossy magazine to promote *American Gigolo*.

He took another series of shots in 1982 which came about almost by accident. They were driving through the Californian desert one day in a Buick when they had a flat tyre. While Gere, in T-shirt and jeans, was jacking up the car, Ritts began shooting his film, and the snaps once again made the front covers of the glossies when *An Officer and a Gentleman* was released. Herb Ritts was a made man.

He became one of the most sought-after photographers in America, who was called upon by the rich and famous, and by the late 1980s he was charging up to $20,000 a day for his services. He has photographed everyone who is anyone, from Madonna to Jack Nicholson, from Michael Jackson to Axl Rose, and from Stephen Hawking to Mikhail Gorbachev. He was the only photographer at Elizabeth Taylor's eighth wedding and the snaps were reportedly sold for $1 million a set.

Unlike Gere of late, Ritts had just gone higher and higher, so busy that his schedule was booked up eighteen months in advance. His static model work is regarded as classic, his fashion pictures are renowned for their electrifying qualities, often bizarre in composition and of a style and social connection that has frequently drawn comparisons with Cecil Beaton. Above all, he has been acclaimed for his celebrity shots of Madonna, Kim Basinger (after she'd appeared with Gere in *No Mercy*), Tina Turner and Brigitte Nielsen.

In fact, it was his erotic nude pictures of Nielsen, published in the December 1987 issue of *Playboy*, that attracted the attention of an up-and-coming young model named Cindy Crawford, who had arrived in Manhattan the previous year to work for the prestigious Elite Agency. Twenty-year-old Cindy described what she felt as she picked up the copy of *Playboy*: 'When I saw what Herb Ritts did with Brigitte Nielsen . . . I thought, Wow, if he can make her look that good, I'd love to see what he could do with me. That's when I decided to go for it.' At that moment, a meeting with Herb Ritts, and ultimately Richard Gere, was on the cards.

Crawford wasn't exactly doing badly, earning around $400,000 in her first year in New York. Her face had already appeared on the front cover of *Vogue* and photographic sessions already booked would ensure that during the first three months of 1988 she would grace the cover of virtually every top magazine in the US, including *Harper's Bazaar*, *Cosmopolitan* and *Mademoiselle* – all this only eighteen months after she first stepped into a swimsuit and posed for a fashion photographer in her home town.

And since she will figure heavily in the remaining chapters of this story, it is as well that we take a look at her origins. Cindy came from a blue-collar background. Born in De Kalb, Illinois, in 1966, she was the middle of three daughters, and had a younger brother who died of leukaemia when he was three. As she would later recall, the child's death almost wrecked her family, and her parents were divorced as she entered her teens. Her father, a plumber, later remarried and eventually went to live in California, although he kept in close touch with his family. Her mother, Jennifer, took two jobs, as a bank receptionist and as a shop assistant at weekends, to make ends meet, and the girls were by necessity independent young kids.

From an early age, Cindy was fending for herself, though her school work did not suffer. She graduated from high school with straight As and won a full scholarship in chemical engineering to Northwestern University. She would probably have done well there too had her looks not quickly taken her beyond the confines of the campus. She had only been at Northwestern one term when, fed up with working in the cornfields for summertime pocket money, she joined fifty other girls in a hair-styling show in Chicago and was spotted by a talent scout for a modelling agency, who suggested that she should try her luck in the fashion world.

Her parents, though wary of her entering a profession so well known for its disappointments, agreed to let her try, and gave her $500 for a portfolio of professional photographs. Initially, she was rejected because of a mole just above her lip – the self-same mole that young girls who wanted to be like Cindy would have copied in tattoo parlours when she became famous. One of the staff at a local modelling agency looked beyond that facial blemish and saw in her face and body the potential that others had missed.

The agency eventually offered her some work, and by the summer of that year, she was earning $500 a day. It was then she decided to drop out of university for full-time modelling. Her career really took off at the age of eighteen when she began working with Chicago's leading fashion photographer, Victor Skrebneski, who became her mentor, her tutor and her guide into the major league. He used her every day in the grinding and often unglamorous world of Chicago modelling, but from him she learned how to pose for the camera, how to look deep into the lens so that her eyes became the focus of any photograph, and above all, with his discipline, how to be a professional: be on time; be immaculate, work hard and never complain.

By then, she was already beginning to commute between Chicago and New York. Subsequently she left Skrebneski after a falling-out, and he refused thereafter to see her or speak to her again. Things that are that strong, he said, cannot just end – they die. In 1985 she moved permanently to New York, and the Manhattan office of Elite Model Management began securing top assignments for her. She travelled the globe: London, Paris, Rome, Milan and all points east. She did a shoot for *Harper's Bazaar* but the magazine editors did not like the way she looked and rejected her as a potential cover girl.

Vogue didn't. In August 1986, she made her first appearance on the cover of the magazine, and never looked back. That edition sold more copies than any other issue in 1986, and *Vogue* immediately booked her for two more. She was in demand for every kind of modelling work, from fashion to cosmetics, in the United States and Europe. Crawford, however, was also sharp and intelligent, and known by all her friends to be fiercely independent.

She also displayed a tendency not to conform to normal rules, and to take risks in her work that others might avoid – as in 1987 when she agreed to appear in a television advertisement for Revlon's Intimate fragrance. It was judged by executives of NBC to be too sexy and was banned from appearing on that network. The commercial, a take-off of a moment in the film *Nine and a Half Weeks*, showed Crawford being subjected to ice cube torture at the hands of her supposed lover. The steamy part – too sexy for NBC – came as the melted water dripped down her *décolletage*.

What Crawford knew by then was that she was one of a dozen leading models vying for position, and she assessed that to go higher, to set herself apart, she needed to market herself.

That was when she saw the Herb Ritts pictures of Brigitte Nielsen – and decided, as she said, to 'go for it'. She made contact with Ritts, who in turn introduced her to *Playboy*. Crawford was quite clear what she wanted: a display of fashion-based photographs in which she would appear in semi-nude and topless poses. *Playboy* executives, of course, were trembling with anticipation. Their photography director, Gary Cole, said: 'Presented with a Ritts–Crawford package, we just said yes, without question. And apart from nailing down a location, we made no other rules. Herb and Cindy would be on their own. You never want to direct a photographer like Herb Ritts. He has his own special vision of erotica and womanhood, his own idea of what he's going after, and we didn't want to interfere with that – we did not even specify colour or black and white. We just said *bon voyage* and sent him on his way.'

The shoot was set on the sands of Kona and Kanapala, Hawaii – a locale which *Playboy* proclaimed 'was perfectly suited to Cindy's volcanic sensuousness', and it lasted only three days.

Ritts decided to shoot in black and white and the results, said Gary Cole, were 'memorable'. They also caused a sensation in the bitchy world of modelling when they were published in the July 1988 issue of *Playboy*, exactly what Crawford had aimed to achieve. At the time, topless was not a word that the fashion industry used. 'I set my own agenda,' she said defiantly. 'I knew people were talking about me in the business, but I didn't go into this with my eyes closed. It was a statement, I'm very professional, and that's part of my success. Some girls don't like to work with me, because I'm all business. A lot of them stay up too late or call in sick. I never do that. The girls that do are giving away some of their power.'

And so Cindy Crawford led the modelling world into bodily exposure in a way previously shunned by the fashion business. 'It was easy to get men's attention,' she said, 'but to earn the respect of other women is a lot harder. But if women are fair they will see that I don't just use this [face].' Before long, others would follow, once Cindy had shown that going topless was not merely the domain of the models who posed for top-shelf magazines.

Like Richard Gere when he was her age, Cindy Crawford had no qualms about displaying her body, and it was one of life's coincidences that the man to whom she chose to reveal this fact was the same photographer who had captured Gere in his most famous poses a decade earlier.

Crawford's decision was controversial and brought much comment and criticism from the leaders of the modelling world, who dismissed her as a fame-mad exhibitionist. In fact they used much the same language that had been employed to describe Gere all those years earlier.

There was, that summer, one other incident which had a curious echo of Richard Gere's own experiences, when he was followed by a fan who had fallen in love with him through his photographs and eventually made contact with him to begin their long relationship.

In Crawford's case, it was a frightening experience. One night in June 1988, she arrived home late after a shoot that had taken her to China. It was well after midnight and she quickly discovered that things in her apartment in Greenwich Village were out of place. Her bed had been slept in, there was fresh food in the refrigerator and her telephone book was missing. As she was searching around, the telephone rang and a male voice on the other end said: 'Don't be mad. I just wanted to make contact.'

It appeared that a fan obsessed by her beauty had managed to get her address by posing as a journalist, and into the apartment building by saying he was a close friend.

He even wangled a set of keys. In the telephone conversation, he said he would come over straight away and introduce himself.

Crawford made an excuse but promised to meet him the following day in a restaurant. In the meantime, she called the police, and when the stalker turned up for their appointment, he was arrested. He was charged with second-degree burglary and sentenced to two to five years' imprisonment. Cindy, nervous and worried, immediately left the apartment for another address and never returned.

Not long afterwards, Herb Ritts's mother Shirley got in touch. She was arranging a barbecue for Elton John and asked if Cindy would like to come along. Cindy said yes. Then Shirley rang Richard Gere and invited him. He agreed, too. Behind her charming smiles, Shirley Ritts was doing a spot of matchmaking. Richard, she told Herb, needed a high-profile and beautiful woman on his arm, and Cindy Crawford might just be the one.

What Shirley was planning, according to one of Cindy's friends in New York who later put the pieces of the jigsaw together, was to bring the world's most wanted female body, metaphorically and commercially speaking, to a union with Richard, whom Shirley thought needed putting back into the limelight and on the path to celebrity again before it was too late. The girl was a dream, but only twenty-two years old. So what's age got to do with it? asked Shirley. She would drag Richard back into the twentieth century, and perhaps stop him going on about that funny man with the shaven head.

Shirley personally made the introduction, and very soon, Gere and Crawford were chatting away to each other. Soon they were dating in conditions of utmost secrecy, almost as if they were a royal couple embarking on a clandestine romance.

In terms of American tabloid interest, of course, it was exactly like that – the hottest model and the once-hot star – and a paparazzi shot of them together would have made any front page. So for months they were seeing each other – albeit spasmodically, because of her increasing workload – without anyone outside their closest circle of friends, sworn to secrecy, realising it. 'Well, yes, it's true my mom pushed them together,' Herb Ritts admitted. 'They got talking and it grew. He's changed her. He's a mature, intelligent guy. Anybody older, you learn if you're open to it. It was an easy relationship. They were sweet and good to be around.'

While Gere's own career continued to languish, Cindy went bounding onwards and upwards. 'She was incredibly aggressive,' said fashion executive Mark Bozek. 'She always wants to be challenged.' And the challenges came thick and fast in the remaining months of 1988 and on into the new year.

The pop singer Prince wrote a song, 'Cindy C.', dedicated to her; she did more sexy picture layouts for male mags including *GQ* and *Sports Illustrated*; she began work on her own swimwear calendar, which would become a best-seller at Christmas 1989; and she appeared on the front covers of more than 200 magazines around the world. To top it all, she signed a multi-million-dollar deal with Revlon, with a contract that extended to her thirtieth birthday, coincidentally following in the footsteps of Lauren Hutton, Gere's co-star in his first major picture, *American Gigolo*.

Cindy also moved into screen media in 1989 when she signed with MTV to present their *House of Style*, a popular fashion magazine, six times a year. Everybody wanted Cindy Crawford, and when the news leaked out in 1989 that she was seeing Gere, the media began a stake-out to try to capture them together. They had little luck.

Whenever the couple travelled together, they got in and out of cars separately so that the paparazzi could not snap them together, and when Crawford appeared on television or in the mass of media interviews that were set up for her after the Revlon deal, she positively refused to talk about her 'friend'. 'It's offensive to me that who I go out with makes me more interesting,' she snapped.

Gere meanwhile remained in consultations with the Dalai Lama as the Tibetan House foundation began planning its own contribution to the Year of Tibet in 1990. His own personal involvement, apart from the various activities and events planned for the year, would be the organisation of a travelling exhibition of work by a collection of the world's leading photographers.

He began making contact with a long list of potential donors whose work could be expected to sell for considerable sums at exhibitions in New York, Los Angeles, London and Japan. And so the dedication to the cause went on, much to the growing annoyance of the Bush administration in Washington. With American politicians and businessmen alike courting Chinese trade opportunities, Gere was a veritable thorn in the side. Every time he spoke about Chinese oppression or voiced his support for the Sandinistas or the El Salvador refugees, Washington winced. Forty years earlier, he would have been hauled before the Un-American Activities Committee.

Gere's image had changed drastically from the old days, mainly because there had been no movie roles to interfere with his cruise towards media acceptance as a man at peace with himself and devoted to a worthwhile project. All of that was about to change again – dramatically. For one thing, it was now common knowledge that he and Cindy were together, and that brought back all the old memories of the sexy Mr Gere.

The spotlight suddenly swung back, and there he was . . . the same Richard Gere, almost forty now, with silvering hair, but still lithe and handsome, and no longer Mr Nasty. He was Nice Guy personified, by all accounts.

And then, just as suddenly, as if by some miracle his name had been plucked from the hat, Hollywood was calling with a proposition, one that would end this warm and tender image that he had spent the last five building for himself: how would he like to play a psychopath cop in a big new movie called *Internal Affairs* – the one, said his agent in not so many words, that would launch him on the comeback trail?

'Well . . .' said Gere. 'I'm not sure.'

He was worried. The nature of the character he was being offered in the new Paramount movie prompted a good deal of soul-searching. He would be cast as Dennis Peck, the sexy, villainous street cop whom he saw as a very negative character, and 'I wasn't sure I wanted that in my life right then', because it would revive references to some of the unpleasant characters he had played in the past, which had caused him a good deal of grief ever since.

But Gere also had to admit to himself that if he was going to make a serious attempt to revive his career, he had to come up with a hit soon – and this movie was being talked of as having that potential. And then there was Cindy. The romance. His money would not last forever. He debated with himself for a while about what to do, though he was still reluctant to play roles that did not sit comfortably with his new spiritual enlightenment.

There must also have been an occasional pang of regret every time he read what Bruce Willis was going to get for his next *Die Hard* sequel, and perhaps the odd twinge when he watched Michael Douglas pick up his Oscar for *Wall Street*.

The indecision was not one-sided, either. Frank Mancuso Junior, who was producing *Internal Affairs*, had been casting his net elsewhere before he went to Gere. According to the film's director, Mike Figgis, Paramount wanted Mel Gibson or Kurt Russell, who were more identifiable with the all-action image. Gary Lucchesi, then president of Paramount's production division, argued that the role was so villainous that they needed a complicated but sexy actor – and it was he who suggested the name of Richard Gere.

Mancuso scratched his head, but eventually agreed. He admitted, 'Richard Gere was not my first choice for the role. When the role Dennis Peck was created, we thought it would be great to get a big movie star to play him and frankly Richard was not big box office at the time. But then we realised that to make this movie work, we needed someone who would push the character as far as we wanted it to go – it was unlikely that we would get a box-office star who would risk doing that. And then the movie would have collapsed around him. So what we needed was not an actor who would not get in the way of the movie, one who would become that character on screen and not be the movie star in the middle of a cop movie. Richard used to have a reputation for taking chances. He also needed a big one.'

The role of Dennis Peck was undoubtedly Gere's roughest since he played the brief but memorable scene as the knife-wielding lover to Diane Keaton in *Looking for Mr Goodbar*. The character is a seemingly respected veteran officer on the force who uses his charm to hide his psychotic tendencies. Behind the friendly smile is a genius running rackets on a massive scale.

The truth of Peck's corrupt past is only revealed when he becomes the subject of an internal investigation by a young police lieutenant, played by Andy Garcia, the bright new star who came to fame in Brian De Palma's *The Untouchables*, in which he held his own against Kevin Costner, Sean Connery and Robert De Niro, and who had just scored a major hit as Michael Douglas's sidekick in *Black Rain*.

Garcia was, in many ways, like Gere in style and approach. His spasmodic early career was perhaps held back by his own determination only to accept roles that he believed in. His portrayal of yet another cop in *Internal Affairs* gave him his most worthwhile challenge to date.

Peck, who kills with cool detachment those who are a threat to him, looks into the Garcia character's life with the same precision with which the young cop is looking into his, and attacks his weakest point – his sexual hang-ups, and a restless wife. As a cold-blooded ladies' man, Peck turns his attentions to the wife, with terrifying results. The story unravels into a taut, uncomfortable thriller whose success is completely dependent on the performance of the principal actors.

Gere, now openly admitting that he needed a success to 'stay viable or they won't let me do this any more', embarked on intense study of the character. He scoured his library and read up the psychology, deciding he would play the role of Peck as a classic force, based upon Shakespeare's Iago, who sets Othello against his own wife. Iago, he surmised, was able to pinpoint Othello's flaw and used it in his manipulations. Peck in his way was not a bitter man, but one who used the same kind of manipulation for control of the situation that confronted him.

Gere found in Mike Figgis a ready supporter of his intentions to base his performance on Peck's psychology. Figgis was a talented British screenwriter and musician taking charge of his first Hollywood project. He had made one film previously, *Stormy Monday*, a dark and moody British gangster yarn with Sting, Melanie Griffith and Tommy Lee Jones, which had some nice touches but had not done well. He, like Gere, had his reputation riding on the outcome, and they went into a huddle straight away with Andy Garcia on how they were going to play it.

Figgis, from a background in experimental theatre, was not averse to improvisation, and they set to with some vigour, giving the film pace and tension. They all got so carried away in one scene that Gere had to be taken to hospital for treatment to severe cuts and bruising. Gere had deeply immersed himself in his role, probably more so than ever before, and because he was the initiator of the film's entire theme of malevolence, he could not fake it – his rage, his evil, had to be believable.

The way he tackled the part surprised everyone, not least Gere himself. 'When I was young playing this kind of role, we were all maniacs. The character becomes your whole life to the exclusion of all else. Now, I've moved on and it was a tough movie for me to make because I don't enjoy hurting anyone. I do not indulge in any kind of violent act. I can't even kill a mosquito.'

For Garcia, it was reminiscent of watching De Niro's raging, virtuoso performance as Al Capone in *The Untouchables*, not for the character similarities but in the explosive intensity and attention to the merest detail of both actors.

Gere looked the part, with his steely-grey hair closely cropped, and his forty-year-old face having lost none of the handsomeness that had made him so sought after in the past. He had a lot of skeletons to shake off with this performance, to rid himself of past memories and bad movies he had played. It really was like starting over again, and just occasionally, there was a flicker of determination in his face that had nothing whatsoever to do with his acting; it was Gere goading himself on. His performance was a skilful rendition that bounced off Garcia's less showy but equally convincing role.

The movie received some good reviews when it opened in New York in January 1990, and although not all the critics were in accord, there was general agreement that Gere was back with his best work since *An Officer and a Gentleman*, and probably his best ever. Even Pauline Kael, who had never been a fan of Gere's, chose on this occasion to applaud his performance: 'You can see why women are drawn to him and why men are taken in. He's heartlessly affable.' Audiences agreed, and the box-office takings boomed away into a major hit.

Chapter Fourteen

He's Back

By the time Gere had finished filming *Internal Affairs*, there had been a fair amount of publicity in the trade press and feature magazines. The word on the Hollywood grapevine was that he was back in business, working well, still handsome and sexy, even when playing evil incarnate. One executive who had shown a particular interest in his revival was Jeffrey Katzenberg, chairman of Disney Studios and the former production boss of Paramount Studios, who had first hired Gere when he was nobody.

He telephoned Gere while he was making *Internal Affairs* and asked him to read the script for a new movie from the Touchstone division of the Disney group. 'It's a kind of *My Fair Lady*,' Katzenberg told him, 'but without the songs.' In other words, it was a kind of *Pygmalion*, without the depth and genius of George Bernard Shaw.

Katzenberg had always taken a personal interest in Gere and the progress of his career. He had first noticed the actor when he made Terry Malick's *Days of Heaven*, and it was Paramount that brought him to notoriety in *American Gigolo* and then *An Officer and a Gentleman*. Katzenberg was also the man who had put *King David* into production and had watched Gere's career go into freefall thereafter. He didn't say so, but perhaps he was now trying to make amends for that embarrassment. 'I was involved with him when he became what Tom Cruise is today, an actor who is also a sex symbol,' said Katzenberg. 'Now I see him as a leading man, though I sometimes wonder whether that's what he wants for himself.'

The big question was, would audiences, who had acquired something of a resistance to his arrogant, sexual cockiness of the past, accept that there had been a transformation? It was a major gamble, for both star and studio. The script Katzenberg sent round had the working title of *3,000*, which was in due course fortuitously changed to *Pretty Woman*.

The 3,000 of the title is the amount in dollars that billionaire businessman Edward offers to a prostitute named Vivian, who will administer sexual pleasures during a weekend in Los Angeles. It was, said Katzenberg, going to be a very big film, and he staked his reputation on Gere's ability to become a star of the 1990s.

Sean Connery, Al Pacino and Tom Selleck had already been touted in the trade press as likely contenders for the role, but the Disney chairman was insistent. He wanted Gere. 'I was absolutely confident about that,' said Katzenberg, who had also predicted that within thirty days of the film's release Gere would be 'as important a leading man as exists in our business'. That was a bold statement, considering the importance, as always in modern Hollywood, of that oft-used word bankability, or, as Sir Ralph Richardson once defined it, the ability to stop the audience from coughing.

Gere's recent past gave no hint of his readiness to return in blockbuster fashion, and his selection for the role raised a good many eyebrows in the trade, as indeed did the fact that Disney, a company founded on the wholesome all-American values of family life, should choose to go overboard on a story whose heroine was a hooker. That particular line of criticism was forestalled by Gere himself when he initiated major changes in the original script to make it a more acceptable light comedy with a happy ending.

Gere had also, once again, been wary about accepting the part because of the way the character had been written. In spite of his precarious standing in Hollywood at the time, and the money that was on offer for the picture, it took the pleadings of his agent Ed Limato and Katzenberg himself to get him to proceed. Katzenberg reminded him of the last time this had happened, when he went down on his knees to Gere and begged him to do *An Officer and a Gentleman.*

The movie mogul attributed Gere's procrastination to his personal conflicts of conscience between art and commerce. He was totally unpredictable as an actor, said Katzenberg. Producers and directors never knew which way he would jump. Limato too had had his patience pushed to the limit in the past, and *Pretty Woman* would be no different.

Gere believed that as originally written the character of Edward Lewis would come across as a cold user who couldn't communicate and who was just out for sexual pleasure. There were dark corners to the character that Gere did not like, and the original story had a 'down' ending – not the glitzy fairy-tale finale that eventually every member of the audience wanted to see. Conversely, he thought that Julia Roberts's character, the prostitute Vivian, had more energy, and overpowered the role of Edward.

Gere voiced his fears to director Garry Marshall who, coincidentally, was a friend from the past. They had first met in 1980 when they were introduced backstage by Marshall's sister Penny after a performance of *Bent.* Marshall knew that Gere had a cool sense of humour that had rarely been seen on screen, and he also knew that it was humour and irony that were needed to inject life into the story.

Gere was unfamiliar with the work of Roberts, who at the time was a virtual unknown. Her latest film, *Steel Magnolias,* was only just coming out, and Gere had to make do with watching her on a tape of her previous movie, *Mystic Pizza.* Although this was not a brilliant picture he thought she was 'terrific'. Marshall and Roberts then flew to New York for a meeting at Gere's house in Greenwich Village. There, in the unlikely setting of his monastic home, surrounded by the paraphernalia of Buddhism, they read through the story of the billionaire and the prostitute and agreed that though a lot of changes had to be made, basically they could make it work.

The rewriting which followed the meeting took full account of Gere's suggestions. Vivian would now be seen as a more intelligent woman, who has resorted to prostitution through bad luck, while Edward would be portrayed as a man who, having picked her up for sex as she stands on a street corner in her eight-inch mini-skirt, then becomes besotted with her.

He indulges himself by giving her the opportunity to become a 'real' woman, adorned in expensive clothes and capable of holding her own among his socialite friends. As the story develops, she in turn will make him think about his own life. He will turn from the ruthless post-yuppie manipulator he has become into a considerate businessman intent on saving the world instead of tearing it apart and selling it off for scrap.

The fleeting similarities to *Pygmalion* were obvious, but the result was a sentimental piece of modern Hollywood, shamelessly based upon an old-fashioned romantic premise. It became the blockbuster of the year, and a best-selling video, regardless of what the critics said. By and large, they took it for what it was, a fairy tale, and audiences responded by turning up in droves. The movie shot to number one in the charts and took $30 million in its first ten days.

Julia Roberts was a made woman, and Gere was back near the top of the pile and sitting on a multi-million-dollar payout, more money than he had ever made from any movie. The film also presented him with one of the most affable portrayals of his career, a veritable nice guy, in the end, who gave the audiences a warm glow as, overcoming his tendency to vertigo, he climbed up to the window of

Julia's seedy apartment and carried her off to dreamland.

The chemistry between the co-stars was a key factor in the film's success, and Roberts acknowledged later that Gere had generously 'given' her the picture which ultimately won her an Oscar nomination. She was the heroine, the focus, while he strolled effortlessly through the story with a wry stolidity which appeared no more demanding than occasionally showing his body and changing his Armani suits. 'He stayed at the low end in performance terms,' said Roberts, 'which is unique to talented people. He made Vivian an interesting character by making Edward show that he found her interesting – otherwise she'd have just seemed like a whacko. He did it for me; he gave me the opportunities even when it meant he himself was standing back. He is an incredibly generous actor.'

This restraint on Gere's part was noticed by his peers but it didn't stop critics and others in the industry from complaining that the film did nothing to alter the perception of Hollywood's general attitude to women; that they were always second-class citizens or cast as mere appendages of men.

While the reviewers might not have put *Pretty Woman* among their top ten best films of the decade, it served Gere's purpose admirably and gave Julia Roberts the kind of career hype that, as events would show, she would have difficulty in repeating. When a movie is so successful, it actually builds a fresh mountain for those involved. It just sits there, saying: Beat that. And *Pretty Woman* would take some beating. Worldwide box-office grosses exceeded $450 million, and that figure would remain as a point of reference for the future. The success of the film would hang like a millstone around the neck of an actor who, unlike, say, Michael Douglas or Sylvester Stallone, was not motivated by the need to stay high in the league table of who's hot.

Even as Gere was back in fashion among the people who mattered in Hollywood, his personal attitudes had barely changed, and his choices, it would soon become clear, had become no more specific in terms of winning box-office acclaim. Further, his deepening friendship with the Dalai Lama and his increasing activism for the Tibetan cause continued to pull him away from the normal workaday routine of a major film actor – that of meetings, script readings, discussion with directors and producers and so on.

None of it seemed to matter that much. Instead, as soon as he had finished filming *Pretty Woman*, he flew off to India and back again almost straight away to meet the Dalai Lama in Norway, where the Tibetan leader was to be presented with the 1989 Nobel Peace Prize.

The rest of 1990 – the Year of Tibet – was punctuated with various events, exhibitions, cultural displays and meetings organised by Tibet House in New York. When Gere went to Canada, soon after the release of *Pretty Woman*, to promote a film about Tibet, he was mobbed by a crowd of enthusiastic fans – right star, wrong movie – who tore his shirt off. Around the same time, he recorded an audio cassette of two volumes of *The Tibetan Book of the Dead*, which the publishers pointed out was a classic of Tibetan wisdom 'intended to be read aloud not only to the dying, but to be studied by the living and applied to everyday life'.

Spiritual concerns aside, Gere's celebrity status had climbed to its highest ever peak as the success of *Pretty Woman* went rebounding around the world, though the interest was heightened by his relationship with Cindy Crawford. Her own career had exploded in the past few months. Her picture was everywhere, her glamour calendar had been a bestseller, she was planning a keep-fit video and her MTV appearances had been stepped up. Gere and Crawford were in constant demand by media writers and broadcasters. While Cindy, by and large, co-operated Gere remained his old reluctant self, aloof and choosy.

In March 1990, when Disney's PR hype for *Pretty Woman* was in full swing, he gave a rare in-depth interview for *Vanity Fair*, published in the May issue. He used the opportunity to expound upon his causes, and to talk in philosophical terms about the pressures of Hollywood, about which he remained sceptical.

When the interview was published, the US tabloids targeted his comments, almost an aside, on the prospect of one day soon becoming a father, from which remark assumptions were drawn that he could soon be setting up home with Ms Crawford. The fact that he had recently been viewing properties in Los Angeles added a further clue. From that moment on, the Richard and Cindy show was rolling, and gathered intensity during the coming months.

They fitted the vision of the American dream perfectly. Two beautiful people apparently – to those looking in, at least – living the most exciting life imaginable. She the Supermodel, with the hair, the face, the body that made her the desire of every man and the envy of every woman; he back in the mould of Superstar, handsome, beguiling, enigmatic, wealthy, the desire of every woman and the envy of every man.

Their appearances together were becoming more frequent, their mentions as a couple in the magazines almost daily. Their schedules kept them apart for weeks on end, but also put them in a permanent spotlight wherever one or the other came to rest, and thus the attention quotient was doubled. Sometimes they would join each other in their individual worlds of fashion and film, the two most glamorous pursuits in the universe outside being a young British royal.

And when they met, the paparazzi kept close watch for those I-love-you glances for which picture editors in a thousand newspaper and magazine offices around the world would pay a fortune; the little touches of personal aside, like a knowing little smile to him, sitting in the front row as she marched down the catwalk of a Karl Lagerfeld show in Paris, or his arm around her waist as they walked into the Oscar ceremony under the glare of camera lights.

They seemed perfectly matched, perfectly in accord, perfectly sculpted with bodies and body language that seduced the great American public – and perfectly set up for life in the goldfish bowl.

Richard and Cindy were, at that time, edging towards centre stage to star in America's own equivalent of the Charles and Diana saga. The Prince and Princess of Wales had something more important at stake, of course, like the future standing of the British monarchy, and in that respect there was no comparison. That did not stop both couples from becoming the reluctant stars of their own parallel soap operas, played out under unprecedented public gaze. The Richard and Cindy affair would have almost as many twists and turns, assisted now and again by media-hungry PR people strategically positioned in the wings to take advantage of any situation that might direct attention to his films or her image and product promotion.

Like Charles and Diana the couple would themselves also throw the occasional log on the fire. Cindy, though exceedingly cautious in interviews about her private life, to the point of refusing to discuss her relationship with Gere, showed little reluctance for expanding her own press coverage. She co-operated with photographers, went on television chat shows and gave interviews for the major journals at the drop of a hat. Gere, meanwhile, remained his usual reticent self.

There were additional elements which gave succour to this growing fascination for the Perfect Couple. Like Charles and Diana, whose stormy marriage and adulterous relationships were slowly being unravelled by a press and public demanding to know the truth, Gere and Crawford would face similar microscopic examination, and specifically over private matters like their own sexuality. That aspect of the scrutiny emerged soon after *Pretty Woman* hit the top, and coincided with the appearance of Gere's interview in *Vanity Fair*. It was inspired by a dirty smear campaign triggered by a deluge of messages over the electronic network, first in the way of untraceable faxes and later via the Internet.

The story alleged that Gere was gay, and that he had recently been admitted to hospital following an accident while indulging in a certain homosexual practice. It was so preposterous that it did not seem to merit even a denial. However, a Los Angeles radio disc jockey – who incidentally said he did not believe the rumours – nonetheless continued to pepper his programme with Richard Gere jokes, and Frank Swertlow, a columnist in the Los Angeles *Daily News*, used the speculation over Gere as his lead item on 1 May 1990. The issue, he said, was not what the rumours alleged, but the lengths to which the people responsible would go to embarrass him.

The controversy reached such a pitch that Gere instructed his publicist, Andrea Jaffe, to break the rule of a lifetime about not commenting on '*supermarché*' stories and record that Richard Gere was the victim of a malicious campaign of slanderous lies. Jaffe added intriguingly: 'You have to look at who is threatened by his success.' The denials were insistent, but the mud stuck hard. This story would not go away.

As for Gere himself, the period was his busiest for years. The promotional effort for *Pretty Woman* had been intertwined with his own projects for the Year of Tibet and attempting to continue his relationship with Cindy Crawford, equally transatlantic in her movements. He was making arrangements for the Dalai Lama to visit New York in September, with the Tibet House organising a whole round of media events along with the social and cultural activities. The political possibilities, however, were decidedly thin and the White House showed little recognition of the visit.

Gere dashed between New York, London and India, and in between on to Paris and Tokyo during the second half of the year. He was working on a couple of new movie projects which would involve him for the first time in the business side: as executive producer on *Final Analysis*, to which he was personally very committed; and in an all-Japanese production of a controversial movie relating to World War II.

Gere had always shown an affinity with the Rising Sun, and a few years earlier he had sponsored a visit to New York by the Japanese national dance troupe, Butoh. His interest in Japan had been revived of late, partly because of his own contacts through his attendance at an Asian peace conference in Tokyo in June 1990, and partly because of the interest shown there in Cindy Crawford, who had become something of a Japanese national monument in recent times.

Through these contacts, he was approached by the famed Japanese film director Akiro Kurosawa, who was making a film whose title translated into English was *Rhapsody in August*. It was to be released in 1991 around the time of the fiftieth anniversary of the Japanese bombing of Pearl Harbor. The director was seeking a leading American actor for the movie in the hope of attracting a US distribution deal, and although he had already decided to approach Gere, he was also surely well aware that Gere was probably the only well-known actor in Hollywood who would even contemplate the project.

First, the artistic community of Hollywood itself was not especially fond of the Japanese at that time because they had been buying up all the studios and the creative companies, along with half the prime real estate of Los Angeles and New York. Quite apart from that, however, was the controversial nature of the film's script. The problem lay in the way that Kurosawa and his writers had interpreted Japanese actions during World War II.

Gere, for his part, seemed prepared to take on the possible wrath of the US veterans of Pearl Harbor and other encounters with the Japanese, on the basis that there were explanations to be made and Kurosawa's film would go some way to making them. His character is central to the movie. He plays a half-Japanese man, the nephew of a woman who survived the bombing of Nagasaki and who is seeking the offspring of her brother who, before the war, left Japan to settle in Hawaii, where he married an American girl. Gere is the catalyst to the film commentary on the vital issues of Pearl Harbor and the bombing of Hiroshima and Nagasaki.

For US audiences, the film would evoke a hostile reaction since they would see it as implying that America was the warmonger of the two nations and making light of the thousands of American deaths at Pearl Harbor and on the infamous death march after the fall of Bataan in the Philippines. Gere found himself speaking lines which in so many words apologised on behalf of America for dropping the atom bombs on Japan.

When the film was released in Japan, it naturally attracted a ready audience and applause for Gere's courage in taking the role. By the time it reached the US, it was insensitively close to the anniversary of Pearl Harbor, and the war veterans came out in force for vocal expressions of their disbelief that Gere should embarrass them by his appearance. Without Pearl Harbor, they said, there would have been no Hiroshima.

Director Kurosawa went before a press conference to explain that his motive in making the film had been to try to gain a better understanding of what had happened. The Japanese, he said, could not show remorse because they were never aware of what was going on. The fact that they have never apologised since, either, seemed to get in the way of his arguments, however, and Kurosawa did not manage to convince a hostile media. Gere went to ground, made no comment and the film was hardly seen in the US. It demonstrated once more the maverick streak in his outlook towards movie-making – offbeat and occasionally offbeam, but quite often commendable if only for *not* going with the flow.

His reasons for making this picture were never quite

clear but in a curious way were bound up with his relationship and devotion to the East, demonstrated once again in May 1991 in California when his two most demanding interests, Hollywood and Tibet, merged for a visit by the Dalai Lama.

Gere brought him there to open an exhibition of The Sacred Art of Tibet at the Asian Art Museum in San Francisco. More than 1,500 people waiting to receive the Dalai Lama's blessing parted like the Red Sea as the holy man in his maroon and saffron robes walked in with Gere at his side. The actor waxed lyrical about the 'affection and joy in the air for the presence of His Holiness' and said it was the best opening he had ever attended. The Dalai Lama, slightly bemused by it all, concurred.

At the time, Gere was already on the West Coast, filming for his next movie. The speculation that his spiritual path had also had an effect on his decisions regarding his work could easily be applied once again. Typically, from experience of recent years, just when he was at the top Gere made selections which were really very hard to understand, even taking into account his little foibles about art and commercialism as described by Jeffrey Katzenberg.

There were two movies in the offing – two he had decided upon, that is. There were actually several more offered after *Internal Affairs* and *Pretty Woman*, but others may have had more obvious potential for success and he avoided them. One he did pick up was a script about a manic depressive named Mr Jones, a character who intrigued him.

There would be a singular drama in itself about getting this picture made. It stretched over the next three years, a tortuous journey which initially started out with the assistance of the British director Mike Figgis, who had led him back to notoriety in *Internal Affairs*.

Gere wanted Figgis to direct *Mr Jones*, and that was the way it started out. But a lot of work had to be done on the script, and Figgis would come and go, along with various other personnel – directors, writers, producers, editors and composers – too numerous to mention. With Gere himself acting as executive producer, and thus for the first time theoretically in charge, it became something of an obsession with him to get this movie made, which he would not actually achieve for some time.

He did move straight ahead with *Final Analysis*, although that too had its teething troubles, both in the script and in the post-production editing. The film was billed as a slick Hitchcockian thriller in which Gere would star with two of the most popular actresses of the moment, Kim Basinger and Uma Thurman. He plays a therapist who begins an intense affair with the sister of one of his patients. She in turn decides she no longer wants her husband around. There is a contrived subplot which involves the question of the sister's sanity, and a lot of very moody photographic work and soft voices.

There was a hint that all had not gone well when, long after director Phil Joanou, a newcomer to Gere's sphere and to the role of movie direction, had delivered his first cut, Warner Brothers asked Gere to return for some reshooting of several takes. It was easy to see why there were doubts. Even the final version was snail-pace slow in parts, and occasionally incomprehensible. Gere himself was monosyllabic, monotonous and unable to raise the temperature. The reviewers, all hyped up for another interesting performance from Gere after *Internal Affairs* and *Pretty Woman*, were mystified about his choice of follow-up. There were very conflicting views about his performance. *Variety* called the film 'a cracking good melodrama in which star power and slick surfaces are all used to potent effect'. Other comments ranged from 'dreary derivative thriller' to 'slick . . . vacuous . . . nothing rings true'.

And the tragedy is that it could have been so good. It is not difficult to imagine Gere reading the first draft of the screenplay and deciding that it had considerable merit. It is very probable that he selected it without contemplating a huge box-office hit, seeing it rather as a moody piece that would have creditable artistic merit – like, for example, a brilliant Martin Scorsese movie that gets huge reviews but doesn't take enough at the box office to cover the cost of his bus fare home. That premise, cinema art at any cost, only works if the performances are electrifying and the movie is riveting. *Final Analysis* failed on both counts.

Chapter Fifteen

Marriage

As the months passed, Richard Gere and Cindy Crawford were following each other around the world, yet they seemed no closer to marriage. Their friends regarded them as a couple and they were talking about all the things couples talk about, like children and houses and where to live. In the autumn of 1991, Gere seemed to be setting his stall out for matrimony when he purchased a property in Los Angeles, a $3.5 million beachfront spread at Malibu Beach, adding one more residence to their collection, which now consisted of his-and-hers apartments in New York and his country retreat on the borders of Connecticut.

It seemed not so much a question of if they would marry, but when and how. They were busy people, but the phrase was trotted out with such regularity that it began to sound like an excuse. Those in their circle who had known him longest were still sceptical. They were the ones who had seen him meditating unflinchingly while mayhem might be going on around him, who had experienced his rubber-band concept of time when an appointment was to be met, who had witnessed him, like a child, infuriatingly impervious to the requirements of others to whom he might not care to speak.

Those who spoke for him, who carried on the pretence

that work and pressure prevented the couple's marriage, would point to the crazy existence they both led, with meetings between them often short and sweet. The life and times of a $20,000-a-day model who had an *ad infinitum* contract with Revlon, another with Pepsi-Cola and the role of a part-time MTV presenter to fit into her schedule, and that of her partner, who was darting between capitals making movies or promoting the Year of Tibet, left little scope for matters personal.

They snatched occasional days away, perhaps visiting her mother or meeting up at one of the New York apartments. Once or twice, when she was in Europe, he would invite her to join him on a trip to the Dalai Lama's headquarters in India. She always refused, saying she would take it one step at a time and that she was not ready to go native. She did, however, finally join him for a week's visit in the early spring of 1991. It was her one and only trip. They lived in a Tibetan refugee camp for a week, eating the local diet of rice, and yoghurt fresh from the yak, and engaging in long, contemplative sessions of ritual meditation, wearing red blindfolds. Cindy did not care for it.

In March 1991 she appeared on the covers of both *Vogue* and *Cosmopolitan*, and by then the front cover tally had exceeded 300 magazines, making her the most successful model of all time. The Cindy Inc. bandwagon was rolling and quite a large entourage had jumped aboard. The couple's lives were separated by their professions and interests, and also by their personal attitudes towards their respective careers.

Gere himself, as had become apparent from his ambivalence to Hollywood over the past few years, was the far more relaxed of the two, and exercised a measure of control over the demands on his time by simply ignoring those with which he did not wish to deal. Crawford, on the other hand, was heading towards the zenith of her years at the top – for a model a notoriously brief period – and was at a stage in her life that was comparable to Gere's two decades earlier.

It was in that area that their age difference was most

noticeable. In the first heady days of success, visions are clouded by the thrill and excitement of it all and by the belief among young stars of public notoriety that there is something vital and important about what they are doing. The need to explore every possible avenue on the climb to the top becomes paramount.

Every day becomes busier than the last, and Cindy was travelling fast on a white-knuckle ride. Gere, on the other hand, had been there, done that, and was *still* wearing the T-shirt. He had passed through the angry young man stage more evidently and publicly than most. He had since retreated into his philosophical, patient and restrained state of existence. He'd spent years analysing his motives, had long ago recognised that the driving ambition of those who reached notoriety at an early age was the attention it brought them, along with the money, and the opportunities, as he put it, for getting laid.

It began with the flattery of recognition and then moved into open pursuit of fame through the child-like syndrome of wanting to be seen *and* heard. It was ambition driven by hedonistic, acquisitive notions that few who enjoy their fame can avoid, and most continue to pursue in later life. Those who tire of it, and all the public scrutiny that goes with it, re-examine their lives. In Gere's case, as we have seen, it took him into spiritual discovery, teaching him how to straighten out his life, but leaving his career on the roller coaster he had climbed aboard in his early twenties.

Crawford was at the beginning of the same journey, and the seventeen-year gap in their ages merely exacerbated the differences in their perception of the future. Gere saw this a challenge for both of them, an opportunity from which they could both benefit, she learning from his experiences and he from the freshness of her approach. Whether that would be a firm enough basis for a union of two vastly different paced individuals remained to be seen.

It was noticeable, for example, that when out together, they both wore similar clothes, much the same style as he had been wearing for years, the jeans, T-shirt and leather jacket look. In fact, one of his reasons for being reluctant about taking the role in *Pretty Woman* was that he did not know how to wear suits any more.

There were the usual areas where age and generation could not easily be bridged, such as the appeal of the loud and lively parties that abound on the periphery of the modelling business, although Crawford herself was, according to some of her colleagues, tediously self-disciplined about getting home early and up with the sun the next day, working out in the gym with her trainer while others were still sleeping.

There were other small incidents where the couple's perception of themselves and their ages differed, and about which their friends teased them. One night, Cindy was reading a book whose central characters were a young student and an older man. Cindy looked up from the page and suggested Gere make a movie of it.

Gere, who knew the book, replied, 'I think I'm getting too old to play college characters.'

'Not that guy,' she replied, 'the other one.'

'You mean the old guy?'

'He's not that old,' she said. 'Perhaps only in his forties.' It was an exchange which Gere has recalled as the moment when he realised that he could no longer play 'young' roles and that younger people viewed him as edging towards his seniority.

Music was another gulf. Gere loved classical music and was also still playing his Bob Dylan and Byrds tapes, strumming along on a guitar from his vast collection or doing a passable impression of B.B. King or, in another mood, jazz guitarist Joe Pass. He had musical tastes with which Cindy had no affinity, and which she could not abide. She loved pop, and had grown up listening to that style of music played on vinyl by her parents, who were only two or three years older than Gere himself. And that also raises the question of parenthood, which was something that kept cropping up in their conversations, long before they were married.

Cindy wanted children, or at least she kept telling everyone she did. First she wanted them quickly, then she changed her mind and said it would be better to get past a certain point in her career – so, not for a few years, until the prime of her modelling had passed and she had moved on into the other regions that interested her. By then, however, Gere would be heading towards fifty, although that was no bar to starting a family, as Jack Nicholson, Warren Beatty and Anthony Quinn had recently proved. 'Cindy has been very vocal about wanting a family,' Gere resignedly told an interviewer from *Vanity Fair*. 'She's always been clear about that, and I think if it was something I didn't want to do, she would reluctantly withdraw from this relationship. Could I exist without kids? Yes. Absolutely. Would I love to have kids with Cindy? Yes, I think that would be fabulous. I know what that would do to her, and I'd love to see that . . . and so I will leave it up to her.'

At the time, the decision about marriage and children remained in constant abeyance because of their respective workloads. A wedding, it was said by intimates of both, had been on the cards for months and put off several times, although it seemed to be edging closer. It was Gere who was unsure. He had taken to questioning friends with families about having kids, and whether it was possible to read while taking care of the baby.

The situation gave rise to strong rumours that he was thinking of giving up acting to concentrate on his Buddhism and become a househusband, but that never seemed a real possibility, despite headlines in a London newspaper claiming 'Gere to quit'. He was content to proceed at his own pace, while keeping Hollywood at a distance.

Though he had occasionally appeared to be on the verge of retirement, friends and associates like Jeffrey Katzenberg were convinced that secretly he enjoyed the star status, regardless of the offhand reluctance with which he greeted most offers of employment. Less kindly intimates even suggested that it was the fear of being overshadowed by Crawford's fame that had made him wary of marriage – that 'he does not want to become another Norman Maine'.

Crawford was certainly becoming more and more famous, increasing her commitments outside modelling. In December 1991, for example, when the latest edition of MTV's *House of Style* programme went out to millions of homes through the MTV cable and satellite channels, she was generally applauded for the articulate manner in which she interviewed her subjects. She brought a gentle irony to the proceedings through her insider knowledge of the fashion world.

In that particular show, she interviewed Jean-Paul Gaultier, known for his anarchic tailoring and ballistic lingerie. 'Have bras and corsets always been part of your look?' she enquired of him with a wry smile, and he confided the story of his grandmother who used to drink vinegar to contract her stomach so that she could pull on her corset. The model Linda Evangelista agreed to submit to a 'day in the life of' piece and made confessions about her work that she would surely not have done with another interviewer. The ratings increased after virtually every one of her shows – and that was perhaps the least demanding of her various roles. Even so, she left no one in any doubt that she wanted to be married.

Gere would only admit that he did not want to lose Crawford, but he wanted to be sure and he also had to put marriage into perspective with his spiritual beliefs, just as he had done with his career, saying quite categorically that it would run in parallel with and one step below his spiritual path.

These were all the considerations that Gere typically weighed up, and upon which he apparently procrastinated for months, while Crawford became increasingly worried that their relationship was going nowhere.

Although she well knew that if their details had been run

through a computer dating agency, they would never have been thrown together, she persevered. 'When Richard and I met,' she said, 'he was forty and wanted to go to India and live in a tent. I was twenty-two and wanted a family and a white fence. Our map didn't match at all. So . . . was I supposed to wait and find someone with a similar agenda or stick with the feelings and try to make the map fit?' She decided on the latter.

Her fears were hardly a good basis for a marriage, but after repeated discussions which took them round in circles, she gave Gere an ultimatum, virtually forcing him either to say yes to marriage or to agree to end their relationship there and then. 'I've got to know,' she told him in front of friends, 'I've got to move on if it ain't happening.'

On 12 December 1991, it happened. They were grabbing some time together before she flew off to her next assignment. He was already working in Los Angeles on the pre-production of what would become the trouble-torn movie *Mr Jones*, and in the early evening they made a spur-of-the-moment decision: Let's do it, now. They could be in Las Vegas in an hour, and married before the night was out without the interruption of the paparazzi. Cindy called Herb Ritts at around 8 p.m. and told him that Richard had proposed.

'We're flying to Las Vegas. You've got to come,' she said. 'Will you be my man of honour – and take the pictures?'

'See you in ten,' screamed Ritts and dashed off to join them. Also going along to witness the event were Gere's long-time agent and friend Ed Limato and another friend, a Disney executive who made the arrangements. He telephoned ahead and booked the ceremony at The Little Church of the West in the midst of the brash neon glitter of Las Vegas Strip. It was a small timber building that Cindy reckoned resembled an International Pancake House and whose past clients included the much-married Judy Garland, Mickey Rooney, Dudley Moore and, fictionally, Elvis to Ann-Margret in *Viva Las Vegas*.

They did not have time to buy rings and so made them out of tinfoil. Then, after a fifteen-minute ceremony costing $510, which the Disney man paid for on his credit card, the wedding party repaired to Denny's fast-food diner for a quiet celebration before flying back to Los Angeles at dawn. Thus the marriage of Ms Cindy Crawford and Mr Richard Gere, which had come so close to being a non-starter, began aptly with a Walt Disney executive as best man and witness to a Mickey Mouse ceremony.

Cindy said she was just happy to be married, regardless of the surroundings or the lack of family and ceremonial trappings. She said she was not even worried that she did not wear a wedding dress, because after modelling so many in the past, it meant nothing to her.

Soon the news was leaked and CNN was broadcasting it to the world – before the couple had even managed to telephone all their relatives. Next morning, it was back to normal. Gere went to work and Cindy drove the car to the carwash and then did some shopping. She came home crying.

'I had about two weeks anguishing about what we had done and the way we had done it,' Cindy later confided. 'I kept crying to myself, "I don't know who you are. Who are you?" I also had this terrible memory of my father leaving us when we were kids and I worried that Richard would do the same.'

Gere became angry: 'I can't believe this. You said marriage would make you happy and now you're completely nutty. I'm not your dad, so don't start laying that one on me.'

Such was the inauspicious start to their so-called wedded bliss. Soon she was flying away again – New York, London, Paris, Milan . . . then back to the US. Secretaries faxed notes and messages from one to the other as they pursued their separate interests. Like all movie stars and models at the time of peak business, social and family life is almost by appointment.

When the star is married to the model, the problems are doubly difficult. How could it be any different? They had always known it would be that way. Some people tried to make it an issue in their lives – suggesting that they weren't really interested in the marriage at all – and that kind of gossip got going almost from the beginning. The truth of the matter, as will become clear in the succeeding pages, was more to do with the schedules of a married couple who were also two of the world's high-fliers, with commitments and diary engagements in a permanent state of conflict. That was their life, the way it was set up, and it could only get worse. Because both were on a roll.

Gere was back in harness with a far greater intensity than had been his style of late. He had already moved his own production company into play, seeking business involvement and a measure of control over his movies, as had been the case with *Final Analysis*, on which he was also executive producer. He had been actively seeking scripts he could initiate himself, and two were already on the drawing board – *Sommersby*, which would be his next film, and *Mr Jones*, a longer-term project which, as we will see, ran into some severe difficulties and would take three years finally to bring to the screen.

In the search for projects which he could be involved in from the beginning, and in which he could have a say in everything from script development to casting, Gere and his production company partner Maggie Wilde had obtained access to a pile of inactive scripts, from which they pulled *Sommersby*. The screenplay had been written by Nicholas Meyer, of *Star Trek II*, *IV* and *VI* fame, and was inspired by the 1982 art-house hit, *The Return of Martin Guerre*.

Meyer recast the sixteenth-century French legend into the era of the American Civil War, when a Confederate soldier returns to his Tennessee plantation and sceptical wife after being listed as missing, presumed dead. Gere discovered that the script was controlled by the co-producers of *Pretty Woman*, Arnon Milchan and Steven Reuther.

Gere had a good relationship with Milchan, an Israeli-born producer six years older than himself. He was a man who, like Gere, was prepared to take risks and did not necessarily follow the Hollywood code of Mammon over all else – as was evident from the list of films he had produced to date. Although *Pretty Woman* had been the outstanding profit-maker of his career, there had been several others which were creditable films but commercial disasters.

He produced Martin Scorsese's very fine *King of Comedy*, with Robert De Niro, which did nothing at the box office but remains one to watch over and over again. He secured the financial wherewithal for Sergio Leone to film his marvellously moody and evocative flop, *Once Upon a Time in America*, also with De Niro. He put Danny DeVito in the driving seat to direct Michael Douglas and Kathleen Turner in *The War of the Roses*, which made money. He also backed two of Terry Gilliam's movies, *Brazil* (again with De Niro in a cameo role) and the heavy loss-maker *The Adventures of Baron Munchhausen*. His were invariably movies which were worth making, and even if some of them didn't make the money men happy, he powered on, providing opportunities for directors and actors to exercise their creative bent.

And so from Gere's point of view, the contact was fortuitous. He called Milchan to ask what was happening to the Sommersby script. Milchan replied: 'Nothing. Let's do it.' The usual conferences and money discussions followed. They studied the list of female stars for the role of the wife and eventually settled upon Jodie Foster. She had recently won an Oscar for *The Silence of the Lambs*, and possessed the particular qualities they were seeking, able to create a strong, sensual female character without overwhelming the movie with her physical attraction.

It would be an expensive film to make, with period settings, costumes, and animals, but they worked to a budget of under $20 million and Milchan put together a trio of backers, with Warner Bros at the helm. Gere, known for his European slant and liking for British directors, had chosen another relative newcomer to Hollywood, Jon Amiel, best known for his direction of the British television series by Dennis Potter, *The Singing Detective.* Gere himself oversaw the script and brought in an additional unbilled writer, Charlie Mitchell, to beef up some of the scenes and provide accuracy in regional dialogue.

Filming began in the spring of 1992 and the unit was transported to western Virginia for an eventful shoot. They had to deal with torrential rain and flash floods, in which Gere became a hero, personally rescuing horses and livestock from probable drowning. 'They were filming a scene when the heavens opened,' said film extra Billy Russell. 'The river which had been swelling after heavy rains all month, burst its banks and all hell broke loose. The cast and crew fled indoors to wait until it had passed, when Gere remembered the horses tied up in a nearby stable. Still wearing his Civil War costume, he waded through the water and by the time we reached the stables, the water was quite high – really dangerous. He untied his own horse and then supervised the removal of all the livestock to a safer area.'

The film opens with Jodie Foster running her plantation single-handed until Gere, as her supposed long-lost husband Jack Sommersby, returns from the war, mysterious, charming and, more especially, very loving. He then has to convince her that he is truly her husband, a fact which appears to be in considerable doubt.

Gere stamped an authority on the role which probably saved the film from disappearing into incredulity. He overcame considerable weaknesses in the script with his convincing performance as a loving family man, yet retaining the possibility that behind his enigmatic charm lurked an outlaw.

There were also some very strong, passionate and moving love scenes, which would be billed by the PR people as a cross between *Gone with the Wind* and *Basic Instinct.* Director Amiel said: 'The love scenes, I think, were very special, even for Richard Gere. They had a lot of sophisticated passion. When he and Jodie watched the rushes, I think even they were surprised by the intensity. You never know how it's going to turn out until you see it on film, really . . .' With such scenes, success depends upon whether the camera likes what it sees, and in this case it picked up the vibes.

Amiel conjectured that Gere, through his Buddhist experiences, had learned how to deal with the possibility of failure, the fear of being made to look ridiculous, which haunted most Hollywood stars like nothing else. Male actors were much more concerned than women about the nature of the emotions they showed on screen, said the director, but Gere had the confidence to play characters in technicolour, in several layers and dimensions. 'He's a great actor now,' said Amiel, 'and often underrated by the critics. They will see he is coming into his prime.'

As with Julia Roberts in *Pretty Woman*, Jodie Foster was equally appreciative of Gere's attentiveness as an actor, as indeed are most who work with him these days. 'There was no angst, no anxiety,' said Foster. 'You don't get him constantly crying on your shoulder saying "Am I OK. Am I OK?" It's not a big emotional hassle. He just lets it happen. Frankly, this surprised me. I had been led to believe it would be different, that he'd be much more confrontational. But he's a really gentle, nice guy, a kind of smouldering person. Even when people do bad things to him, he's too cool to get mad. He just jokes about it, defends himself with witty remarks. It was good. There is, of course, the bad boy side to him . . . the side that makes him want to see how far he can go with you. We were complete opposites. I go on these fast-talking tirades, he was so laid back.'

Sommersby was a surprisingly effective film, if dawdling and restrained – typical Gere – in parts. Perhaps most controversially of all, the hero is killed off, hanged for a murder he did not commit. The film surprised some of the critics, who did not rate it: 'Fails to generate any sense of tragedy or passion . . . mistaking seriousness for profundity and aloofness for sophistication,' said *Sight and Sound*. But who cared what the critics said? It earned $150 million, which made everyone concerned very happy, and especially Gere, who had a slice of the percentages.

Gere had been busy making his movie, away on location for four months and then in post-production for another two. Cindy was here, there and everywhere. They were separated for weeks on end and had to make an effort to meet, like taking a plane halfway across America for a one-night stand. Half complaining, half delighted, Gere said: 'Cindy is more famous than I am.' Perhaps he meant more of a celebrity. Flashback to July 1992:

'Cindy . . .'

'Over, here . . . Cindee . . .'

The surrounds of the Ziegfeld Theater on West 54th Street are crowded with so many paparazzi that it might be Princess Diana arm in arm with Elizabeth Taylor they are expecting. It is the première of the movie *A League of Their Own*, starring Madonna and Geena Davis. The stars rush inside, surrounded and protected by their minders, and then the cry goes up, 'Here's Cindy . . .' The crowd surge forward and the flashes are popping in the evening gloom, a hundred, maybe more, cameramen falling over themselves to get a shot.

Cindy steps out of her limo and marches forward in a slinky, backless black dress with spaghetti straps and a *décolletage* which also gives great exposure to her front. As the snappers cry out for her attention, she obliges. She turns, flicks her head so that her hair hangs loose and casual, puts her hand on her left hip and selects one of the provocative poses from her catalogue of modelling positions. Other famous names, meanwhile, slip unnoticed into the theatre.

Arc lights for the television cameras brighten the street and the lenses zoom in on the star. Cindy is there not just as a celebrity; she is also hosting a special programme in her *House of Style* series for MTV. She is surrounded by a posse of helpers and PR people. Everyone is in on the act: her managers, her aids from Revlon, some people from Pepsi-Cola and of course the producers of the MTV show. The latter are telling anyone who will listen that Cindy is a pioneer of fashion reporting on television. Her show is soaring in the ratings among the forty-eight million US subscribers to the channel, and according to a wordy study of fashion television by the *New York Times*, it reflects the 'symbiotic relationship that has sprung up between music and style. MTV videos have made musicians more conscious of their images and have trained audiences to expect a new look with every album.'

Now everyone wants Cindy. Why? She has her own explanation ready. 'People like to see me not as an ice princess, but as one of them. Plus, I'm an insider. They trust me.' She also keeps a firm control of that image, resisting some of the more ridiculous PR stunts. When Revlon executives suggest she wears a baseball jacket and jeans for the première of *A League of Their Own* – about the war-time all-girl baseball teams – she refuses point-blank and reminds them that the Revlon image is not one of teenage casual but is stylish, elegant and womanly. She is right, they admit, and so she arrives elegant and slinky.

After the film, the party move to the Tavern on the Green where MTV have set up a tent for Crawford to interview the stars for her show. They are wheeled in, one after another, Tom Hanks among them, for uncontroversial chatter. When it is all over and time to leave, Crawford heads for the street, surrounded by her bodyguards and minders who have been forewarned that there is still a crowd outside.

Cindy discovers her limo has not arrived, and she is left waiting. The crowd surge forward, clutching copies of magazines with her on the front, and glossy photographs that they want her to sign. She obliges for a good five minutes, and even as she gets into the car, a woman thrusts a photograph forward and pleads for her autograph, 'for my dying grandmother'.

She is *the* celebrity. At the MTV awards soon afterwards, the hierarchy of the international pop scene are lost in the crush when Cindy arrives. Annie Lennox receives no more than a polite ovation, Mick Jagger slips in almost unnoticed. Then, the thousands of fans and the photographers in the crush outside go wild as Cindy, in classic Gianni Versace gown, and hair bundled high on her head, draws up looking the absolute star after the parade of oddly dressed, peculiarly coiffured members of rock's royalty.

'Strike a pose,' yells a photographer, and as ever, she stands statuette-still for a minute or more while a thousand flashes light up the sky. People in the crowd are yelling her name and she walks back towards them as they thrust forward photographs and calendars for her to sign. A throng of radio reporters shove their hand mikes towards her and she gives them all a soundbite.

As she enters the theatre to begin her evening of hostessing, a huge bunch of red roses is handed to her. They are from her husband and she reads the card aloud: 'I love you desperately. Have fun tonight. Richard.' And with her snow-white teeth glistening as she beams a great smile, she dashes inside to go to work.

Gere was still busy; 1992 was his fullest year for a long time. He was anguishing over the other movie which he had initiated – a script pulled from the same pile of inactive screenplays from which he had retrieved *Sommersby* and which he had been working on for months. It was another intense situation, at times traumatic. He was deeply involved and could not let go.

The film script was *Mr Jones* – with Gere himself in the title role – another therapist v. patient movie, like *Final Analysis*, only this time Gere was the patient and the international Swedish actress Lena Olin, barely known in the US, his Ingrid Bergman-like therapist. Again, it was not difficult to see why this movie had attracted Gere and why he persevered with it as its star and executive producer. With all the bad luck he suffered while making it, others might have been inclined to get off at the next stop. But he assessed that it had the potential for greatness – just as he did with *Final Analysis*, which in the end failed to meet expectations.

Both, had they turned out right, could have provided him with the long-awaited Oscar. He was not at fault in the selection, but the execution of the production and the making of *Mr Jones* was a sorry tale of Hollywood-type woe that afflicts movies that get out of control. For various reasons too many and too complicated to list, but largely due to personality clashes and differences of opinion at virtually every stage of the creative process, the following tally of personnel came and went during the history of his near-three-year stop-and-start production of *Mr Jones*: nine producers, two directors (plus some unofficial helpers who stuck their oar in), six writers, three editors and three composers. The film went through five cuts before a final print was accepted for release, and its release date was put back three times.

The story is this: Gere's character Mr Jones cons his way into a job by convincing a construction site boss that he is an expert roofer. He is nothing of the sort, but uses the situation in which he finds himself in an attempt to learn to fly, without an aircraft or other mechanical means. He is rushed immediately to an institution where Lena Olin, as the therapist, issues a diagnosis that he is a manic depressive and begins treatment. The whole business develops into melodrama as Olin gets romantically involved with her patient.

Gere maintained that it was always his intention that the film should not be based upon bedroom exploits, an element now so commonplace in mainstream movies that it had lost its impact and meaning. He wanted to depict the 'trust and intimacy behind a relationship' rather than the actual consummation of it. 'If sex is gratuitous,' he ventured, 'you get embarrassed and *Mr Jones* is not about sex. It is about an illness, that of manic depression. It is intended to reach a lot of people who don't know they have this problem, or friends or relatives who are displaying the symptoms.'

Unfortunately, in his endeavours to make a movie about a relationship, the story and the film became bogged down by good intentions. Few movies that deal with medical matters or physical disabilities manage to capture the imagination of audiences. Penny Marshall did, to some degree, with Robin Williams and Robert De Niro in *Awakenings* though it was barely a hit movie, while De Niro's workout with Jane Fonda in *Stanley and Iris* – about an illiterate blue-collar worker – was a disaster. In fact, there were a lot of throwbacks in *Mr Jones* to past movies, with hints of Jack Nicholson in *One Flew Over the Cuckoo's Nest* and Matthew Modine in *Birdy*. It wasn't anywhere near as good as either, but always had that underlying possibility that it just might have been.

Mike Figgis, the director who was on the credits, had struggled on in vain to make the film worthwhile. But with an earnest script that on occasions had the audience laughing in the wrong places – always a danger with tales of so-called movie-loonies – truth and reason became obscure. 'I don't know about Mr Jones, but I myself became very depressed,' said Figgis. 'But Richard never lost his spirit or his sense of humour.'

However, the reaction to *Mr Jones* when it finally opened in October 1993, two years after it first went into production, was quite devastating, and although some acknowledged that Gere had given measured and interesting characterisation, the movie turned out all wrong. Financially, it wasn't as bad as it might have been, grossing $8.5 million, but because of his managerial and financial involvement, it hurt Gere more than any of his past failures. 'I was very disappointed it did not work,' he admitted. 'I've had films that I didn't like and didn't do well and I didn't care, frankly. When you fail at this level, with everyone watching, it can hurt bad.' Then he turned philosophical again and confirmed that it was easier for him to deal with now: 'It's all impermanence . . . it's all in the flow.' Without question, Buddhism had helped him to find the positive in every situation so that he could handle it.

But could he? 'I don't think *Mr Jones* hurt him,' said Sherry Lansing, chairman and chief executive officer of Paramount Motion Picture Group, which had been Gere's most regular employer throughout his career. 'His talent is so clearly at its peak.'

Chapter Sixteen

Who's Gay?

Storm clouds are gathering, there may be trouble ahead, the writing is on the wall. Within a year of the wedding, the clichés were edging into the reportage and, to add another, pieces of a jigsaw of emotions were being slotted into place. One other oft-recurring phrase first made its appearance in the autumn of 1992, that their marriage was actually a sham. Almost from the moment they flew to The Little Church in the West, it was being rumoured that the marriage was a cover-up for their true sexual orientation, and it was being compared to Rock Hudson's union with his agent's secretary, Phyllis Gates, at a time when *Hollywood Confidential* magazine was about to run 'evidence' of his homosexuality.

Gere gay? Cindy lesbian or bisexual? The history, as we have seen in earlier chapters, went back to Gere's youth, with all the innuendo that surrounded him at the time he made *American Gigolo*. It died down for a while but the renewed speculation about him really started with the faxed smear campaign which alleged that after performing a homosexual act with a gerbil in a plastic bag, he had been rushed to hospital to have it removed from his rectum.

Totally untrue, but the story had been broadcast far and wide over the electronic airwaves and into the myth and folklore of the Internet. In New York, Los Angeles, San Francisco, people claimed proof of the rumour, one citing a former roommate who saw X-rays, another a friend whose cousin worked at the hospital and had actually held the tongs to extract the rodent. Gere and the gerbil jokes became bar-room banter, and were alluded to on local radio stations and TV programmes. At half-time in the 1992 Superbowl, two comedy characters from *In Living Color* laughed about Gere's marriage, and one sniggered: 'Wouldn't you like to see that gerbil in a wedding dress?'

Someone even offered a $50,000 reward for proof that the story was true. No one came forward to claim it. When one interviewer finally plucked up the courage to mention it to Cindy, in one of her many media conversations, she replied: 'I know what the truth is. Richard's publicist [Pat Kingsley] wondered if he should make a statement about it. He said, "Why should I even acknowledge it?" We laughed at first. But it became seriously disconcerting. Then we let it go. What other choice did we have, short of a medical examination?'

Gere had ridden out the allegations about him being gay before, and even if he did have inclinations in that direction, what difference did it make? It was not as if he was denying it, like Rock Hudson did for his entire professional life, but he wasn't admitting it either. He simply refused to discuss his personal feelings publicly. He felt he should not even have to consider such a step. Anyway, there had been no public disclosures, no young men, or even older ones, from his past coming out with a kiss-and-tell.

So when the stories started to appear, they were hung on the flimsiest of facts, unlike the time when Brando told Truman Capote that he'd experienced homosexual relationships because he had to test himself and his artistic way of life, or the way James Dean used to say, 'What's the point of going through life with one hand tied behind your back?'

As far as Gere was concerned, the case for the prosecution rested largely on the fact that his female relationships had been few and there had been enduring friendships with male acquaintances. The same list of about four or five former girlfriends was trotted out each time some writer or other tried to put together a catalogue of his conquests – *à la* Warren Beatty. But he was no Beatty. Apart from Penny Milford and Sylvia Martins, there had been no one special, and Gere found himself having to explain over and over again that he was a very monogamous creature. What the rest of Hollywood did in their spare time was no concern of his.

Then they would point to the fact that even after their marriage, he and Cindy maintained their own bachelor apartments in New York. He found it irksome to have to explain that it was a matter of convenience, and fitted their personal career arrangements.

The innuendo did not stop him becoming very active in supporting gay-related causes. He was an outspoken orator on gay rights and an ardent worker for AIDS charities. It did not seem to matter to those who queried this association that he was one among dozens of showbiz people who had rushed to display their solidarity with the movement after Rock Hudson's death and as the virus went on to claim increasing numbers in the world of entertainment.

Gere had never been afraid of such advocacy. Remember, he played the lead in *Bent* on Broadway when few actors would have touched the role. He continued to remain upfront about gay rights while others in his profession cowered as the AIDS backlash flared in the mid-1980s. He became a committed AIDS campaigner and supported AIDS relief organisations almost from their inception. So did Cindy. She was involved with P-FLAG – Parents and Friends of Lesbians and Gays. So what?

Further discussion was inspired when in 1992 Gere agreed to appear in the television movie being made by HBO, *And the Band Played On*, joining a cast list which would eventually include Ian McKellen, Matthew Modine, Alan Alda, Steve Martin and Phil Collins. But the rest of them did not get the same kind of nudge, nudge, wink, wink attention that Gere received. Directed by Roger Spottiswode, the movie was an adaptation of Randy Shilts's true account of the beginnings of the AIDS crisis. The subplot was a medical thriller about the teams who discovered HIV, overlaid by the cameo roles of celebrities ever eager to show their sympathy with the cause.

In the HBO film, Gere himself played the role of a choreographer struck down by AIDS at the peak of his career. The part was inspired by the story of the Broadway director and choreographer Michael Bennett, who died of AIDS in 1987. Steve Martin was his grieving brother and Phil Collins appeared as the owner of a San Francisco bath-house. The movie wasn't that terrific, as it turned out, but it caused a good deal of comment and served the purpose of attracting attention to the AIDS relief movement. But Gere's role in it was invariably singled out.

The 'risk' for Gere, as perceived by the pundits, was that he had associated himself with the main 'gay' role in the movie. This was sufficient in some quarters to pursue the theory of probability by association. He, meanwhile, gave openly and frankly his reasons for agreeing to a professionally risky role: 'I need to contribute something towards an understanding of why and how this disease is spreading.'

He repeated his commitment later that year at a star-studded AIDS fund-raiser in San Francisco where he was supposed to appear with his wife. Cindy, however, was delayed and he began the sit-down meal without her, placed between *Vogue* editor Anna Wintour and the co-star of his next movie, Sharon Stone. Midway through the meal, he had to leave to collect Cindy from the airport, but their cars passed and when they finally met up back at the AIDS benefit, they made their entrance together. Gere said he hadn't seen his wife for two weeks, and demanded to have 'every camera in this room on us'.

At a press conference for the benefit, at which he took centre stage, Gere said emotionally: 'We all have friends and relatives who have been infected. I've just found out about three more of my friends. One died and two more are on the edge.' And referring to the death of actor Anthony Perkins from an AIDS-related illness the previous month, he said: 'These are very, very sad times. My emotions well up over Tony. I'd known him for twenty years. No one is escaping this. It touches us all and the government is not doing enough to find a cure.'

There were two other poignant deaths that he referred to without naming the victims. Tina Chow, the designer, with whom he had been friends for years, had died of an AIDS-related illness which she contracted from a lover, while Joan Marshall, who had befriended him when he first came to Hollywood, was another recent victim. Joan, former wife of director Hal Ashby, had contracted HIV from a transfusion of infected blood.

Gere had visited her many times as she neared her death, and often left in tears. 'She was a giver,' said Gere. 'Not one of the takers who abound in this place. When I first arrived, she went out of her way to introduce me to people who made things happen. When I had problems, the first person I would call was Joan and she was always there. When she told me she had contracted AIDS, it was as though somebody had hit me in the face with a hammer. I could not understand how something like this could happen. But she never complained, not once. Her courage was an absolute lesson in dignity . . . she is one of the reasons why I must help.'

But the sadness of these losses was unknown to the public at large and conveniently ignored by certain sections of the media, who were displaying a growing boldness in their questions to both Gere and Cindy about their reasons for their high-profile association with gay causes. Gere was asked by one reporter if he had a 'special interest' in the benefit, a coded enquiry as to whether or not he was gay, and he replied: 'Every American, man or woman, straight or gay, has a special interest.'

Rumour and fact were merged so that the whole question

of the sexuality of the couple became the fascination and preoccupation of writers, the tabloids and America's 1990s phenomenon, the proliferation of television gossip programmes, plus a fair few of their friends and, eventually, the public at large.

The intrigue was fuelled by enigmatic contributions from Gere and Crawford themselves. Increasingly, instead of discreet enquiries as to their feelings for one another, the couple found themselves confronted by full-on questions along the lines of 'Are you gay?' The answers they gave were never straightforward, and so enigma grew into mystery, and mystery into assumption.

This progression assumed new momentum and the issues became altogether more cloudy when Crawford made some seemingly startling comments during an interview with the British *Elle* magazine in the summer of 1992, after recent rumours of her having been seen smooching with two other women were pursued. 'Who cares?' she snapped back. 'Besides, I've got the cleanest image in the world so it's good if there is a little dirt about me.' And on lesbianism itself she went on: 'I think it's a safe way to explore sexuality in this age of AIDS. I've heard a lot about it from my friends and I know it's just them looking for a kick.'

As far as the rumours about her husband were concerned, she said: 'Richard is clear about what he is and if people think he is gay he would not give a fuck because he wouldn't mind if he was.' It is said by those close to them at the time that Gere was not very happy that his wife should go on record about their personal lives in this way, because as he knew from personal experience, statements like that would not be the end of the matter, merely the beginning. And he was right.

The world and his wife homed in on their 'remarkable marriage', and if Cindy's first outburst on the subject might have been dismissed as an off-the-cuff remark which she had made without much thought for the consequences, the same could not be said for her continuing discourse on the subject. 'I find it kind of funny,' she said in yet another interview, 'that I've not been married very long and all of a sudden I'm a lesbian and my husband's a homosexual. We must be the happiest gay couple around.'

At this point the mood changed and a subplot developed in the real-life saga of the Crawford–Gere relationship. In November 1992, Cindy allowed it to be known that she was writing a contribution to the jacket blurb for a new book entitled *The Lesbian and Gay Parenting Handbook* by April Martin, scheduled for publication by HarperCollins in a few months' time. 'The vision of two pregnant women walking down the street holding hands blows me away,' she said in serious fashion to Rob Tannenbaum from the men's magazine *Details*, who just happened to be around at the time because he had been invited by Cindy's publicist to do a follow-me-around piece for the Christmas issue. 'There's so little love around – why are we gonna brand it as bad? We should support people loving each other.'

Was Cindy going over the top? And if so, why? Her family was worried and her friends in the fashion game were giggling. Every time Crawford spoke, some mention of gay rights or gay love seemed to creep into the reportage. What happened next must be viewed with a certain degree of cynicism; perhaps someone had spotted the commercial advantages of this particular rolling stone, gathering speed – and moss. Certainly the word exploitation springs to mind.

In the new year of 1993, while Gere was working on his film commitments, there was a round-table conference between Cindy, her PR people and her managers. A remarkable chain of events followed, and whether Gere was involved at any level of the discussions is unknown, though probably his input was very little. One insider put him in the passenger seat of this particular journey from the word go.

What happened was this: Herb Ritts, who had played such a significant part in both their careers with his overtly sensual snaps, came up with an 'amazing idea' for a pictorial essay that he would sell to *Vanity Fair*. He laid it out before Cindy – a photographic session with her and the self-declared lesbian, Canadian country and western singer k.d. lang.

The choice of k.d. was clearly the key, the object being to achieve maximum shock impact – teaming Supermodel Cindy, the American dream girl and international sex symbol, with one of the pop world's most militant gay activists. In what has been described by one close to Ritts as a wild fantasy of same-gender titillation, model and singer would be photographed in dozens of provocative poses.

It would be sensational. And k.d. lang was delighted when the scenario was relayed to her. She agreed without hesitation, so long as she did not have to take *her* clothes off. Ritts had Crawford dressed in a skimpy black teddy and spike-heeled ankle boots, while k.d. lang was decked out in a man's pin-striped suit for a photographic spoof of a famous Norman Rockwell drawing.

In one shot, k.d. was sitting in a barber's chair with shaving cream around her chin, seemingly in ecstasy with her head resting on the model's left breast while the pouting Crawford, with eyes closed, appeared to be shaving her. In another, still with remnants of the shaving cream about her face, k.d. lay back in the chair, face to face with Crawford, who was astride her; imagination was not necessary. But what caused even greater interest were the carefully contrived facial expressions of both women, which had needed take after take to get exactly right.

The editors of *Vanity Fair* pored over the pictures with glee. They were as controversial as the now world-famous photograph of Demi Moore, nude and in the latter stages of pregnancy, which *VF* had whacked across its cover the previous year. The shaving photograph was to be used on the cover of the August 1993 issue and was reproduced around the world. Graydon Carter, editor-in-chief of *Vanity Fair*, said, 'I have no idea why Cindy Crawford agreed to be photographed in this way. What is important, however, is that lesbian chic has simply exploded. Sexual politics is as much part of where the nineties are right now.'

In fact, the trend had been started two years earlier by Madonna, in her male-attired photographs with the American comedienne Sandra Bernhard, with whom she was said to be having an affair at the time as she was seeing Warren Beatty. But as with David Bowie's shock tactics in the 1970s when gay-look bands like Village People and Sweet flourished, those around her merely said that Madonna's apparent interest in bisexuality was a highly tuned PR operation aimed at enhancing her career. It was a good point to bear in mind.

If that was the aim as Herb Ritts and Cindy Crawford planned the photographic session with k.d. lang, it worked. The publicity was internationally huge for all concerned. It must also have had the nod of approval from Revlon, whose tightly drawn contract gave them a voice in Cindy's extramural activities and a parental eye over her personal and social habits. Nor did it end there.

Later in the year, and after an adequate interlude in which Cindy was once again seen in high profile in the sexiest of classic modelling situations, *Rolling Stone* bought an outstanding portfolio of Herb Ritts photographs for its December issue, which pictured Crawford dressed and made up to look like various famous stars, including Marilyn Monroe, Brigitte Bardot, Bo Derek and Tina Turner. But the one which attracted most attention, again securing international coverage, was Cindy as George Michael, dressed in male clothes and replete with quiff, designer stubble and snarling mouth.

Why George Michael, who had himself been the subject of unfounded rumours about his sexual preference? No explanations were forthcoming, although Cindy had appeared in one of his videos and was supposedly a good friend.

The editorial accompanying the photographs also addressed the subject of lesbianism. In it Cindy repeated her view that it was a safer way for young women to explore their sexuality. Then the article quickly switched the focus to her husband. 'Richard has obviously been accused of being gay,' said Crawford. 'Why? Because he has a lot of gay friends? It's amazing to me, considering the number of women he's associated with. Like, when does he have time to be gay?'

Stunning, controversial photographs; quote after quote on the subject of homosexuality – the cynics among us might not be entirely convinced by the protestations of 'the world's most beautiful woman' that she and her husband had been wronged, hounded and insulted by an aggressive media on both sides of the Atlantic who were repeating vicious slanders against them, alleging that one or other of them – or perhaps both – was gay.

Those who were anxious to retain the goodwill of Cindy's PR people dutifully recorded their shock and horror at such smears. Yet close research of the articles in which Cindy Crawford had co-operated in recent months showed that invariably she had been vocal on the subject of homosexuality, and her PR machine had certainly set none of the normal parameters of questioning common with celebrities. All they were concerned with was limiting questions about the dreaded mole, which Cindy was fed up with discussing. It was almost as if they were inviting the media to continue the controversy – though Gere's co-operation was noticeably lacking.

Throughout this time, Gere had been buried away on location or in film studios, work which he interspersed with the occasional visit to the Dalai Lama, whose spiritual calming he surely needed. However, in the autumn of 1993, at a time when he was promoting two new movies, he agreed to give a rare interview to a writer from *Vanity Fair*, with the prospect that he would be featured on the front cover – just as Cindy had been in the summer with k.d. lang, except that his would be a solo head shot. The piece dealt with his career and spiritual beliefs but inevitably, after all that had gone before in the preceding months, the questioning turned eventually to his own sexuality. Was he gay?

Gere refused to answer in direct terms. Instead, he gave what must rate as one of the most well-rehearsed 'off-the-cuff' responses to that question ever seen in print. To answer the question with a yes or no, he said, would cast an implicit male judgement on others. 'It doesn't matter if you're straight or gay,' he told the *VF* interviewer. 'Cosmically, there's nothing wrong with being heterosexual, homosexual, or omnisexual – with being anything, as long as you don't hurt anybody, yourself included. The accusation is meaningless and whether it's true or false is no one's business. I know who I am; what difference does it make what anyone thinks? This kind of silly prejudice cripples everyone – the people who think them, and the people they lay their judgements on. It's insane. It's schoolyard stuff, real kid stuff. But if you start to take a defensive mode and say, "No, I'm not," it gives credence to the idea that there's something wrong with it, and there's nothing wrong with it. I have no interest in putting myself in a category. My best friends in the world are gay, and I also have heterosexual friends. Why would I ever put myself in a category that would lay judgement on friends of mine?

'If I was a leopard and someone came up and started screaming, "You're a cow," is a leopard going to be uptight about this? He knows he's a leopard. He's going to think, "What silly people." '

Gere, with his noncommittal response, was clearly dismayed that the question should keep on arising. He could not have been pleased, either, about Cindy's PR stunts, of a kind he had used himself years ago but which, judging by his own words to *Vanity Fair*, went against everything he now stood for. The world, not just him, had changed. AIDS was an issue, but not the sole one. This was about the freedom of the individual and civil rights, and to have to answer accusations of being of any particular sexual persuasion was invasive and unwarranted.

Whose life was it anyway? Gere was an unhappy man, and the circle who ultimately controlled his wife's schedule, the style of her promotional efforts or quantity of her engagements, were not among his favourite people at that time, either.

The coincidence of all this – and this time it was a coincidence – was that it clashed with Gere's latest film. From the publicity angle this was fortuitous in the extreme, but on another level it was rather disconcerting because the basis of the movie was the good old-fashioned theme of the heterosexual yearnings of a man in mid-life crisis. Furthermore, it involved him in an encounter with Sharon Stone, the hottest property in Hollywood at the time. Stone, as it happened, was also getting 'very pissed off' with the commercially orientated hype concerning her own sexual ambiguities as displayed when playing the role of Catherine Tramell, Michael Douglas's mysterious bisexual lover in *Basic Instinct*. This was the movie that launched her career with the steamiest couplings ever seen in a mainstream movie, not to mention her leg-crossing revelations minus knickers.

She leapt to 'overnight' stardom after almost fifteen years in the business, during which time she had been confined to playing bit parts and dumb blondes in B-movies. Now, she suddenly needed a ring of bodyguards every time she ventured out of the house.

Since then, and in spite of her personal fears of becoming a top-shelf star, she had agreed to disrobe again, for producer Robert Evans in his comeback movie, *Sliver*, his first since he was blackballed by Hollywood after the *Cotton Club* débâcle. The new movie, which had been his obsession ever since, was a voyeuristic thriller released amid much ballyhoo but failing to match the high hopes and expectations at the box office.

Stone turned down *Sliver* several times but Evans was nothing if not persistent, largely because he had been advised by those in the know that a sexy movie with Sharon Stone in the lead would be guaranteed to take $75 million at the box office. It didn't, but hope still springs eternal in Hollywood.

Eventually, she took his $6 million plus a snip of the percentages and made the film, though she remained sceptical. 'I am sick of Catherine Tramell,' she said. 'And I'm fed up with people gawping at my tits.' She felt the same about *Sliver* and castigated herself afterwards for doing the film that *Variety* dismissed as 'all flash and no sizzle'. She now earnestly wanted to shake off the fleshy image and her fictional lesbian past but found herself in exactly the same predicament that Gere faced after his bare-all roles of the early 1980s – except that she had no time to let the dust settle.

She was thirty-six years old and, as she herself said, that was old in Hollywood. She unashamedly organised her own remarkable self-promotional relaunch to kill that sex-only perception and to try to convince those in power that she had greater talent than merely lifting her skirt. It sounded an awfully familiar pleading. She ditched the bare-breasted picture of herself sucking an ice-cube which had been on the front cover of *Playboy* and scrubbed all references to sex from the biographical notes in her PR pack.

She found the movie she wanted, and decided to go all out for it; make or break. The film she chose was *Intersection*, and Richard Gere and director Mark Rydell had just begun casting the female roles when she telephoned.

She asked director Rydell, best known for *On Golden Pond*, if she could read for him for a role in his new film. Rydell said that he had not previously considered her because frankly he shared the view of many around Hollywood that although she had earned acres of media coverage after *Basic Instinct*, she had yet to prove herself as a talented actress, and was for the time being best in the buff.

Rydell said he would get back to her, but never did. She telephoned again, and again and again and again, before he agreed to let her read for him. Even then, he was expecting her to test for the sexier of the two female roles in the love triangle around which the film is built, that of a journalist girlfriend of Gere's character whose principal scene appears at the beginning of the film, when she is seen naked in bed. 'No, no,' cried Stone. 'I don't want that part . . . I want to read for the wife.'

Rydell was surprised, because the role did not require the actress to strip, and there was only one love scene for her – and she even kept her clothes on for that. The part called for the portrayal of a frigid woman, betrayed by her architect husband. And so the reading began, and Rydell admitted: 'I was stunned. I expected a moderate piece of work, but she was terrific. She read four scenes, and then we gave her the most dramatic moment of the picture when she had to collapse and come apart at the seams when her husband announces he is leaving her. It was a remarkable performance.'

Sharon Stone's readings for Rydell lasted five hours. They had a long discussion about her own ambitions and her fears – especially her worry that she would end up becoming a caricature of herself, which, in another way, is what happened to Gere all those years ago. At the end of it, Rydell and Gere agreed to sign her for the part of the wife. She went home happy, convinced that she had finally left Catherine Tramell far behind.

They went to work and filmed the movie with speed and professionalism. But at the end of the day, would it be the hot property that Hollywood had been predicting when they learned that Gere was teaming up with Stone? The plot had a decent ring to it; perhaps to some, a familiar one. It was based upon Claude Sautet's 1970 French melodrama, *Les Choses de la Vie*, glitzily transformed by Rydell.

Gere plays the wealthy architect, Vincent Eastman, and Stone his glamorous but standoffish wife who is also his partner in business. The movie follows their lives and their work and shows the wife smooth-talking their clients at the office while remaining cold and unapproachable at home. Vincent eventually takes a mistress, the vibrant young Olivia, played by the Canadian actress of Yugoslavian descent, Lolita Davidovich. Though separated, Gere and Stone still have to work together every day in their business, she clawing to get him back and his mistress passionately attempting to retain his affections. Finally, he is forced to choose, but having made his decision, he changes his mind while driving at eighty miles an hour in his Mercedes Roadster. Fate takes a hand, and he crashes.

The basic flaw of the film, which is supposed to be an upmarket morality tale, is that the audience is expected to have some sympathy for Gere's rich and comfortable character. Unlike his performances in *Pretty Woman* and *Sommersby*, when he won the audience over, this time the script did not give him the opportunity to do it.

Stone, meanwhile, tried hard, too hard, to downplay her sexuality, and though she had considerable presence, she was never quite convincing as the emotionally tormented wife. Catherine Tramell would not go away that easily. It was a showy picture for two stars with their own particular hang-ups about Hollywood, by no means uninteresting but lacking real heart. Still, it performed moderately well at the box office, taking $20 million in the US alone and eventually earning more than $50 million.

Sex sells all, as Cindy Crawford and Richard Gere knew only too well. The problem was, in their case, and certainly hers, it could all rebound in the most unfortunate way.

Chapter Seventeen

Where Are We Sleeping Tonight?

They had long since been labelled Hollywood's Golden Couple, the talk of Los Angeles, but they were no nearer a settled life. They had between them the security of millions of dollars flowing in but there was little anchor to their marriage because of their movements. Cindy was changing and Gere didn't like it. In the space of a year, her whole being as a celebrity had been put through the mangle of high finance, from which she emerged as the supreme image-maker of marketing: the glossy, glitzy, glamorous, hair-blowing-in-the-wind-machine personality with more than a touch of sexual mystery, around whom multi-billion-dollar merchandising campaigns were built. She was no longer a mere model, or even a Supermodel. What she had become was a Celebrity with a capital C, guided and controlled by men in suits as only America knows how. She was in full swing now, in her stride and earning an estimated $12 million a year.

Gone were the slippers-by-the-fire ambitions of a young wife who had declared in 1992, 'I want a family. More than anything I want kids and sort of feel like that's the thing I'm going to be best at, being a mother.' She'd changed her mind. Twelve million dollars a year? Kids could wait.

They had it all. Everything anyone could want . . . and

houses? They could take their pick: two apartments in New York, his country retreat in Westchester, the beach house at Malibu and now, after Cindy's pleadings for a residence which befitted their status, they had bought a magnificent Georgian mansion, costing $4.5 million, in the most exclusive region of Bel-Air, complete with a grand *Gone with the Wind* staircase, bedrooms galore, and swimming pool set in a secluded acre. So much for the monastic existence that Gere had once enjoyed. The only snag was, they were too busy to live in their new palace. Weeks passed before they even found time to choose the furniture.

Cindy was being stolen away, lured by the suits and the excitement of *fame*, and neither of them realised it. But here was the irony: as she was getting into her stride, Gere would have preferred for them to retreat back into the shadows of celebrity life. She admitted: 'Richard likes to think he is an artist. He doesn't like the word "commercial". But that's not me. I've got to get out there . . . this is my time.' Indeed it was.

She herself had become the ultimate commodity – assigned to a life the opposite of that which Richard Gere had established in his closed, private, meditative world during the past decade. He had fought tooth and nail to keep the media and Hollywood at bay. To him, commercialism and materialism were still dirty words, regardless of the paradox of him wallowing in the millions earned from his recent films. As Jeffrey Katzenberg said, when Disney tried to sign Gere for *Pretty Woman*: 'Don't mention money. Talk about the script and the art of the movie. Richard is not interested in money.'

Now, everything his wife was involved in carried the stench of the dollar; it was all marketing and promotion gone mad, push, push, push. Around her was a ring of steel which even Gere himself could barely penetrate. Company executives and publicists, with their private planes and stretch limos, champagne and red roses, carried her to one promotional event after another, one interview situation to the next, and Cindy brought Gere to the point of apoplexy with her policy of talking about the matters which he had put out of bounds to journalists almost from the moment they began seeking him out.

In his entire career, he had hardly ever appeared on television chat shows – and one of those was to promote the relief work in Nicaragua. He had turned down hundreds of requests. His media interviews were few in comparison to most Hollywood stars, and to this day were always notoriously and uncompromisingly light on personal detail, to the point that there was a widely accepted health warning for interviewers who actually managed to get to see him: Don't ask him about Tibet.

Cindy, on the other hand, was on chat show after chat show – Oprah Winfrey, Arsenio Hall, all the big television hosts booked her in America, and in England she appeared on Des O'Connor's show – plus her own increasingly popular television show *House of Style*. Barely a week went by when she was not featured in one of the top glossies. She had only one competitor at the time whose face could also be guaranteed to sell thousands of extra copies, and that was Princess Diana. Crawford gave a clue as to the outside control over the media situation when she mentioned in an offguard moment that Revlon had 'decided' that she should only appear on the covers of leading magazines, and that she should be selective when granting interviews.

This 'instruction' also indicated the way that she could virtually pick and choose those to be favoured by her presence. There were enough magazines and newspapers above the middle-market line to keep her in front of the public and the market which Revlon aimed at, without resorting to co-operation with the bottom half of the publishing world and the gossipy television shows.

Even so, she always obliged writers with some decent copy that would ensure hefty, usually respectful, coverage and glamour layouts, just as she always obliged the cameramen who shouted out, 'Strike a pose, Cindy' whenever she turned up at an opening or a promotional event.

Few interviews passed without Richard, or the gay issues being mentioned, as much as she may have tried to avoid it. Here it comes again: 'Is it easier to be friends with gay men?' Meaning, is Richard gay? She pauses and fires back: 'I have a lot of gay friends because there is a lot of homosexuality in this business. I hang out with the ones who are fun.' But who was using whom?

She has been well schooled in the art of interviewing and giving interviews. It is important. Skilful writers could lead her into all kinds of traps just now and the suits are worried. Similarly, when she is on the other side of the mike, mischievous people might be tempted to have a laugh at her expense. It's easy to imagine the scenario of her tuition, because it is reflected in the way she operates:

'Be calm and gracious, like a princess – that's what you are; remember that. Not high and mighty, but not the girl next door either. Keep it cool. Small-town girl made good, and it shows. Kids need to identify. A little cleavage, not too much. Keep the chat light and fluffy, but sensible. Never laugh or giggle. Throw your head back now and again, keep the hair big and natural. Smile enigmatically at difficult questions and talk about something else. A trick: talk about yourself in the third person and throw in a touch of dirt, like, "When I get up in the morning, I'm just me. Once they do the makeover, I see Cindy Crawford. I don't mind. I created her myself . . . She doesn't get upset, just nods her head, grits her teeth, gets on with the job and doesn't say 'fuck' in public." The mags like that word.

'Good. Now talk about the books you are reading, Lillian Hellman's always a good choice. Mention going into therapy for treatment for the ulcer you are suffering through pressure, and that the therapist recommended you read Camille Paglia's *Sex, Art, and American Culture*. That's good. Or talk about Naomi Wolf's *The Beauty Myth*, and argue against her claim that women are oppressed by the marketing ploy of beauty in fashion and advertising.

'Tell them you're a reluctant icon, that you don't want to be that girl in the room everyone looks at and that for sure it's fun now and again, but sometimes it's hell. Tell them you're a feminist at heart and that you hated all those purple descriptions in men's mags about your pouting lips, moist and parted by the tongue, and beautifully rounded breasts, and hope they don't ask why, then, did you pose nude for *Playboy*? If they do, tell them it was a point in your career that you passed through and you want to leave all that behind. Talk about your ambitions, that you want to be the Barbara Walters of the nineties and interview all those famous people; get serious.'

Gere stood back, aghast. The horrendous publicity throughout 1993, which centred around the allegations that the couple were gay, followed by Herb Ritts's sensational photographs, was merely a beginning. Never in his life had he been subjected to such relentless scrutiny that so disturbed the spiritual peace and tranquil existence he longed for.

That was very evident one day in the summer of 1993, when *Playboy* came to interview Cindy. Gere had been against it from the start, because the *Playboy* interview is still renowned for being akin to a public visit to a psychoanalyst, when all the subject's personal thoughts, fears and emotions come tumbling forth, prised loose by the deeply researched questioning of a senior editor. Gere personally would not even contemplate a *Playboy* interview, but Cindy had, and he was not pleased.

Playboy contributing editor David Rensin had arranged to do the interview at the couple's new mansion, and was ushered in to find Cindy sitting by the pool waiting for him. 'Soon after we began,' said Rensin, 'Gere came home and ambled over to say hi. An hour later, he returned to say, "I want my wife. The interview's over." I bargained for more time. Later Gere and Crawford tooled around their kitchen discussing schedules. Suddenly Gere said, "By the way, I'm going to knock up my wife tonight." Crawford winced.'

Gere had made his point with ironic clarity. He didn't like having a senior *Playboy* writer talking to his wife and even less that he was actually inside his home. That was another broken rule – he virtually never let writers into his house; fewer than half a dozen in his life had got past the threshold. He usually booked a hotel room on the occasions he agreed to give an interview. Anyway, Cindy obviously got the message. That particular interview turned out to be one of innocuous discourse about fashion. Richard Gere was mentioned once, and then only in passing.

The build-up to Gere's apparent antagonism towards Cindy's publicity explosion and transformation into media figurine came throughout 1993 and on into 1994 as she began to downgrade her modelling in favour of product endorsement, personal appearances and television work. She was busier than ever, but the catwalk was the least of her concerns.

She had moved on.

Modelling, she was telling everyone, had ceased to be a challenge. But the men in suits controlled her more than she knew, and certainly had a far greater influence on her career development than Gere himself. Work for Revlon, Pepsi-Cola, MTV, Kay Jewellers and various others in which she appeared as a celebrity rather than a model kept her permanently on the hop.

Half the time, she was just the front woman for a promotion, like the day Pepsi hired her to hostess an outing for 250 area retailers at a racetrack outside New York. She spent the day mingling, posing for photographs with the suits, signing autographs, dining with the top brass, and handing out the prizes. Then, saucily grabbing the microphone, she giggled: 'It's a twenty-inch', and everyone laughed, while she smiled sweetly and said under her breath, 'Pass the sick bucket.' It was so demeaning. At the stroke of eight, her stint done, the white limo appeared from nowhere and spirited her away. Another day, another twenty grand.

The suits were happy to pay. They could quote figures at each other about percentage increases in turnover on products that Cindy endorsed. Graphs and charts monitored her involvement. Revlon openly admitted that controversy did not hurt sales because Cindy had her strongest following in the sixteen-to-twenty-four age group. 'She's off the charts with young consumers,' said the company's product manager, Jerry Levin. The media magazine, *Adweek*, in its own examination of the Crawford phenomenon, identified that her success was partly due to the publicity about her alleged sexual ambiguity, which matched the concerns of a young generation on whom there were all kinds of pressures about sex.

This was entirely born out by a test-market survey conducted by Kay Jewellers, who were on the brink of signing a lucrative endorsement contract with Cindy at the time she appeared on the cover of *Vanity Fair* with k.d. lang. Some worried Kay executives were ready to ditch her. So they went out into the marketplace and conducted a vox pop which produced startling results – most people were not concerned, and those who were troubled did not blame Cindy, believing she must have been tricked into it.

So Kay signed and put Cindy to work, and their sales shot up by ten per cent in the following twelve months. Every agent in New York would confirm that Cindy had a major effect on the sales of all the products she was publicly associated with, and now she had left Naomi Campbell, Linda Evangelista and the rest way behind. 'She is the Jackie O. of modelling,' said her agent, Ann Veltri at Elite.

She was also a hard-headed businesswoman, and by mid-1993 she and her managers were moving towards business enterprise and the formation of various offshoots of Cindy Inc. Numerous additions were planned for her business portfolio. Among them was the fitness video which she completed with the help of her trainer, Radu. Fitness tapes were all the rage with celebrities. *Jane Fonda's Workout* was followed by a dozen others. Cindy's was billed as something extra-special: *Shape Your Body and Work Out.*

Taking a leaf from her husband's book, she announced that she had appointed herself the executive producer of the fitness film so that she could have control of it from filming to editing. Having completed the hundred-minute tape, it was launched amid tremendous hype. And now her image was switched to the health and fitness pages and major newspapers devoted acres of space to reviews of her 'film'. The *New York Times* even gave it a half-page, and writer Janet Maslin recognised immediately that this was more than just an instruction manual for fitness freaks.

There was Cindy in her skimpy sports gear, going through her personal programme of exercises, glistening occasionally with perspiration. 'She creates an interesting ambiguity,' wrote Maslin in a serious tone, 'one that is chiefly expressed through setting and costume. Will she be seen by the sea in that tiny black swimsuit? Will she be in colour or black and white? We are meant to care desperately . . . Although all Cindy seemingly does, as the centrepiece of this minimalist character study, is to work out and drink water, she manages to infuse the action with powerful emotions. (Many of those emotions will no doubt be experienced by viewers who, strictly for study purposes, watch this film at home.)'

Point taken, but the *Library Journal*, in its review, made no bones about it: 'The overuse of close-ups and repeated shots of her cleavage make this as much a showcase for her body as a serious workout programme.'

Cindy travelled the globe promoting the video, which sold out in spite of comments by Cher, her rival in the fitness-tape business, who claimed that some of her suggested exercises might actually be dangerous. Then came Cindy Crawford, the sequel – a second video entitled *The Next Challenge*, released a few months later. This too was subjected to criticism, by reviewers who felt that some of the exercises were unsafe for home viewers. Between them, however, the two tapes sold five million copies worldwide – with gross sales approaching $100 million. Cindy donated a large chunk of her earnings to leukaemia charities in memory of her brother.

She would also establish what her business manager described as a 'business relationship' with Planet Hollywood, the fast-food restaurant chain owned jointly by Sylvester Stallone, Bruce Willis and Arnold Schwarzenegger. Gere himself was not invited. 'We are not a dog and pony act,' Cindy would say.

In fact, by the end of 1993 there was already a clear and deliberate division between Crawford's personal and her business life. Gere was not even mentioned in the biographical notes of her press pack because her managers felt her appeal was reaching a different generation from his. As one bluntly said, 'Her fans do not look at Cindy and say, "Oh . . . she's married to Richard Gere." Some of them, a lot of them, don't even know who he is. And that's a fact. So basically they are appealing to two separate groups in the orientation of product targeting.' It's adspeak – but it tells the story.

Gere was not a consideration as far as Cindy's managers were concerned. They said he did not understand the movement of her career, and claimed that he did not place a great long-term value on it because he would say that it was no longer based upon artistic merit. There were arguments, and on some occasions, but not many, he won. He didn't like the Cindy calendar, those twelve sexy swimsuit shots which she had produced since 1989, and which had made her the bestselling pin-up of all time. The 1993 version went on sale with the news that this would be the last one, and consequently it was in great demand.

No explanation was given as to why she would not be producing another. It was, however, because her husband did not want garage mechanics and truck drivers in greasy-spoon cafés ogling her body in this rather common way. Evidently, he was becoming increasingly fed up with the massive coverage she was achieving across the whole spectrum of the international media.

Crawford's fame had grown so rapidly, and to such an extent, that it threatened to eclipse his own. His production company partner Maggie Wilde confirmed that he would often pick up a magazine, stare at it wistfully and declare: 'Cindy's more famous than I am! They come out to see Cindy.' Yet it was not the idea of her fame that concerned him, or that it presented an attack on his own ego. His concerns were about the intrusions that her success had brought into their personal lives, both in the open discussion of matters he considered private and in the simple day-to-day aspect of living together.

There was absolutely nothing normal about their lifestyle. 'I never thought marriage would require so much patience,' he declared. 'I had no fucking idea, and it's a great lesson, especially for someone like me. I've had a great life, a really great ride, and if I don't like something, I move on. That hasn't been without a certain toll. But when you make this commitment you don't just walk. The lessons of patience I have begun to learn in marriage are probably the greatest spiritual lesson I've learned in my lifetime thus far.'

Close friends were continuing to swear that Gere and Crawford were still deeply in love, and that the pressure of work had been a mere passing phase that they would overcome. However, it was a fact that they were seeing less and less of each other, and because of conflicting schedules communication was often done by secretaries and faxes. Gere's assistant to Crawford's secretary, for example: 'Richard wants to know which house she's sleeping in tonight, and he'll try to get there.'

Weeks passed without the couple seeing each other. They were always on planes, one going one way, one going the other. Cindy estimated that by the end of 1993 she had clocked up 500,000 frequent-flier miles. There were also some silly games going on in the background. An eagle-eyed photographer had captured Cindy in the company of a hunky Puerto Rican singer named Chayanne, and closer inspection, by magnifying glass, revealed that she wasn't wearing her wedding ring. Memo to paparazzi: Fall in behind the pair of them.

It was too late. Gere had already left the country for China, where he had been invited to attend the première of *Sommersby* in Canton on 14 November 1993. This was a matter of major importance to him. The Chinese were allowing into their country one of their most outspoken critics, the man who had for years passionately denounced them as murderers and despots over their treatment of the Tibetan nation.

Gere saw it as the opportunity finally to visit the forbidden country itself. Perhaps there had never been a time when he needed that spiritual revitalisation more than he did now. The trip was prearranged and, once in China, carefully planned. The Chinese were watching him, of course, because Gere was not merely some Hollywood actor out on a promotion jaunt. He was acting ambassador for the exiled Tibetan spiritual leader. They all knew that.

After the première in Canton, he travelled on to Peking to attend a film festival and from there headed towards the Tibetan heartland. On 1 December, it was announced in Los Angeles that Richard Gere was missing, and the news wires flashed the story of Hollywood fears for the safety of the star. People in Los Angeles were quoted as saying they were very concerned for his well-being.

There were stories with sinister undertones suggesting that the Chinese could have arrested him, or even done him in. Then it was thought possible that he had had an accident, that he had fallen off a snow-covered mountain. Newspapers around the world headlined the story: 'HOLLYWOOD FEARS WORST AS GERE GOES MISSING'. It was an embarrassing, silly situation that wrongly, from his point of view at least, had the air of a publicity stunt.

The truth was that on 26 November, Gere set off on a journey to discover the roots of his spiritual beliefs and view for himself what remained of the traditions of the nation for whom he had been campaigning for almost twenty years. He hired the services of Tenzin, a twenty-one-year-old guide who, when he was not showing the tourists around, helped run his mother's teashop. They rented a pair of bicycles and spent a couple of days touring around the decrepit streets of the Tibetan capital, Lhasa, 12,000 feet above sea level. Tenzin also took him off into the hills, where he met nomadic tribesmen and sought out a few of the remaining temples and monasteries around Lhasa. The inmates he greeted there knew nothing of his fame and were even more surprised to learn that he brought greetings from their leader, the Dalai Lama himself.

Gere did not entirely forgo his comforts. He stayed at the city's Holiday Inn, though it was not exactly the kind of luxury he was used to. It was a touch down-at-heel, having been run by a corrupt Chinese government department for years, and had only partial central heating to ward off the freezing temperatures. He had the best room in the place – the £180-a-night Tibetan suite, with canopied bed and traditional painted furniture.

In the evenings, he would join the handful of other Western tourists in the hotel coffee shop. Another American guest, Gino Wernikoff, a retired advertising consultant living in Thailand, remembered: 'He ate with us a couple of times. But he was pretty busy. Apparently, meetings had been set up for him with people in Buddhist circles and he had a lot of courtesy calls to make for the Dalai Lama. It was obviously a diplomatic mission for him. But he's a great guy – very friendly and unpretentious.'

The Holiday Inn marketing manager, Peter Horlemans, said that Gere was keen on keeping the visit private. When one of the hotel staff asked if they could take a photograph of him, he declined apologetically and said he did not want any fuss. He made numerous telephone calls, which were apparently bugged by the Chinese police, and then on 5 December, he and two friends rented a four-wheel drive off-road Toyota with driver, and set off on the hazardous 580-mile journey to Kathmandu, Nepal, over some of the highest and most treacherous mountain roads in the world.

The journey is usually completed in about three days, given decent weather conditions, but Gere took an extra day, stopping over at Buddhist monasteries on the way and spending time in true Tibetan meditation. He finally reached Kathmandu on 9 December and from there flew on to Tokyo, where he caught a plane back to Los Angeles.

The trip represented one of the most significant experiences of his life, but the shenanigans in Hollywood over his alleged 'disappearance' had left him looking a bit of a fool. Someone in his circle, either a film company PR or one of the fashion publicists at Cindy's end, had fed the story to a Los Angeles-based news agency with such dramatic details that the tale was soon flashed on to television and around the world. Gere knew nothing of its being leaked until someone told him in Tokyo that half the globe was looking for him. He laughed, at first, and then realised that someone somewhere had been manipulating a perfectly straightforward situation for unknown reasons. Games were definitely being played by someone, and for a time one could almost feel sorry for him.

Chapter Eighteen

Year of the Split

With all their millions, their showy lifestyle and their materialistic environs, it was difficult not to view the Richard and Cindy show with more than a modicum of distaste, and it is clear that even Gere himself was not exactly revelling in the publicity. There was also something rather irksome about their outward appearance of smugness, the smiles that when they were together said, 'Aren't we terrific?' They worked hard and had collected several accolades for their support of various causes, but they pursued their daily existence attended by every luxury, surrounded by flatterers and sycophants, who were also carving their own slice off the bountiful turkey. Why should they not give some of it back?

The new year of 1994 promised more of the same. Gere had two new film projects in the offing, one of which would take him to Britain for a four-month shoot with Sean Connery in an Arthurian tale entitled *First Knight.*

Cindy had a ridiculously hefty schedule already in prospect, and for a married couple who had found it necessary to keep on reassuring the public of their enduring love, it looked as if they would have even less time to prove it, even to each other.

There was talk of a movie for her too. It looked as if she

was planning finally to make the jump across the great divide that few in her profession have successfully achieved – from catwalk to Hollywood, the ultimate switch. The names of those models who have successfully made the transition to post-modelling celebrity are few. Lauren Hutton, of course, did it and was helped to sustain her visitation to the acting profession by her appearance in the Gere movie, *American Gigolo*. In recent times, Andie MacDowell, Rene Russo and Elle McPherson have also been successful.

Crawford, however, did not see the move into films as a one-dimensional state for the future, merely part of the overall business plan for Cindy Inc. She had become one of the most famous women in the world, spoken of in the same breath as Gere's co-stars of recent times, Julia Roberts and Sharon Stone, but did her husband warn her that fame isn't the only ingredient? In fact, it's the worst one, because the world is watching. But by all accounts, Crawford is a tough businesswoman who knows her own mind and does not need the words of her agents and managers to convince her that it would be foolish to look to Hollywood as the final destination for her future life in the public eye.

There was competition enough among actresses in the movie industry and not enough decent starring roles to go around, even for them. It was a source of wonderment to some that she even wanted to try, and risk being made to look silly. Why? Cindy, as one of the original supermodels, had made millions, and yet was willing to put herself through the torture of making movies and risk falling flat on her face. She had witnessed the traumas of her husband's movie career, and knew there were no guarantees that hers would be any different in that bitchy, back-biting world of Tinseltown. Despite the possible pitfalls, however, it was duly announced in the summer of 1994 that she would co-star in a movie being produced by the famed film-maker Joel Silver, the man who had failed to convince Gere himself to take the lead in *Die Hard*.

Silver was a high-flier and a Hollywood veteran – with a

long list of mass-market successes to his name: the *Lethal Weapon*, *Predator* and, of course, *Die Hard* series, to name but a few. He announced that Cindy would appear in his new sexy thriller, *Fair Game*, opposite William Baldwin. She would take the role of a management consultant who becomes tangled up with a murder. Filming would begin in late autumn for release in 1995.

Cindy was putting herself on the line. Who can tell what drives the already famous, already wealthy stars of showbiz and fashion into going that extra mile? More intriguing is their fallibility in failing to spot the potholes in the road ahead into which they may fall, even though they are surrounded by highly paid advisers, PR consultants, publicists and other assorted information controllers.

Once upon a time, the big studios had publicity people whose job it was to invent stories about their stars just to ensure they got their names in the papers around the time of a new movie going on release. That is no longer as prevalent but the studio gossip system is still in place, in a more whispered way, and keeps a whole gaggle of tabloid reporters occupied.

Then there are the inexplicable publicity gaffes from celebrities themselves who seem intent on creating their own forthcoming troubles. So often, they simply create a rod for their own backs, and it is quickly taken up. Sometimes it appears that they are deliberately pointing the muck-rakers and tabloids directly to the things that they would rather not discuss in public. Cindy had dropped a few indiscretions here and there, a strategy that had the look of naivety, but was obviously not. A psychologist might say that she had a hidden desire to bring about a confrontation in her marriage and chose to enforce it by certain means, perhaps almost subconsciously.

What we are leading to is this: at the very time when their marriage was under a microscope, Crawford agreed to a magazine request to keep a diary of her week, so that readers might see how hard she worked. Fair enough. But Cindy also made it very personal, with some rather poignant entries which were certain to inspire a rush of blood to the heads of a hundred tabloid editors.

'Wednesday, 5.45 a.m.,' she wrote. 'Kiss Richard goodbye. He's leaving on a two-and-a-half-week trip to India today. He barely opens his eyes . . .

'Thursday, 12 a.m. Go to sleep chatting about life [to her mother and sister]. It's hard for them to understand my life – like why I'm here and Richard is in India – but sometimes, the Midwestern girl in me doesn't understand it either.'

Under normal circumstances, this would be fairly innocuous stuff, but not in their particular goldfish bowl. Suddenly, everyone was looking in – again – anguishing and analysing, turning up the old chestnuts and bringing them back into play. Did Cindy really imagine, as she wrote those few words about Richard barely noticing that she had kissed him, that they would float past unnoticed?

Whatever her intentions, the ferrets were soon scratching at the door. In April, the French weekly tabloid, *Voici*, published an article which stated outright, without ifs, buts or maybes, that the marriage was a sham, that Gere preferred men and that Crawford 'played at ambiguity with her female pals'. Furthermore, said *Voici*, their marriage of convenience was about to end. For once, the mode of calmness in crisis learned during his study of Buddhism deserted Gere. He was furious and immediately began plotting his revenge. A retraction, it soon became apparent, would not be forthcoming, and although a legal action under French privacy laws was a possibility, it would entail both him and Cindy having to go to France to give evidence.

Cindy was all for letting it drop. Gere felt he had to pursue it. One close friend reported that he was angered not so much by the allegations that he was gay as by the fact that the article in effect accused him and Cindy of lying about their marriage. He rampaged around for days trying to find a way to resolve his anger, and then hit upon the idea of placing a very large advertisement in the most respectable of European newspapers to make an all-embracing denial of the basic accusations in the article, and to restate and confirm the couple's own sexuality and their undying love for one another!

Cindy did not like that idea either. She ran it past a couple of her advisers. What they told her is known only to them. But they surely saw the possibilities of danger ahead. Far from solving anything, to tackle the situation with this kind of action would probably exacerbate the situation. It would bring their marriage and their sexuality back into focus. There would be miles of newsprint devoted to it. It did not matter what the advertisement said, the result would be the same – media overkill. If, on the other hand, they simply ignored the *Voici* article, the story would eventually be proved wrong by their continued devotion to each other, and would soon be forgotten, just like all the other similar articles.

Gere, however, would not be pacified, and to those in his circle there seemed a determination about him that they had never seen before. It was as if the French article had made him snap, the final straw after years of continuing innuendo and smear dating back to his early days in New York and the smouldering sexpot pictures that became glamour pin-ups for gays.

Even as he sat brooding in his study about what to do, the gossips were putting pen to paper alleging that Cindy was seeing Rande Gerber, the handsome owner of Manhattan's Whiskey. Gere's tough publicist Pat Kingsley weighed in with a firm denial: 'All this is totally false. They are just friends.'

That may well have been the case, or not, depending on who you believed. Regardless of these irritations, Gere was preparing to wheel out his cannon: the masterstroke, an unprecedented public denial of everything that *Voici* had claimed, a remarkable personal statement to say, 'I'm innocent' which would only be capped by Prince Charles when he told Jonathan Dimbleby in a television interview, 'I'm guilty'.

Gere spent hours working on his statement, and then, through the offices of Columbia TriStar pictures, booked space in *The Times* for its edition of 6 May 1994. A full-page advertisement was negotiated at a cost of £17,500. The advertising department of *The Times* was not told of the content and believed it would be a promotion for a film. The copy was produced at the very last minute and read as follows:

A PERSONAL STATEMENT
by
Richard Gere and Cindy Crawford

For some reason unknown to us, there has been an enormous amount of speculation in Europe lately concerning the state of our marriage. This stems from a very crude, ignorant and libellous 'article' in a French tabloid. We both feel quite foolish responding to such nonsense, but since it seems to have reached some sort of critical mass, here's our statement to correct the falsehoods and rumours and hope it will alleviate the concerns of our friends and fans.

We got married because we love each other and we decided to make a life together. We are heterosexual and monogamous and take our commitment to each other very seriously. There is not and never has been a pre-nuptial agreement of any kind. Reports of a divorce are totally false. There are no plans, nor have there ever been any plans for divorce. We remain very married. We both look forward to having a family. Richard is not abandoning his career. He is starting a film in July with others to follow.

We continue to support 'difficult' causes such as AIDS research and treatment, Tibetan independence, cultural and tribal survival, international human rights, gay and lesbian rights, ecology, leukaemia research and treatment, democracy movements, disarmament, non-violence and anything else we wish to support irrespective of what the tabloids try to imply.

> Now, that said, we do feel we have a basic right to privacy and deserve to have that respected like anyone else. Marriage is hard enough without all this negative speculation. Thoughts and words are very powerful, so please be responsible, truthful and kind.

Phew! So the world could breathe again. Everything that had been said about them was a pack of lies which, incidentally, readers of *The Times* probably knew nothing about in the first place. That 'enormous amount of speculation' had passed them by, as it had countless other millions who were not avid readers of tabloids and fanzines and to whom the marital woes of an ageing Hollywood star and his megamodel wife were of minimal interest.

The statement brought a hailstorm of publicity around the globe, as Gere had surely known would be the case. It would have been easy to imagine it as a huge publicity effort, which the old studio PRs could not have done better, but of course it wasn't. The fact remained, however, that whatever nullifying effect he believed might be achieved by such a sensational outburst, there was nothing more certain from the outset than that the statement would be overshadowed by the torrent of coverage and analysis that would follow in its wake.

In effect, Gere was asking the media to record their pleadings that all was well in the Bel-Air mansion, or the Malibu beach house, or the country retreat in Westchester, or their apartments in New York, or wherever else their heads came to rest. Acceptance of that claim lasted about five minutes. Even the serious broadsheet newspapers began to wade into 'the inconsistencies in their expostulation', as the *Daily Telegraph* put it.

Having said that, it is quite possible that Gere's gamble might have paid off. He certainly persuaded himself that once the furore about the statement had died down, so would the constant references to their alleged 'sham' marriage. It was exactly the same principle which Prince

Charles applied when he dropped his few bombshells about his marital infidelity and more or less succeeded in putting the 'investigations' into his private life behind him. They rumble on, of course, but not with quite the same intensity as might otherwise have been the case.

Gere might well have achieved the same effect, except that within days of the advertisement appearing, the Cindy factor was coming back into play with considerable impact. Two days after the advertisement was published, Crawford took off for a ranch in Colorado, and then went to the Greenhouse Spa in Dallas, Texas, with her mother. According to friends she was very upset. One person close to her management made clear her feelings about the *Times* advert: 'Cindy found it humiliating. She thought it looked desperate and of course it did. In my opinion that was the real end.'

When she returned to New York, Crawford went back to work. She was already booked to appear on the *Tonight* show, nationwide across America, and the host Jay Leno told her as soon as she arrived at the NBC studios in New York, sweeping past a crowd of autograph-hunting fans as she arrived with her entourage of PRs, that he could not avoid mentioning the statement. She pleaded for brevity.

But that wasn't all. Cindy was accompanied on her journey to NBC by Cathy Horyn, a star journalist from *Vanity Fair* who had just been charged with the task of writing one more major, incisive exploration of the life and times of the supermodel. To accompany her piece, the ever-present Herb Ritts had taken another set of stunning photographs of Cindy, one of which had her apparently sitting inside a huge shell. In a pose after Botticelli's *Venus*, it gave the impression that she was naked, her minute bikini swimsuit being hidden by the position of her long legs. Another shot showed her lying full length on a couch cuddling a live seal. The set was taken by Ritts exclusively for *Vanity Fair*, and would in due course be reproduced around the world.

What would cause the most interest in this latest essay on Cindy were her own comments on the advertisement in *The Times*, and the state of their marriage – comments which all but cancelled out the effect of Gere's 'Personal Statement'. Cathy Horyn slipped the quotations into her piece quietly and without a hint of sensationalism, almost with a touch of mystery, as if it were a prelude to later developments. Cindy, she revealed, had 'reservations about running the ad' and only went with it because her husband had 'different things at stake'.

Cindy went on to admit that there were 'growing pains' in her marriage as she tried to define herself and handle her booming career. 'For my relationship, especially now that I am twenty-eight, I expect more,' she said. 'It really is hard to know when it's your turn to say "I need this. This is about me." Especially for women because we're used to being accommodating . . . When I was twenty-two I didn't know who I was or what I wanted. I wanted just to make everyone happy. And then you think, "Wait a minute, this is for the rest of my life. I better start changing things I'm not happy about." I haven't figured everything out but at least I know that I don't have to want what everyone else thinks I should want.'

The magazine article itself, meanwhile, was supportive and appeared to be deliberately low-key. 'Being wholesome in the high life of fashion,' wrote Horyn, 'may not sound like much of a recommendation but far from limiting Crawford, her clean-scrubbed sensibleness serves only to reinforce her mass appeal. For all her Hollywood vapour – the handsome actor husband, the four houses coast to coast, the beautiful clothes, and soaring career – she is still fundamentally that most American of goddesses.' Cindy's mother, meanwhile, was quoted as saying that her daughter 'wasn't happy'.

Cindy's comments were picked up and reproduced everywhere. They were open-ended and inconclusive and set the gossiping tongues wagging again. Gere's attempt at foreclosure on media speculation went out of the window overnight when *Vanity Fair*'s latest Cindy issue hit the streets at the beginning of July. Once again the media moved in on America's own so-called fairy-tale couple.

By this time, Gere was in England, preparing to begin filming his next movie, *First Knight*, a $30 million production in which he was cast as King Arthur's champion, Sir Lancelot. He became an obvious and immediate target for the paparazzi. They followed him day and night and he did nothing to damp down the speculation when he was discovered late at night dining with his friend and colleague Uma Thurman, with whom he had co-starred in *Final Analysis*.

The hounds really began to snap at his heels when it was later discovered that he was seeing a twenty-two-year-old model, Laura Bailey, whom he met in July at a reception for the Dalai Lama at Grosvenor House. Laura, the classic, fair-haired English rose, was the daughter of an Oxford academic. She shared Gere's philosophical and spiritual interests and they went on meeting through the summer and into the autumn. They were seen dining regularly in London and also flew out to the French Riviera, with Gere facing down the paparazzi with a confident and abrasive air that reminded the old snappers among them of the man they once knew and hated.

In September, the news of Gere's friendship with Laura leaked out, and damage limitation operations were set in motion, with his publicists demanding to be heard. Gere and Laura were just good, spiritual friends, they insisted. Cindy prepared to dash off to see her husband. She told her PR people at a fashion shoot in New York that it was urgent that she get to London. It was probably the ending of the marriage that had to be discussed.

If rumour and conjecture are to be believed, Gere tried to patch things up after he finished filming in November, and Laura, his constant companion for the past four months, tearfully urged him not to end his marriage. Even Laura's father weighed in, with comments about his disappointment that his daughter, who had a first-class honours degree in

English and had been the star of her year at Southampton University, had given up the potential to become a 'perfect academic' for this palaver in London.

In the middle of the breathless coverage about his romantic intentions, Gere himself fuelled the mêlée with some further thoughts on the rumours that he was gay. He memorably chose the evening of a gay festival – the 1994 Stonewall Equality Show in aid of the homosexual lobby group, at London's Royal Albert Hall – for what he jokingly described as his new declaration. The event, hosted in part by Sir Ian McKellen, who presented a parade of a hundred UK athletes who had represented Britain in the Gay Games in New York the previous June, was attended by many luminaries of the gay rights movement, along with other supporters like Tony Blair, leader of the Labour Party. Elton John, Sting and the drag star Lily Savage were among the performers.

Gere appeared before the audience of 5,500, the largest gay ticket event in Britain's history, to rapturous applause. 'I think in honour of all this, I should make a statement,' he said. 'You've all heard some rumours about me over the years . . . and I guess this is the moment to do it.' With the hall now totally silent with anticipation of an astounding announcement, he went on: 'My name is Richard Gere . . . and I am . . . a lesbian.'

The joke did not go down at all well.

More seriously, however, the hugely public married life of 'the world's most glamorous couple' was already all over bar the formalities – such as telling the newspapers that Mr and Mrs Richard Gere were no longer living together. The couple who had, by their own actions and those of their publicity-hungry employers, exposed their thoughts, opened their hearts and latterly lived their lives in the columns of *Vanity Fair* et al., now had to perform one last task which was to reveal that they had separated.

They had actually decided to split up in July – soon after Cindy had dropped those little hints to Cathy Horyn about expecting more from her relationship. Their publicist issued a joint statement on 1 December 1994, confirming their separation: 'This personal and painful decision was made between us in July. Since that time, we have been trying to work things out. But due to recent conjecture in the press, we have decided to make a statement at this time. There are no present plans for a divorce.'

The dalliances of Gere and the dates of Cindy did not have a great bearing on their separation. Their relationship was built on shifting sand and there was always the threat that it would sink. He was very possessive; she was reluctant to take on the merest resemblance of being a wife in the sense of home cooking and slippers by the fire. In fact, they were regular customers at the takeaway near their Malibu beach house.

All of those things got in the way of a settled marriage, but friends will confirm that what really killed it was the massive hype that they had been sucked into, almost unaware of how it would all explode in their faces. Cindy always reckoned she was hard-headed enough to make her own decisions, and Gere had long ago demonstrated that he would dance to no one's tune. Then, as the PR settled on him for *Pretty Woman* and on her for being the superstar megamodel of the nineties, they were spun into the fairy tale, surrounded on all sides by the suits and the sycophants who bound them up into an unrivalled marketing package, with each interrelated with the other – of that the PR people made sure.

The stunts, the magazine covers, the publicity interviews, Crawford's whistle-stop existence as she was bounced from one assignment to the next, unable even to call Gere, locked away on location for one of his movies – these were the killer ingredients. His work alone was sufficient to test the strength of any marriage, as dozens of stars and showbusiness celebrities will testify; when the other partner has an even busier schedule, the marriage is virtually dead in the water for weeks, sometimes months on end and has to be rebuilt over and over again against a backdrop of smouldering resentment and mutual suspicions.

The knockout blow was Cindy's decision to go into movies herself. Gere's displeasure at her displaying more of her body than was necessary in her swimwear calendar was just a foretaste of his greater unhappiness that his wife might go into a sharp Hollywood production where the key element would be sex, blatantly exploiting her body for the sake of a fast buck. Joel Silver, one of Hollywood's most commercially orientated producers – and co-instigator of the sex-based movie *Sliver* that Sharon Stone ended up hating herself for making – had already tried to get Cindy to co-star in *Demolition Man* with Sylvester Stallone.

For one thing, Gere and Stallone weren't the best of pals. A few months earlier, in November 1994, while at a party at Elton John's house, the two stars had had a furious row, with Gere openly accusing Stallone – within the hearing of other guests, including Princess Diana – of sleeping with his wife. That was a by-product of the suspicions that had built up.

By then, Cindy had long since committed herself to Joel Silver, and all Gere's original fears about exploitation were, he felt, about to be realised. By December 1994 Cindy was clearing the decks for her move into movies. Silver, who counts the accumulated box-office and video sales of his films in billions, had teamed her up with the rugged William Baldwin, who had not long ago recovered from the experience of some heavy fictional sex with Sharon Stone in *Sliver*.

On this venture, *Fair Game*, Silver was splashing out $30 million-plus of Warner Brothers' money, and so had much riding on his decision to risk the unknown acting prowess of the world's most famous model. All eyes would be on her in that direction, although as Gere predicted, thespian ability seemed to be a lesser part of the financial equation than her fame. 'I am not out to make cinematic history here,' Silver admitted in defence of his decision to build a big-money extravaganza around an untested talent. 'The point is, she has an unbelievable media awareness throughout the world. She also has an incredibly young male awareness and these films that we do are young male movies. I've tried for a long time to get her to do this. I really wanted her very much for *Demolition Man*.'

And so, as ever, the promotion of Cindy Crawford, movie star, rested not so much on her abilities or otherwise as an actress, but on her power to generate the dollars, a fact not lost on Cindy herself. 'I have no illusions why I am here,' she said from the location shoot in Florida. 'But I weighed it up . . . what was the worst thing that could happen to me? That the movie would be a big flop and I could be terrible. Who says I have to be good at everything I do?'

She had a built-in diversion away from close examination of her first-time acting efforts, of course, because in all Joel Silver movies the action and the pyrotechnics, the screaming car chases and the incendiary explosions, are as important as the stars, and in *Fair Game*, he ensures that the tradition is continued, even if the plot is a touch familiar.

Cindy plays a Miami family lawyer, Kate McQuean, who becomes caught up with William Baldwin's homicide detective in a battle against a renegade KGB gang, fronted by Steven Berkoff. The promised big bangs in the action are certain to cover many flaws, and the sexual activity will also divert the eye, especially when Baldwin takes Crawford across the bonnet of a car while travelling on a freight train. But Cindy an actress? By the time these words are in print, we shall know the answer.

The his-and-hers movies are scheduled to appear within months of each other, Gere in *First Knight* and Crawford in *Fair Game*. Even in their now separate lives, the two will remain intertwined publicly for some time to come, and when the dust has finally settled on this most scrutinised of unions, it will be interesting to discover if Gere retreats back into his peaceful, spiritually calming shell, where he had been hiding for virtually the whole of the second half of the

1980s, until that fateful day when Shirley Ritts invited him to meet Cindy Crawford at a barbecue.

The Dalai Lama will get more of his time now; that is for certain. But also perhaps moviegoers might at last be shown an actor of greater consistency than Gere has managed to achieve in the past. The ups and downs of his life and career have been largely self-induced or self-inflicted. As Michael Douglas once said, power in Hollywood is the ability to make choices, so Gere supposedly had all the power that he needed.

In one of the few similarities he does possess to Robert De Niro, Gere largely shunned the glitz and glamour of Hollywood, after his early experiences. Like De Niro, he spent half his life rejecting big-money offers to appear in ultra-commercial movies. He made some interesting choices of work, some so low-key as to be beyond comprehension. It was as if, with sufficient money in the bank for a single man to survive on for years ahead, he did not especially want to put his head above the parapet, because when he did it invariably became a target.

Even the old antagonistic streak, the precociousness and the arrogance, had largely slipped away from his public persona; he had taken on the appearance of being a much nicer guy to know and meet, a man at peace with the world and content to coast along, working now and then, between his trips to India. Even his old enemies in the media were beginning to acknowledge it. He still kept himself pretty much to himself and that was the way it remained until he met Cindy – and made *Pretty Woman*. In two moves he was drawn to the epicentre of the kind of world and hype he had been trying for almost a decade to avoid.

Before he knew it, the Hollywood sluicegate had opened up, and millions of dollars came pouring forth into his lap, from the massive $450 million take on *Pretty Woman*, and the abundant riches arising from his financial involvement in his next three movies. Some considered that given the ups and downs of his career, this resurgence was barely deserved, especially by one of such fickle talent. Gere has never had much to boast about in terms of acting achievement since the early days on Broadway. And his latest movie, *First Knight*, would not rectify that situation. But there is no doubt that he has a competent winning manner, as proved by the statistics quoted at the beginning of this book, produced by *Empire* magazine.

He remains a very bankable leading man, of a style and quality which these days is fairly unusual. The experience of working with Julia Roberts, Sharon Stone and Jodie Foster – three of Hollywood's most highly paid and admired actresses – and then marrying the world's most successful model, was to bring Gere to a new level of recognition by one generation that had forgotten him, and another that had never heard of him.

How can he fail?

Filmography

Report to the Commissioner United Artists, 1974
(GB title *Operation Undercover*)
Director: Milton Katselas; screenplay: Abby Mann and Ernest Tidyman (novel: James Mills); photography: Mario Tosi. Cast: Michael Moriarty, Yaphet Kotto, Susan Blakely, Hector Elizondo, Tony King, Richard Gere.

Baby Blue Marine Columbia, 1976
Director: John Hancock; screenplay: Stanford Whitmore; photography: Laszlo Kovacs. Cast: Jan-Michael Vincent, Glynnis O'Connor, Katherine Helmond, Dana Elcar, Bert Remsen, Richard Gere.

Looking for Mr Goodbar Paramount, 1977
Director and screenplay: Richard Brooks (novel: Judith Rossner); photography: William A. Fraker. Cast: Diane Keaton, Tuesday Weld, William Atherton, Richard Kiley, Richard Gere.

Bloodbrothers Warner, 1978
Director: Robert Mulligan; screenplay: Walter Newman (novel: Richard Price); photography: Robert Surtees. Cast: Paul Sorvino, Tony Lo Bianco, Richard Gere, Lelia Goldoni, Marilu Henner.

Days of Heaven Paramount, 1978
Director and screenplay: Terrence Malick; photography: Nestor Almendros. Cast: Richard Gere, Brooke Adams, Sam Shepard, Linda Manz.

Yanks United Artists/CIP, 1979
Director: John Schlesinger; screenplay: Colin Welland and Walter Bernstein; photography: Dick Bush. Cast: Vanessa Redgrave, Richard Gere, William Devane, Lisa Eichhorn, Rachel Roberts, Chick Vennera.

RICHARD GERE

American Gigolo Paramount, 1980
Director and screenplay: Paul Schrader; photography: John Bailey. Cast: Richard Gere, Lauren Hutton, Hector Elizondo, Nina Van Pallandt.

An Officer and a Gentleman Paramount, 1982
Director: Taylor Hackford; screenplay: Douglas Day Stewart; photography: Donald Thorin. Cast: Richard Gere, Debra Winger, Louis Gossett Jr, David Keith, Lisa Blount, Lisa Eilbacher.

Breathless Miko/Martin Erlichman, 1983
Director: James McBride; screenplay: Kit Carson and James McBride; photography: Richard H. Kline. Cast: Richard Gere, Valerie Kaprisky, William Tepper, John P. Ryan, Art Metrano.

The Honorary Consul World Film Services/Paramount, 1983
(US title *Beyond the Limit*)
Director: John MacKenzie; screenplay: Christopher Hampton (novel: Graham Greene); photography: Phil Meheux. Cast: Michael Caine, Richard Gere, Bob Hoskins, Elpidia Carrillo, Joaquim de Almeida.

The Cotton Club Zoetrope/Robert Evans, 1984
Director: Francis Ford Coppola; screenplay: William Kennedy and Francis Ford Coppola; photography: Stephen Goldblatt. Cast: Richard Gere, Diane Lane, Gregory Hines, Lonette McKee, Bob Hoskins, Fred Gwynne, Nicolas Cage, James Remar, Allen Garfield, Gwen Verdon.

King David Paramount, 1985
Director: Bruce Beresford; screenplay: Andrew Birkin and James Costigan; photography: Donald McAlpine. Cast: Richard Gere, Edward Woodward, Denis Quilley, Jack Klaff, Cherie Lunghi, Alice Krige, Hurd Hatfield, John Castle, Niall Buggy.

Power TCF, 1985
Director: Sidney Lumet; screenplay: David Himmelstein; photography: Andrzej Bartkowiak. Cast: Richard Gere, Julie Christie, Gene Hackman, Kate Capshaw, Denzel Washington, E.G. Marshall, Beatrice Straight, Fritz Weaver, Michael Learned.

No Mercy Tri-Star, 1986
Director: Richard Pearce; screenplay: Jim Carabatsos; photography: Michael Brault. Cast: Richard Gere, Kim Basinger, Jeroen Krabbe, George Dzundza, Gary Basaraba, William Atherton.

Miles From Home Fox/Braveworld/Cinecom, 1988
Director: Gary Sinise; screenplay: Chris Gerolmo; photography: Elliot Davis. Cast: Richard Gere, Kevin Anderson, Brian Dennehy, Jason Campbell, Austin Bamgarner, Larry Poling, Terry Kinney, Penelope Ann Miller, Helen Hunt, John Malkovich.

Internal Affairs UIP/Paramount, 1990
Director: Mike Figgis; screenplay: Henry Bean; photography: John A. Alonso. Cast: Richard Gere, Andy Garcia, Nancy Travis, Laurie Metcalf, Richard Bradford, William Baldwin, Michael Beach.

Pretty Woman Buena Vista/Touchstone, 1990
Director: Garry Marshall; screenplay: J.F. Lawton; photography: Charles Minsky. Cast: Richard Gere, Julia Roberts, Ralph Bellamy, Jason Alexander, Laura San Giacomo, Hector Elizondo.

Rhapsody in August Palace/Shochiku, 1990
(Japanese title *Hachigatsu-no-Kyoshikyoku)*
Director and screenplay: Akira Kurosawa (novel: Kiyoko Murata); photography: Takao Saito and Masaharu Ueda. Cast: Richard Gere, Sachiko Murase, Hisashi Igawa, Narumi Kayashima, Tomoko Ohtakara, Mitsunori Isaki.

Final Analysis Warner, 1992
Director: Phil Joanou; screenplay: Wesley Strick (from a story by Robert Berger and Wesley Strick); photography: Jordan Cronenweth. Cast: Richard Gere, Kim Basinger, Uma Thurman, Eric Roberts, Paul Guilfoyle, Keith David, Robert Harper.

Sommersby Warner, 1992
Director: Jon Amiel; screenplay: Nicholas Meyer and Sarah Kernochan; photography: Philippe Rousselot. Cast: Richard Gere, Jodie Foster, Bill Pullman, James Earl Jones, Lanny Flaherty, William Windom, Wendell Wellman, Brett Kelley.

Mr Jones Columbia, 1993
Director: Mike Figgis; screenplay: Eric Roth and Michael Chrisofer; photography: Juan Ruiz-Anchia. Cast: Richard Gere, Lena Olin, Anne Bancroft, Tom Irwin, Bruce Altman.

And the Band Played On HBO production for television, 1993
Director: Roger Spottiswoode. Cast: Matthew Modine, Alan Alda, Ian McKellen, Richard Gere, Steve Martin, Phil Collins.

Intersection Paramount, 1994
Director: Mark Rydell; screenplay: David Rayfiel and Marshall Brickman; photography: Vilmos Zsigmond. Cast: Richard Gere, Sharon Stone, Lolita Davidovich, Martin Landau.

First Knight Columbia, 1995
Director: Jerry Zucker; screenplay: William Nicholson (from a story by Lorne Cameron, David Hoselton and William Nicholson); photography: Adam Greenberg. Cast: Sean Connery, Richard Gere, Julia Ormond, Ben Cross.

Index

Notes: RG is used as an abbreviation for Richard Gere, and CC for Cindy Crawford. All references are to Richard Gere unless otherwise specified. The names of some films are abbreviated in places to save space, eg *Mr Goodbar*.